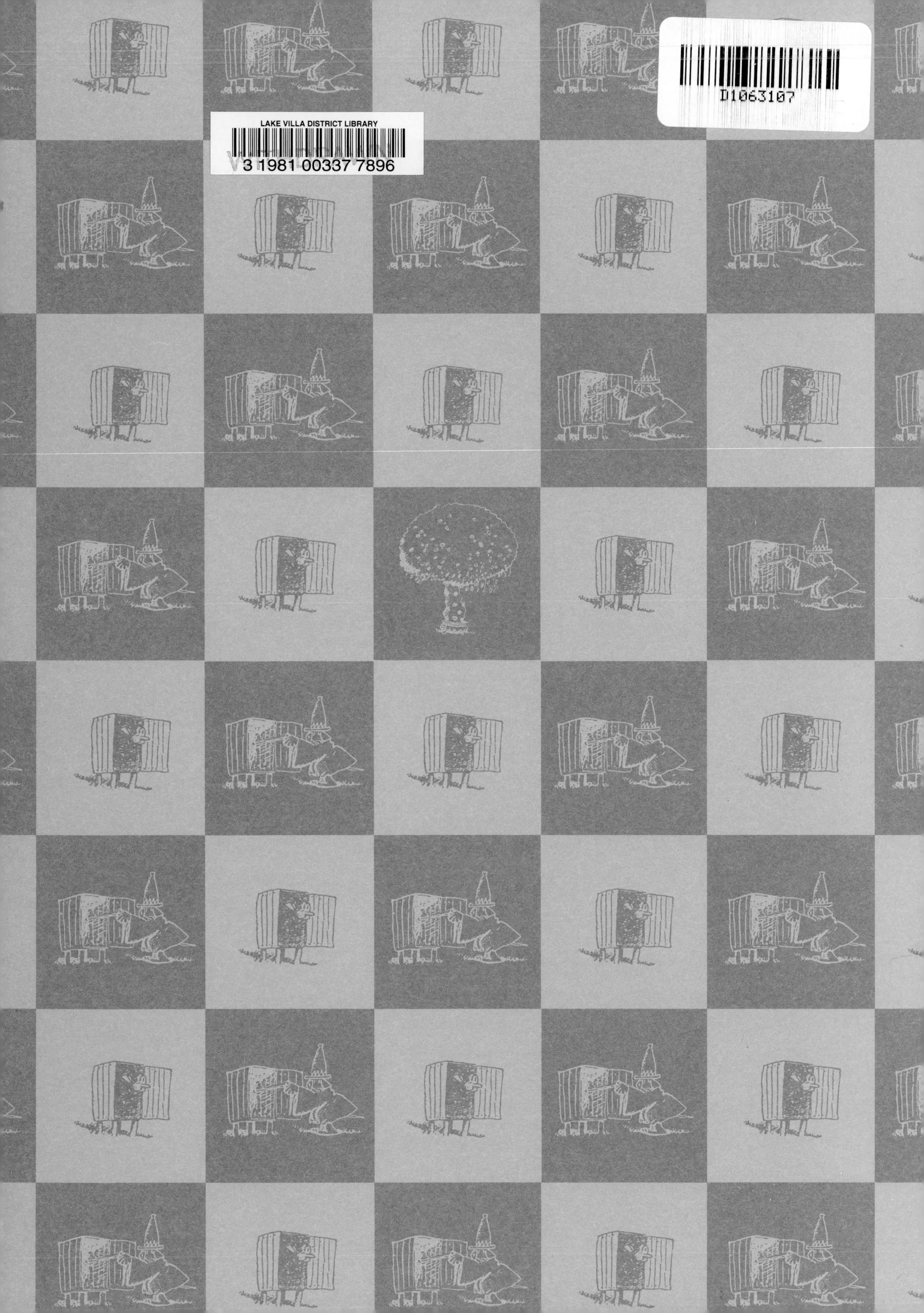

George Herriman

By George Herriman.

(himself!)

Undeleted by Censor.

New York, Aug. 23, 1917 (via U. S. Mails). Dear Dead-Line:—As to age, we might say that we're skating a pretty loose hoof in the finale of our thirty-sixth year, sparring for time and wind to make a classified entry into our thirty-seventh. From then on we don't care what becomes of us.

We were born out in Los Angeles, Cal., and raised on plain skimmed milk taken out of a gourd bottle—glass ones being too expensive and high-toned them days—and whether it was the milk, or that we inhaled a few gourd seeds, it seems like we did not get a fair start—being a trifle anaemic and stubby, and also addicted to rheumatism. However, fifteen years ago we blew the old pueblo, cheated Mr. Santa Fe and Mr. Erie out of carfare, and landed in N. Y.—twenty-two days short of a bath, but full of ambish.

For what we have inflicted upon the poor public in the way of "Comics" we humbly beg pardon. If we had crust enough to go back into the dark ages, we could dig up a lot of Coarse Work, but if you'll only stand for Baron Bean and Krazy Kat a little while longer, it'll just mean that we'll be able to give the family its regular rations until they're able to shift for themselves, and turn a helping hand for the maintenance of the "Ole Man."

Well, adios. We're now going to perpetrate another one. Ever thine,

Geo. Herriman,
New York Evening Journal.

[Editorial Note.—George Herriman's comics have for years past commanded the daily laughter of all readers of the Hearst chain of newspapers, through which they have been syndicated from the very first. Herriman is astoundingly prolific; a rapid worker with a personal fund of unfailingly spontaneous humor. His humor, like his sketching, affects a naive *grotesquerie*, bordering closely upon the blatantly absurd. As one said to us the other day: "His work is so bad that it's really damn good! He's so silly that I *have* to look at his stuff—and am mad at myself afterwards for laughing over it."

Everybody recalls the furore occasioned by his "Daffydills" eight or nine years ago. They were widely copied and quoted; passed into the national, if ephemeral, vernacular of the day and still are embalmed therein. Other series equally as good preceded them. His most popular current daily and Sunday comics include the "Krazy Kat" strip and "Baron Bean," both of which are herewith illustrated. We're for you, George H.!]

An article from the September, 1917 issue of *The Dead-line*,
a "Magazine of and by Newspaper Men and Other Professional Writers for
Fellows of Their Own Kind," and on whose advisory board George Herriman
served. It perspicaciously anticipated its readership: amongst articles about
press clubs, famous newspapermen, and pictures of girls in bathing suits
were also ads warning of the dangers of alcohol poisoning.

Strangely, Herriman's style is described as "so bad that it's really damn good!"
(Does this invective suggest that Herriman might've once
been considered almost ... "punk"?)

Note also that the photograph is obviously from the same "session"
which appeared in our 1925-26 volume.
Courtesy of, and many thanks to, Mr. Rob Stolzer.

KRAZY & IGNATZ.

by George Herriman.

"Necromancy by the Blue Bean Bush."

Compounding the Complete Full-Page Comic Strips,
with some extra Rarities.

1933-34.

Edited by Bill Blackbeard and Derya Ataker.

Fantagraphics Books, SEATTLE.

KRAZY KAT *by H*

Published by Fantagraphics Books.
7563 Lake City Way North East,
Seattle, Washington, 98115, United States of America.

Edited and annotated by Bill Blackbeard and Derya Ataker.
Except where noted, all research materials appear courtesy of the San Francisco Academy of Cartoon Art.
Design, decoration, and some cutlines by Chris Ware.
Production assistance and scanning by Paul Baresh.
Promoted by Eric Reynolds.
Published by Gary Groth and Kim Thompson.

First Fantagraphics Books edition: November 2004.

ISBN 1-56097-620-9.

Printed in Canada by WestCan Printing Group, Winnipeg, Manitoba.

Special thanks to Robert L. Beerbohm and Rob Stolzer
for their generous help in assembling this volume.

KRAZY & IGNATZ.

NO KIDDING ...
We've Run Out of Kats!

Introduction
by Bill Blackbeard.

Er, black-and-white *Krazy Kat* Sunday pages, that is. We've culled all that we could find through mid-1934 (when reference sources petered out, a year before returning in full-color glory in two afternoon Hearst papers), lifting them from the microfilm of obscure small-town papers and thriving metropolitan dailies alike, wherever the errant, short-lived fancy of this or that editor brought Coconino County to hallucinatory life in their papers for a few weeks or even (gasp!) months. What we found in 1933 through 1934 is engagingly laid out in the following pages, painstakingly restored from microfilm where all printed record had long since gone to landfill. Some pages, alas, show their source material more than others and resisted any further "massaging" to bring them up to the crisp splendor of those shot from original tearsheets; we hope that loyal readers will be forgiving.

The strictly editorial "we" cited above is largely, of course, our remarkable one-man Kat page hunter and preservationist/restorer, Derya Ataker, who shares the editorial byline of this and the preceding K&I volume. Derya refused to believe that the strange dumping of the Krazy Kat black-and-white Sundays from the Hearst papers that had, in some cases, carried the Herriman feature for a decade or more, meant that the strip had vanished *in toto* from all newspaper pages beginning in 1933. Surviving originals, dated by Herriman or King Features Syndicate from much of the bereft period, showed that proofs taken from these had indeed gone out — *somewhere.* Derya doggedly went about finding out where.

Months of diligent digging (replete with dismal dead ends when a just-discovered source would drop its new feature after only a few weeks), finally garnered far more Kat pages from the '30s than anyone had seriously expected, suggesting that more might very well eventually be found from similarly rigorous searching — and will be printed, when exhumed, in forthcoming volumes of this series.

A further word about the 1933-1934 run of strips contained herein: More than half of them were apparently never printed in their original large-scale format. By the year 1934 the *New York Evening Journal* was the only newspaper found that had continued with the Sundays. Unfortunately the page had been truncated to daily strip format. Consequently, Herriman's unusual framing and panel work were committed to the depths of oblivion. In August 1934, unhappily, the *Evening Journal* gave up this odd exercise and the Sunday page dropped out of sight altogether, only to be reborn and flourish in color in June 1935, in exactly two (count 'em, two) Hearst papers including the *Journal.*

Even after a comprehensive study of the earlier years' full-page spreads, the original layouts of the 1933-34 Sundays could only be guessed at. Regardless, following the tedious recovery from available microfilm, each truncated comic was cut and remounted by Derya to resemble Herriman's past compositions and diverse paneling as close as it was determinable. During this laborious process, selective omissions and additions to the artwork were unavoidable. On the other hand, the alterations were quite necessary to somehow reverse what was done to these comics by the meddling editors of the *Journal*. In order to reprint the Herriman *Kat* in its full-page glory, artistic liberties were taken only with total respect and utmost love for George Herriman's work. (See page 111 for a complete list of strips thus "reduxed," for both this and the previous volume.) Should any of these "reconstructed" strips turn up in their original forms, they will also be collected in future volumes.

The primary content of the next several volumes of K&I will be the color Sunday tabloid pages Herriman turned out beginning in mid-1935 for two Hearst evening sports dailies published in New York and Chicago. Here, Herriman's employer-champion felt sure, the fifteen other color pages of his new tabloid Saturday comic section would so engage the relatively lowbrow attentions of his sports-fan readers (with the rambunctious doings of Brick Bradford, Mandrake the Magician, Buck Rogers, Radio Patrol, and the like) that there would be few if any complaints about one single "incomprehensible" comic page amid the boisterous plenty the new section supplied. (Too often before had the surreal antics of the Coconino resident driven the black-and-white Sunday format KK pages out of Hearst and other papers, following torrents of complaints from readers who felt the papers' editors were making fun of their sane and sensible readers with this large, multi-paneled farrago of lunacy. Yet the same general body of readers voiced few mutters of discontent when the daily *Krazy Kat* ran amid ten to twelve other similarly sized strips for decades.) The calculated mix happily did the trick, and *Krazy Kat* in gorgeous rainbow raiment saw regular print in these two papers from 1935 until Herriman's death in 1944.

Starting with the next volume of K&I, then (1935-1936), Herriman's weekend Kat tabloid page will appear here in sumptuous color, without any breaks in published continuity, together with a colorful array of other Herriman Sunday features, hand-tinted original drawings, and — possibly — additional rescued black-and-white pages for your delectation.

We'll look for all of yez, then, in the wondrous Katboodle of kolor pages coming from Fantagraphics in K&I 1935-36, late in the year 2005!

And finally, in response to those who have clamored for a hardcover Kat, let it be known that the five volumes published to date by Fantagraphics — covering a full decade of Sundays, from 1925 to 1934 — is being collected as one ineffable hardcover book, to also be designed by Mr. Chris Ware. This will be a limited edition of only 1,000 copies, available from the publisher and a select group of comics shoppes.

Above: Herriman himself makes an appearance in the September 3rd, 1931 daily "Krazy." Note cufflink.
Following pages: These five 1909 examples of an early Herriman strip in Sunday half-page format all contain vignettes of Krazy at home with the Dingbats — who here appear in a rural locale.

→ Mary's Home From College ←

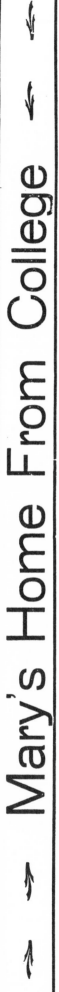

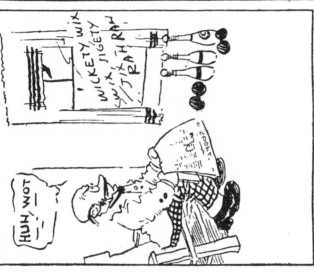

Mary's Home From College

Copyright, 1909, by American-Journal-Examiner

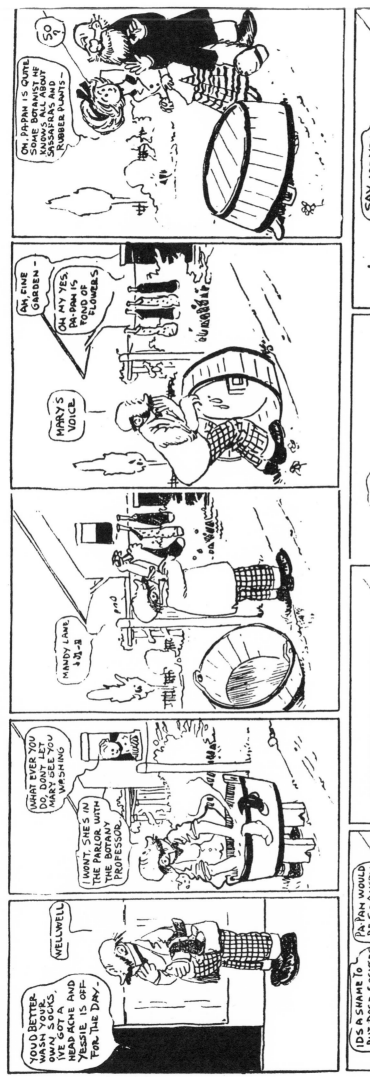

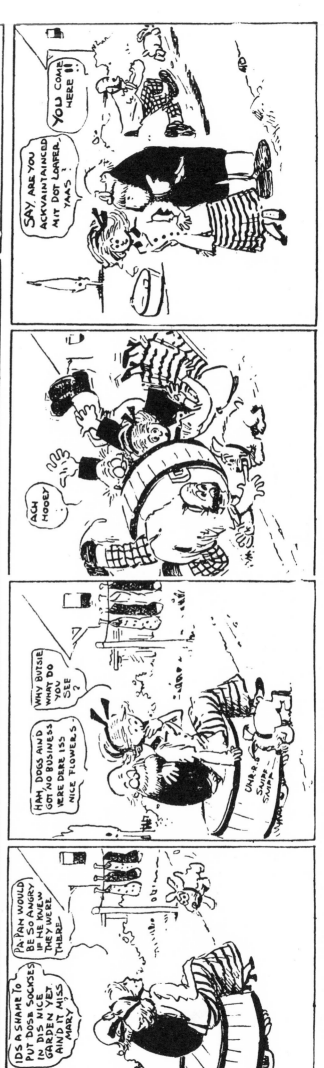

Mary's Home From College

Mary's Home From College

MARY'S HOME FROM COLLEGE

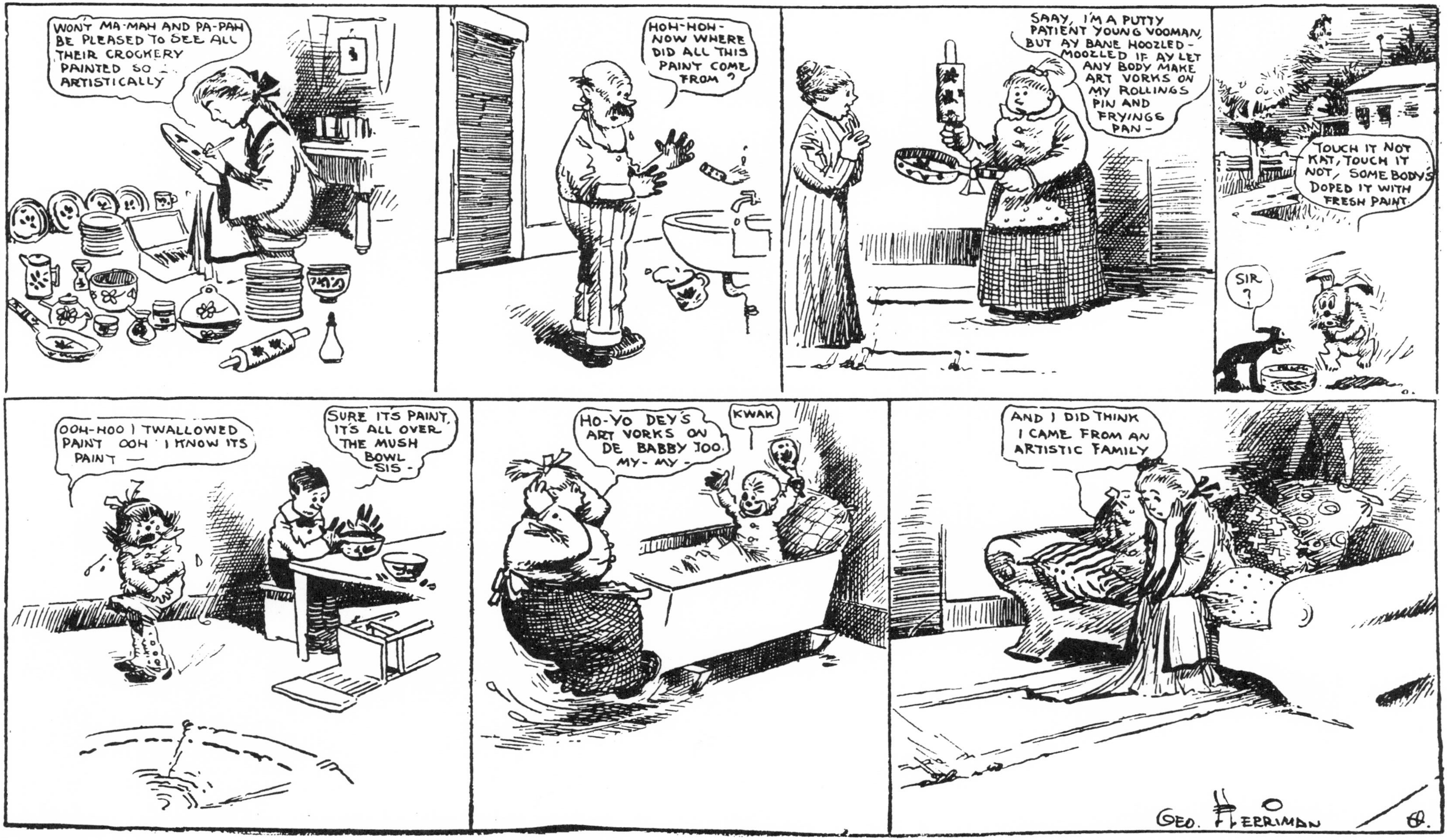
WON'T MA-MAH AND PA-PAH BE PLEASED TO SEE ALL THEIR CROCKERY PAINTED SO ARTISTICALLY
HOH-HOH- NOW WHERE DID ALL THIS PAINT COME FROM ?
SAAY, I'M A PUTTY PATIENT YOUNG VOOMAN, BUT AY BANE HOOZLED-MOOZLED IF AY LET ANY BODY MAKE ART VORKS ON MY ROLLINGS PIN AND FRYINGS PAN-
TOUCH IT NOT KAT, TOUCH IT NOT, SOME BODY'S DOPED IT WITH FRESH PAINT.
SIR ?
OOH-HOO I TWALLOWED PAINT OOH I KNOW ITS PAINT —
SURE ITS PAINT, IT'S ALL OVER THE MUSH BOWL SIS -
HO-YO DEY'S ART VORKS ON DE BABBY TOO. MY- MY -
KWAK
AND I DID THINK I CAME FROM AN ARTISTIC FAMILY
GEO. HERRIMAN

MRS. GEORGE HERRIMAN says that the famous creator of Krazy Kat simply will not part with an old suit of clothes. The suggestion drives him mad!

MRS. F. B. OPPER says that the famous creator of "Happy Hooligan" is invariably serene save when someone changes the precise arrangement of his personal belongings, and then ——!

MRS. RUSS WESTOVER confides the fact that Russ hates seeds in oranges; becomes frantic over squeaks in his car and can't bear to see "Tillie" in the same dress more than once!

MRS. R. L. GOLDBERG whispers that "Rube" has a vicious hatred for spinach and rocking chairs—and flies into a rage at the bare suggestion that he part with an old pair of shoes.

MRS. T. A. DORGAN telegraphs in to say that TAD has but one pet aversion—the well known housefly!

MRS. JIMMY MURPHY says: "Jimmy gets white in the face at the sight of a doughnut and sees red when offered a ham sandwich."

MRS. JAMES G. SWINNERTON avers that Jimmy loathes "bell bottom" breeches, cologne, bobbed hair and half-baked pugilists.

HAVE COMIC ARTISTS "COMIC ARTISTIC TEMPERAMENT"?
THE WIVES OF THE "COMICKERS" SAY YES!

The July, 1923 issue of *Circulation* — a King Features promotional magazine — featured photographs of some of the syndicate's most popular "cartoonist wives," Mabel Herriman included. Apparently, back then, cartoonists had little trouble finding mates. Courtesy of and thanks to Robert L. Beerbohm.

Drawn especially for THE DEAD-LINE *by Herriman, of the N. Y. Journal.*

DEMPSEY "UNDER WRAPS" IN FINAL SPARR

Apropos the "Grande Battaille" -:- -:-

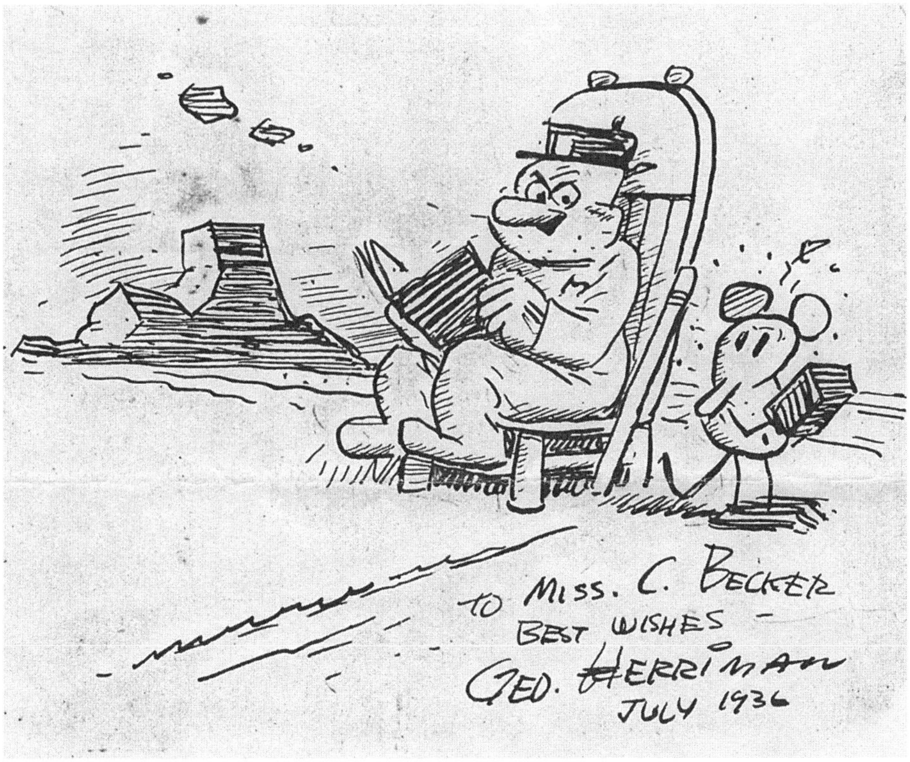
TO MISS. C. BECKER
BEST WISHES
GEO. HERRIMAN
JULY 1936

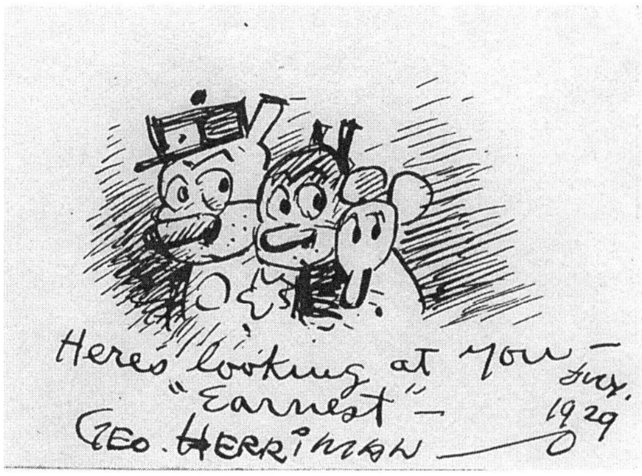
Here's looking at You—
"Earnest"—
GEO. HERRIMAN
July 1929

These two cartoons are typical of the postcard drawings Herriman would send to fans who wrote him over the years. With a possible eye on future archivists, he was kind enough to date every one.

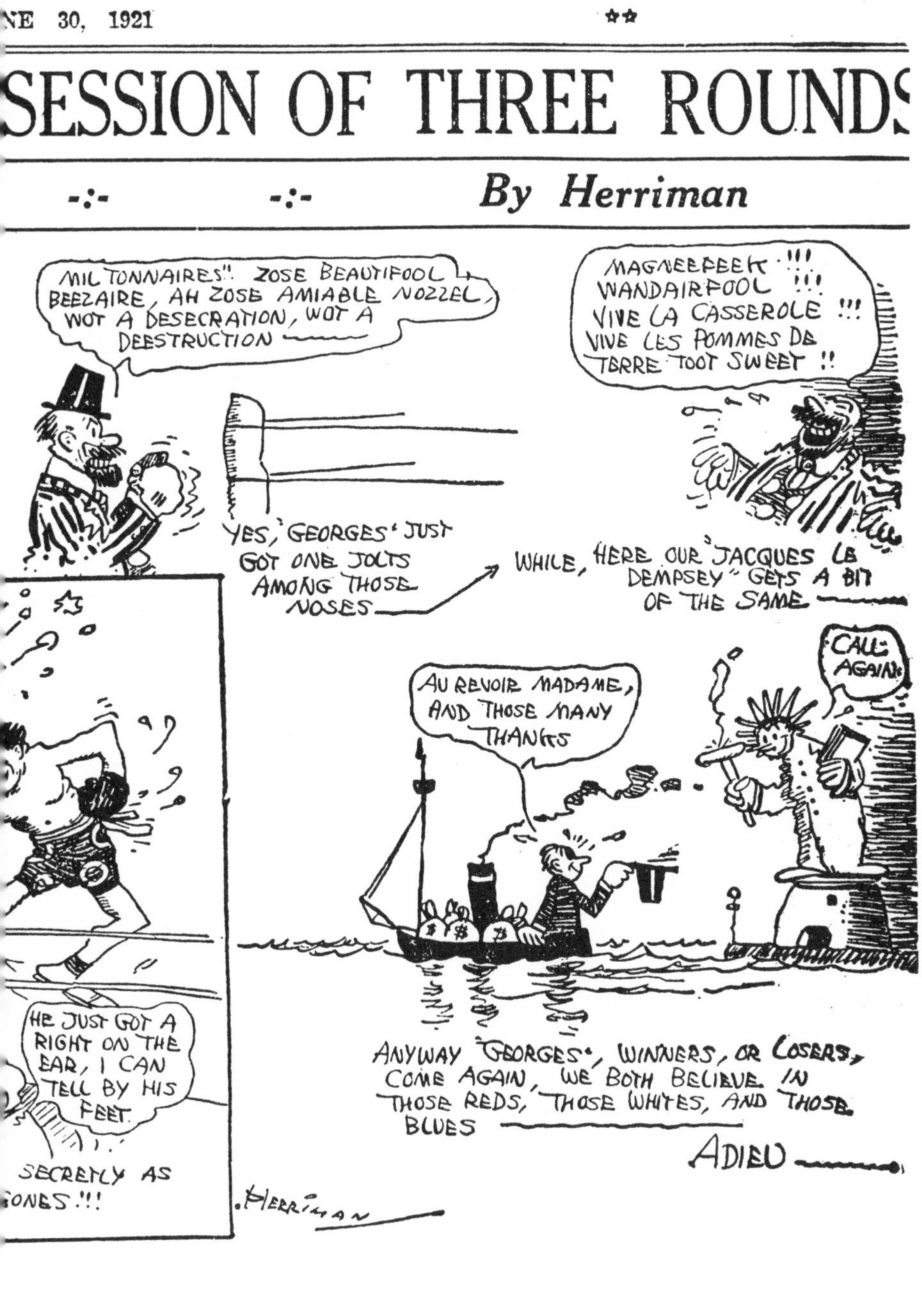
NE 30, 1921
SESSION OF THREE ROUNDS
By Herriman
MIL TONNAIRES". ZOSE BEAUTIFOOL BEEZAIRE, AH ZOSE AMIABLE NOZZEL, WOT A DESECRATION, WOT A DEESTRUCTION
MAGNEEFEEK !!! WANDAIRFOOL !!! VIVE LA CASSEROLE !!! VIVE LES POMMES DE TERRE TOOT SWEET !!
YES, "GEORGES" JUST GOT ONE JOLTS AMONG THOSE NOSES
WHILE, HERE OUR "JACQUES LE DEMPSEY" GETS A BIT OF THE SAME
CALL AGAIN
AU REVOIR MADAME, AND THOSE MANY THANKS
HE JUST GOT A RIGHT ON THE EAR, I CAN TELL BY HIS FEET
SECRETLY AS
ONES !!!
ANYWAY "GEORGES", WINNERS, OR LOSERS, COME AGAIN, WE BOTH BELIEVE IN THOSE REDS, THOSE WHITES, AND THOSE BLUES
ADIEU
HERRIMAN

Far Left: A drawing done exclusively for the same 1917 issue of "The Dead-line" which contributed this volume's frontispiece. One wonders whether Herriman's hastily-scrawled notes at the bottom were really intended for publication, however. Thanks again to Mr. Rob Stolzer for the loan of this rarity.

Left: Our Krazy enters a Herriman sports page for the *New York American* of June 30, 1921, followed by the master's graphic reflections on the pending world heavyweight boxing championship bout which took take place three days later, on July 2nd, focussing on the French candidate, Georges Carpentier.

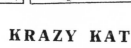
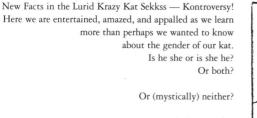

New Facts in the Lurid Krazy Kat Sekkss — Kontroversy!
Here we are entertained, amazed, and appalled as we learn
more than perhaps we wanted to know
about the gender of our kat.
Is he she or is she he?
Or both?

Or (mystically) neither?

It is to ponder.

KRAZY KAT

By Herriman

16.

KRAZY KAT **By Herriman**

THAT TIGER TEA IS GOING TO MAKE THAT KAT RICH — RICH BEYOND THE DREAMS OF AVERAGE —
YES, MOMMY
AND WE MUST ADOPT HIM IN OUR FAMILY.
YES, MOMMY.
WE MUST MAKE HIM A RELATIVE
UNCLE KRAZY — OR AUNT KRAZY — - MOMMY ?
SUIT YOURSELVES
HERRIMAN
9-8

KRAZY KAT **By Herriman**

NOW THAT WE HAVE DECIDED TO TAKE THAT KAT INTO OUR FAMILY AS A RELATIVE — WHAT HAVE YOU CHILDREN MADE UP YOUR MINDS TO CALL HIM — UNCLE KRAZY OR AUNT KRAZY
?
WE'LL SEE.
UNCLE KRAZY — OH - UNCLE KRAZY —
HE WONT ANSWER.
AUNT KRAZY —
KOLLIN ME, DOLLINS ?
HERRIMAN
© 1936, King Features Syndicate, Inc., World rights reserved
9-9

THE AMOURS OF MARIE ANNE MAGEE

THE AMOURS OF MARIE ANNE MAGEE

Here and on the following pages is a complete early Herriman comic strip, apparently sold as a package to interested newspapers by Herriman himself. This daily panel romance was printed in a small town newspaper in the fall of 1907, as dated, but was probably drawn at a somewhat earlier date.

THE AMOURS OF MARIE ANNE MAGEE

THE AMOURS OF MARIE ANNE MAGEE

THE AMOURS OF MARIE ANNE MAGEE

THE AMOURS OF MARIE ANNE MAGEE

THE AMOURS OF MARIE ANNE MAGEE

THE AMOURS OF MARIE ANNE MAGEE

THE AMOURS OF MARIE ANNE MAGEE

Assigned to Herriman and Billy De Beck in the late twenties, this daily gag panel appeared on the Hearst daily comic pages for about three years. Here we have a look at a Hearst paper comic artist bullpen and a painful peek at the Old South à la Garge.

Two Cars Keeping Peace in Family

George Herriman, famous cartoonist, originator of "Krazy Kat," likes harmony in his family, so he purchased two cars—both 1930 Buicks. Pictured here is the satisfied couple in front of their attractive Hollywood home. At the left is the artist's impression of just what is going to happen on his first trip to the cactus land—the home of his picture folk.

CAKES TO KRAZY KAT

HOW ARTIST ESCAPED THE BAKERY

None other than George Herriman, creator of the whimsical "Krazy Kat," which frolics in The Journal every week-day.

By George Herriman
Creator of "Krazy Kat," a premier Journal feature.

THIRTY-SIX years ago we started to exist in a humble way out in Los Angeles, and had we been properly chaperoned we might just as well have been at the head of the bakers' trust, or drawing down a fat income from a patent non-skid doughnut, but we were left to blaze our own trail, which accounts for why we are today making dots and dashes, and calling them comic pictures.

Our father tried to tell us in his learned way not to forsake the bakery for art. Bread, said he, the world must have and will forever cry for, but art, while a few cry for it, still it allays neither hunger nor thirst.

There are a thousand bakeshops and bun emporiums to one art shop, and nobody ever sees any art wagons on the highways, but look at all the bread busses and the bun cabs we see dashing about at all hours answering the wild calls of a starving populace.

But, sinner that we were, we persisted, and we remembered, when we left the old home town 16 years ago for the big village

of the Harlem, our parent's farewell words were: "Don't forget how to stencil doughnuts!"

However, when we look back on our career, and view with emotion how we might have been a "bun baron" sending thin loaves of bread down the river and having them come back heavy money, and having to dodge our own coffeecake trucks, and sitting up nights worrying about our millions, we feel that when we answer the big roll call we'd rather plead guilty to having worried the dear public with our "Krazy Kat" than having dealt them out 2 cents' worth of near bread, and nicked them 6 cents for it.

The papers have been awful kind to us and stand for a lot of sad stuff, and if some day they decide that they would look a great deal better without our art in it—then—and only then will we fall—we'll dig up the old union card, polish it up a bit and take our seat on the "bread wagon."

For bread we must have, while "art," well, nobody ever gets up much of an appetite for "art," so "adios," see you in the paper tomorrow.

A Word from One Famous Humorist about the New Famous Laugh Resort

"STUMBLE INN"

Far left and left: Nicely framed by newspaper staff artists of the era, these two journalistic scoops on Herriman at home (11/17/29) and at the drawing board (1/22/29) have been rescued from the grip of old newsprint for your delectation.

Above: A "house ad" for *Stumble Inn,* from *Circulation,* March, 1923. Thanks again to Robert L. Beerbohm.

DARKTOWN ARISTOCRACY CAUGHT IN THE SWIRL.

THE skating craze has struck darktown. Brer Slayton, one of the leaders of the negro aristocracy, has opened a rink where the color line is strictly drawn.

Every time the colored orchestra strikes up rag time, the colored Four Hundred goes down with a wild bump from the effect of trying to cake walk on wheels.

A rough house almost started the other night when two black actors from the Orpheum butted in and tried to put on airs. They could hardly notice any of the admiring colored people at all.

There was no occasion for uppishness on their part because an air of chaste elegance pervades the place.

As you come into that zone you begin to notice there is some society event of peculiar refinement going on.

There is a humming, grinding noise upon the air, and the cars are laden with colored people in warm clothes. You are received with great ceremony. Mister Slayton's father-in-law stands at the door with shining pate and a fine long coat.

He waves aside your money/ with great formality.

"Back to the ticket office," he says, as you prance back to the outside of the building and poke in your coin through the window, you are bewildered to see the same genial face of the Slayton pa-in-law gleaming through. When he sells you the ticket, he hops around to the door and takes it away from you again.

However, there is nothing like doing things up in style.

Slayton himself stands majestically in the middle of the floor while the skaters weave with subtle, insinuating grace about him. He is fat and genial and of such elegance that the wonder is the Orpheum actors were not overawed.

They are alleged to have gone in with their noses in the air and an expression of such disdain as to be almost maddening.

A seal-brown man with a wonderful long-tailed Prince Albert coat leaned against the rail with a dauncy air of languor that is considered to be the finest thing known east of San Pedro street. To see him wearily munching pop corn out of a bag in this attitude is worth going far to see.

The actorines and the actors swept right by him without a pause. It was thought that the star skater would have them going sure.

He cut a pigeon wing and then slid by on one skate at a time, behind, this way and that—just the most graceful thing—but one of them brushed right by him never noticing the way he was gliding with both heels together and his toes turned out.

When one of them turned away from the belle with the transparent sleeves, that was the limit. When you didn't notice how she was skating, the end came.

The next time they came sailing disdainfully around, somebody remarked crushingly that he had heard darkey shouters were all out of date anyhow.

A little fat boy was so impressed by their proximity that his feet suddenly slid out from under him and they all went down in a heap, most of the rest of the rinkers falling on top as they came by, neatly landing on the bunch.

After this they were gouged in the ribs, and crushing remarks were handed them.

Bumps are more contagious here than in the other rinks. They don't bother about trained instructors; they just climb upon a pair of skates and start. One lean, sad-eyed black boy won the championship. It seemed to take him in spasms. He would sneak cautiously along as though he suspected his feet. Suddenly his worst suspicions would be realized when they would both go up into the air and the floor would shake. With an injured look he would climb cautiously up again, but teeter over forward; then backward. A sudden panic would send him an instinct to make for the dry ground by the chairs. He would fall nineteen times getting to the edge, and at last finish the hazardous journey on his hands and knees, dragging his terrible skates behind him.

EVENING WITH THE HINDU'

Christ Episcopal Church, T' and Flower streets, has array interesting evening on life in Monday evening, at which t' two native speakers. M' Banarjee of Calcutta, conditions surrounding widows in India. Acc toms of her country married at the ag' had a wonderfu' tell the history mission and s native Hind speaker is Christian and inte The lc invit'

When Garge worked for the *Los Angeles Times* in 1906, he covered the city oddities with both typewriter and penpoint. Although sans byline, this "Darktown" text was almost certainly written by Herriman. The art, of course, is Gargeous.

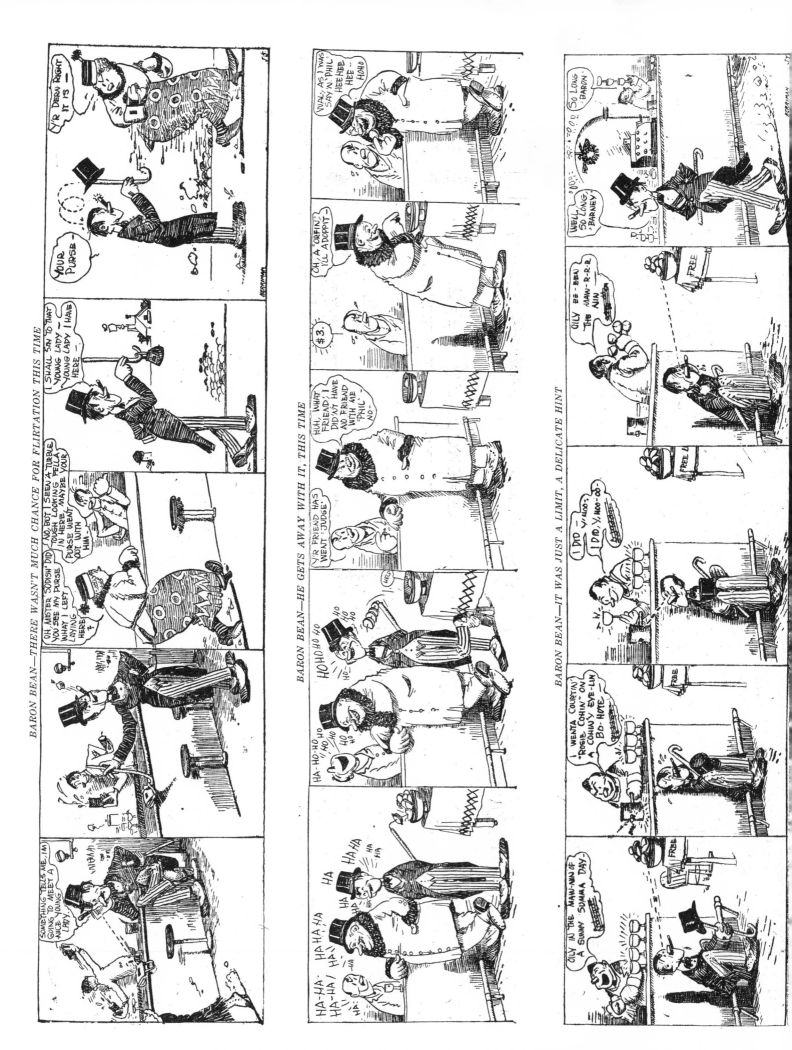

This page: *Baron Bean* from January 5th, 6th, and 7th, 1916; opposite: January 8th, 10th, and 11th, 1916.
The first two or three strips are almost certainly not by Herriman. Apart from the lack of authentic signature, the figures and compositions
are uncharacteristically awkward — though the drawing improves as the week wears on. Contradicting the generally accepted notion that
Herriman rarely, if ever, used a "ghost," these strips ask — who was it here? Collection C. Ware.

BARON BEAN—SHOWING THAT FIVE PERCENT HASN'T BEEN EXTRACTED FROM THIS BEAN

BARON BEAN—HE WAS GOOD WHEN HE HAD IT

BARON BEAN—WHICH MADE THEM EVEN ALL AROUND

BARON BEAN—AND NOW GRIMES WISHES IT MORE THAN EVER

BARON BEAN—AND NOW GRIMES WISHES IT MORE THAN EVER

BARON BEAN—THIS DUCK HAS MIGHTY LONG LEGS

Baron Bean from February 24th, 26th, and March 6th, 1916.

Readers, please note: an Ignatz "dingbat" placed
below a strip indicates a relevant or related footnote
at the volume's end for that particular selection,
all to be found in the "Ignatz Debaffler" section.

1933.

Readers, please note: an Ignatz "dingbat" placed
below a strip indicates a relevant or related footnote
at the volume's end for that particular selection,
all to be found in the "Ignatz Debaffler" section.

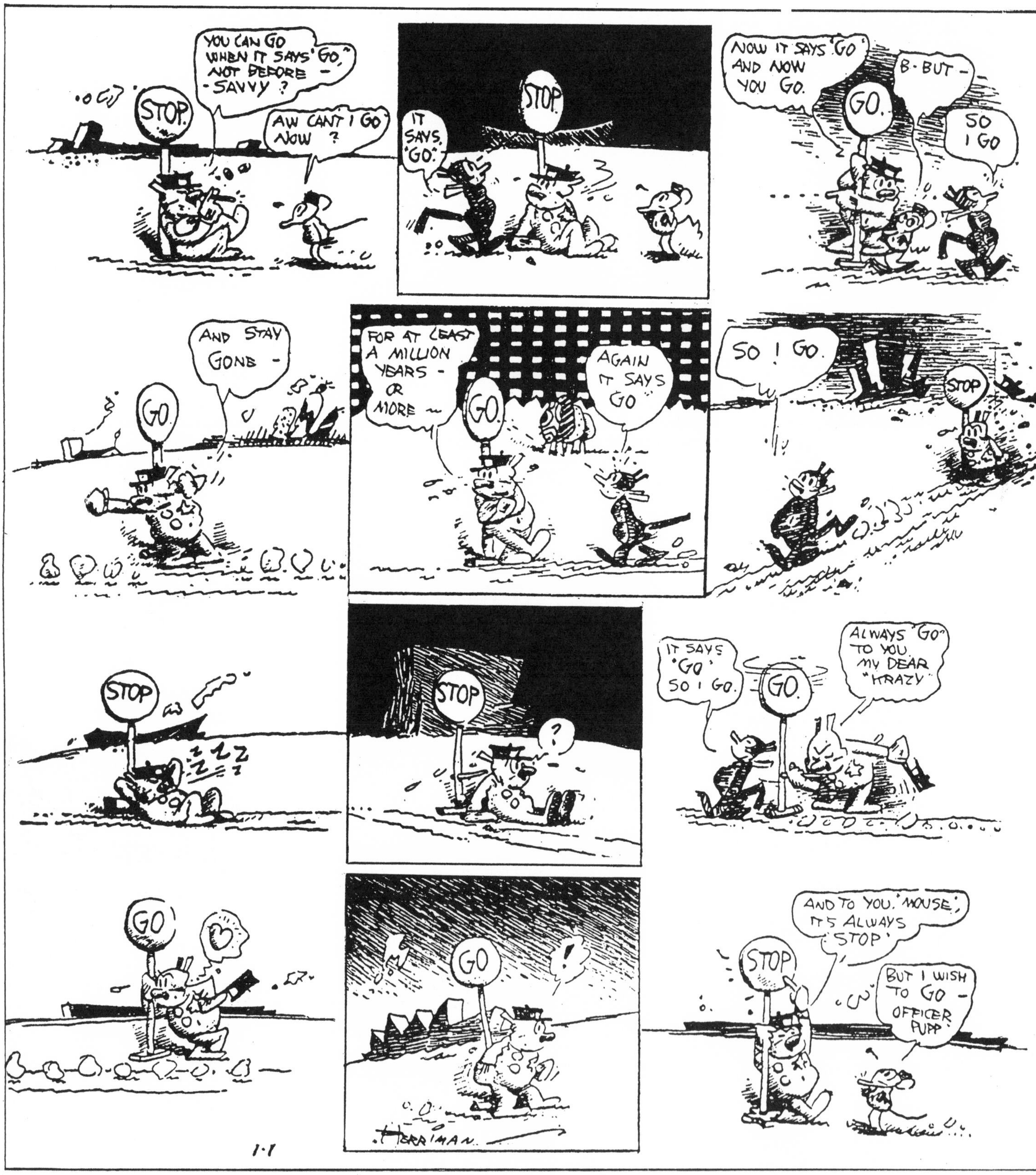
YOU CAN GO WHEN IT SAYS "GO," NOT BEFORE - SAVVY ?
AW CAN'T I GO NOW ?
STOP
IT SAYS "GO."
STOP
NOW IT SAYS "GO" AND NOW YOU GO.
B-BUT -
SO I GO
GO.
AND STAY GONE -
GO
FOR AT LEAST A MILLION YEARS - OR MORE -
AGAIN IT SAYS GO
GO.
SO ! GO.
STOP
STOP
STOP
?
IT SAYS "GO" SO I GO.
ALWAYS "GO" TO YOU, MY DEAR "KRAZY"
GO.
GO
GO
!
AND TO YOU, "MOUSE," IT'S ALWAYS "STOP"
BUT I WISH TO GO - OFFICER PUPP
STOP
HERRIMAN
1·1

January 1st, 1933.

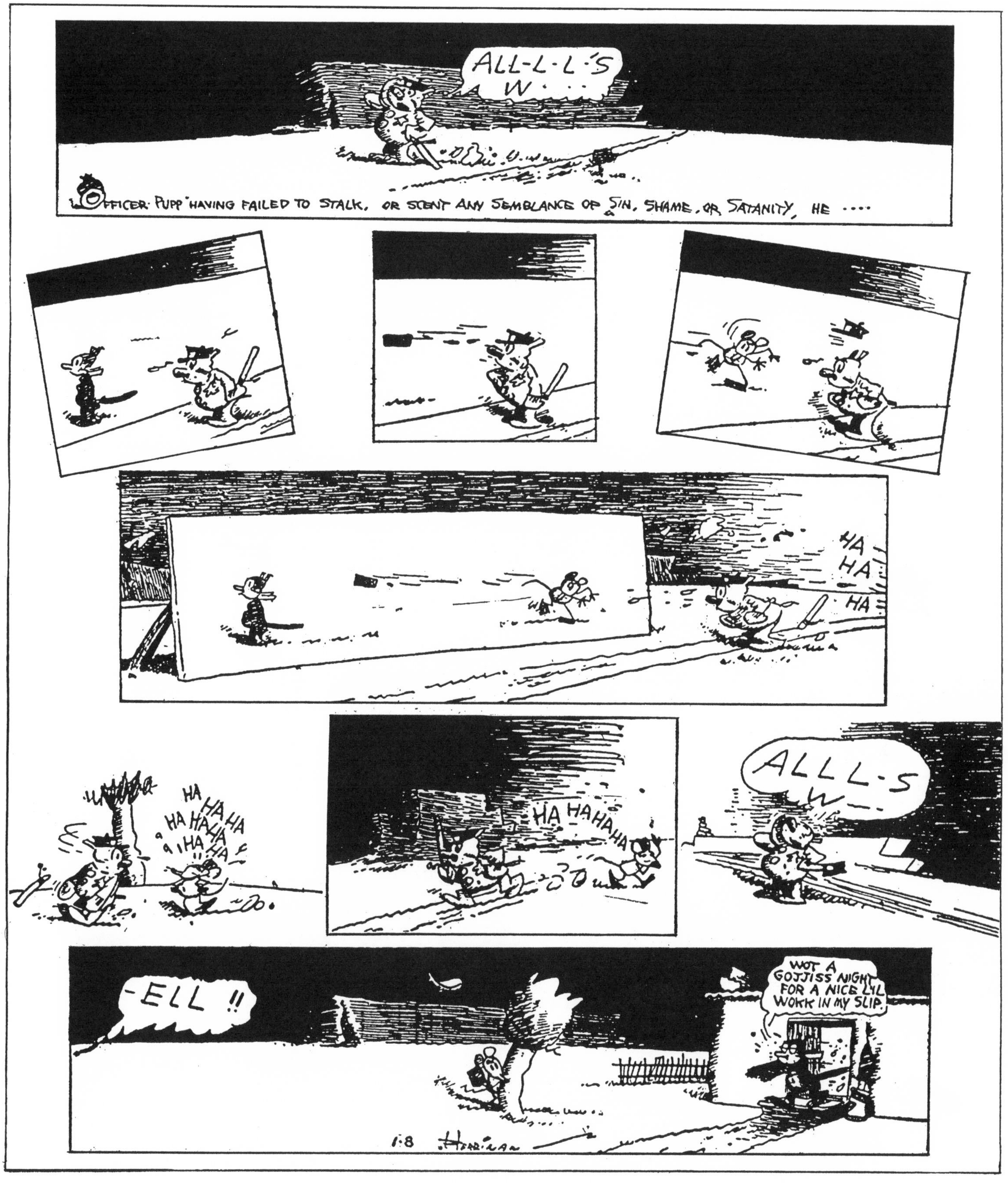
ALL-L-L'S W....
Officer Pupp having failed to stalk, or scent any semblance of sin, shame, or satanity, he ....
HA HA HA
HA HA HA HA HA HA HA
HA HA HA HA HA
ALLL-S W
-ELL !!
WOT A GOJJISS NIGHT FOR A NICE LI'L WOKK IN MY SLIP

January 8th, 1933.

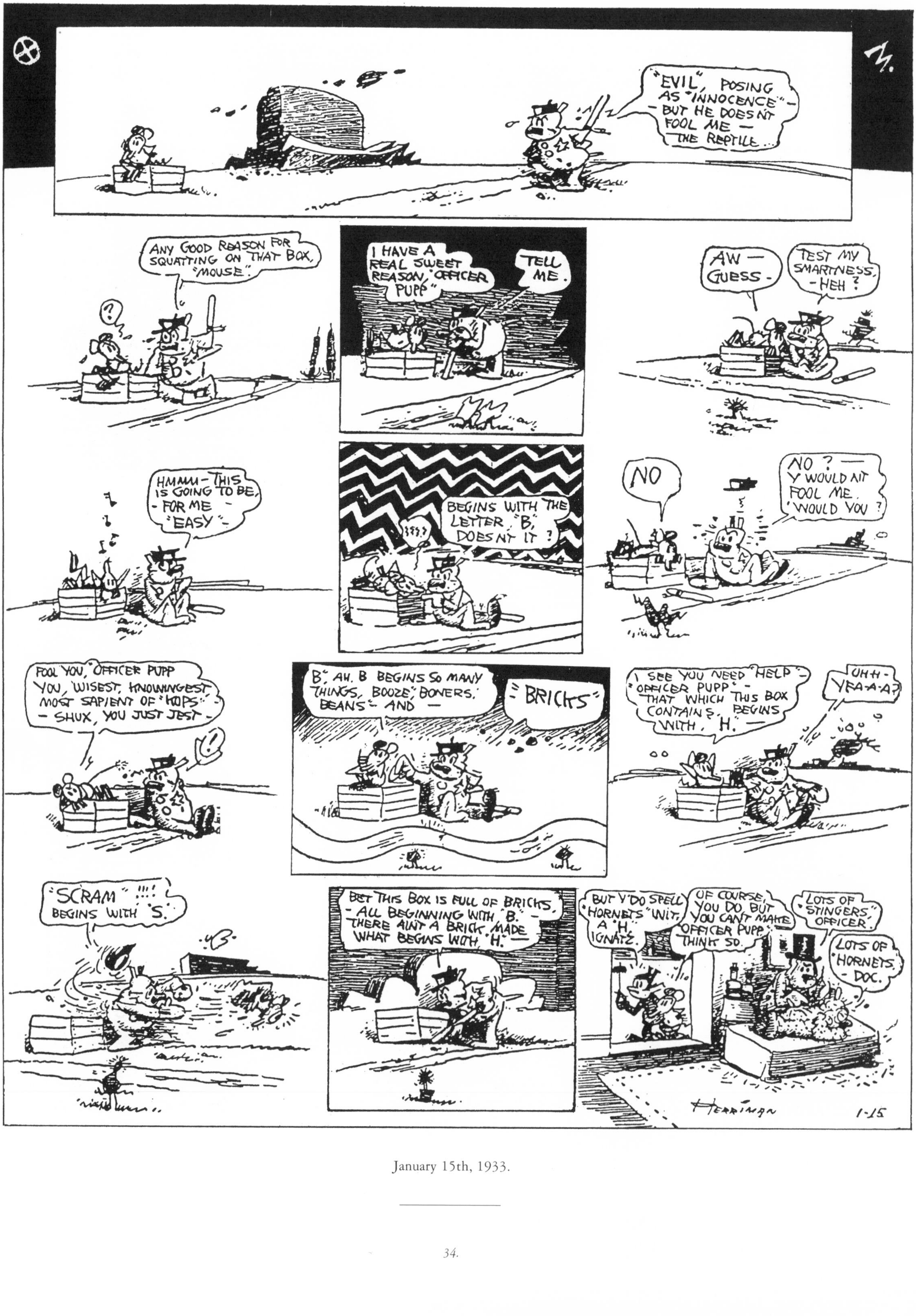
"EVIL", POSING AS "INNOCENCE" - BUT HE DOESN'T FOOL ME - THE REPTILE.
ANY GOOD REASON FOR SQUATTING ON THAT BOX, "MOUSE".
I HAVE A REAL SWEET REASON, "OFFICER PUPP"
TELL ME.
AW - GUESS -
TEST MY SMARTNESS, - HEH ?
HMMM - THIS IS GOING TO BE, - FOR ME - EASY -
BEGINS WITH THE LETTER "B", DOESN'T IT ?
NO
NO ? - Y WOULDN'T FOOL ME, WOULD YOU ?
FOOL YOU, "OFFICER PUPP" YOU, WISEST, KNOWINGEST, MOST SAPIENT OF "KOPS" - SHUX, YOU JUST JEST -
"B", AH. B BEGINS SO MANY THINGS, BOOZE, BONERS, BEANS - AND -
BRICKS
I SEE YOU NEED "HELP" - "OFFICER PUPP" - THAT WHICH THIS BOX CONTAINS, BEGINS WITH "H." -
UHH - YEA-A-A?
"SCRAM" !!!! BEGINS WITH "S."
BET THIS BOX IS FULL OF BRICKS - ALL BEGINNING WITH "B." - THERE AIN'T A BRICK MADE WHAT BEGINS WITH "H."
BUT Y'DO SPELL "HORNETS" WIT A "H." IGNATZ.
OF COURSE, YOU DO, BUT YOU CAN'T MAKE OFFICER PUPP THINK SO.
LOTS OF "STINGERS" OFFICER.
LOTS OF "HORNETS" - DOC.
HERRIMAN
1-15

January 15th, 1933.

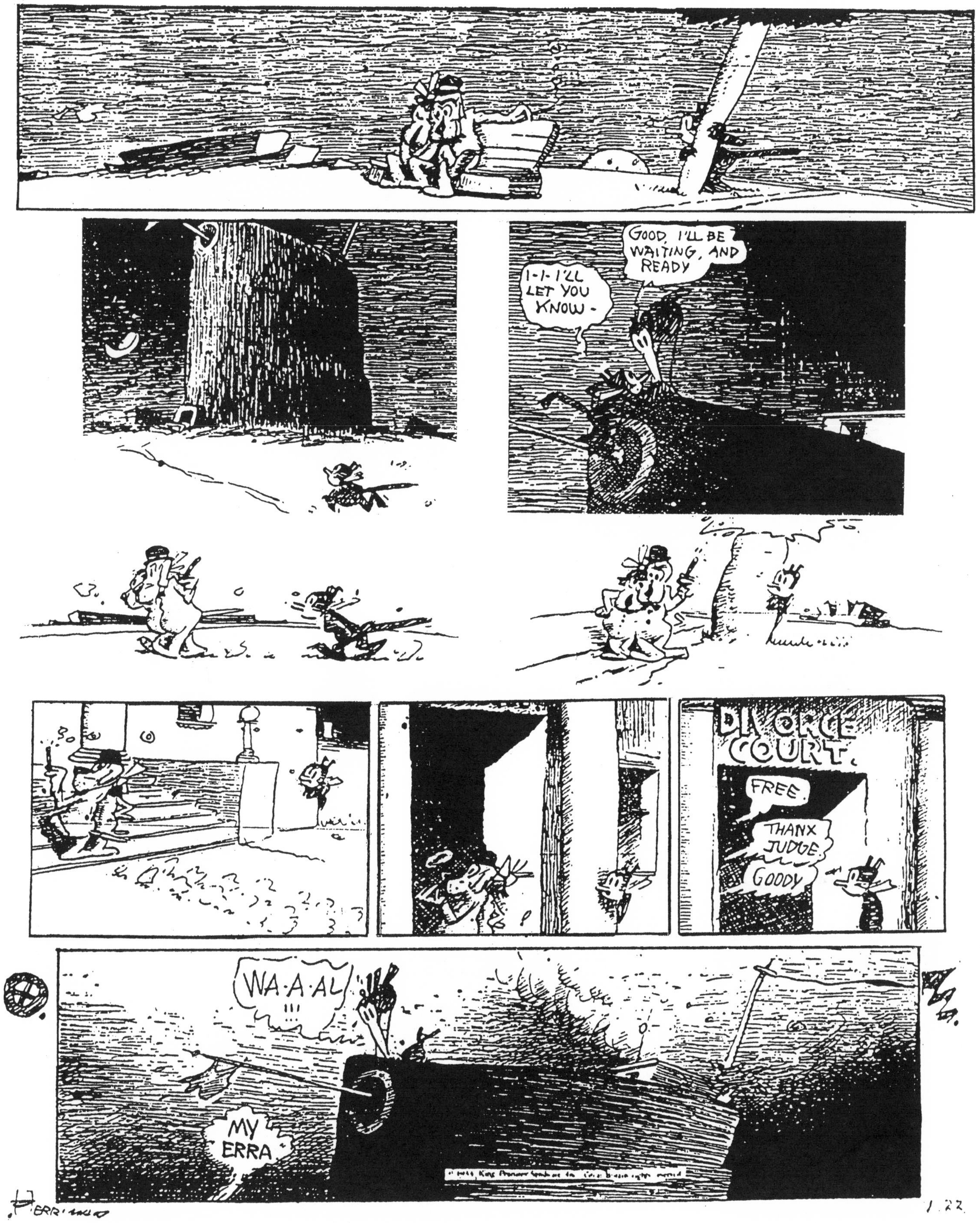
I-I-I'LL LET YOU KNOW-
GOOD, I'LL BE WAITING, AND READY
DI ORCE COURT.
FREE
THANX JUDGE
GOODY
WA-A-AL !!!
MY ERRA
1.22

January 22nd, 1934.

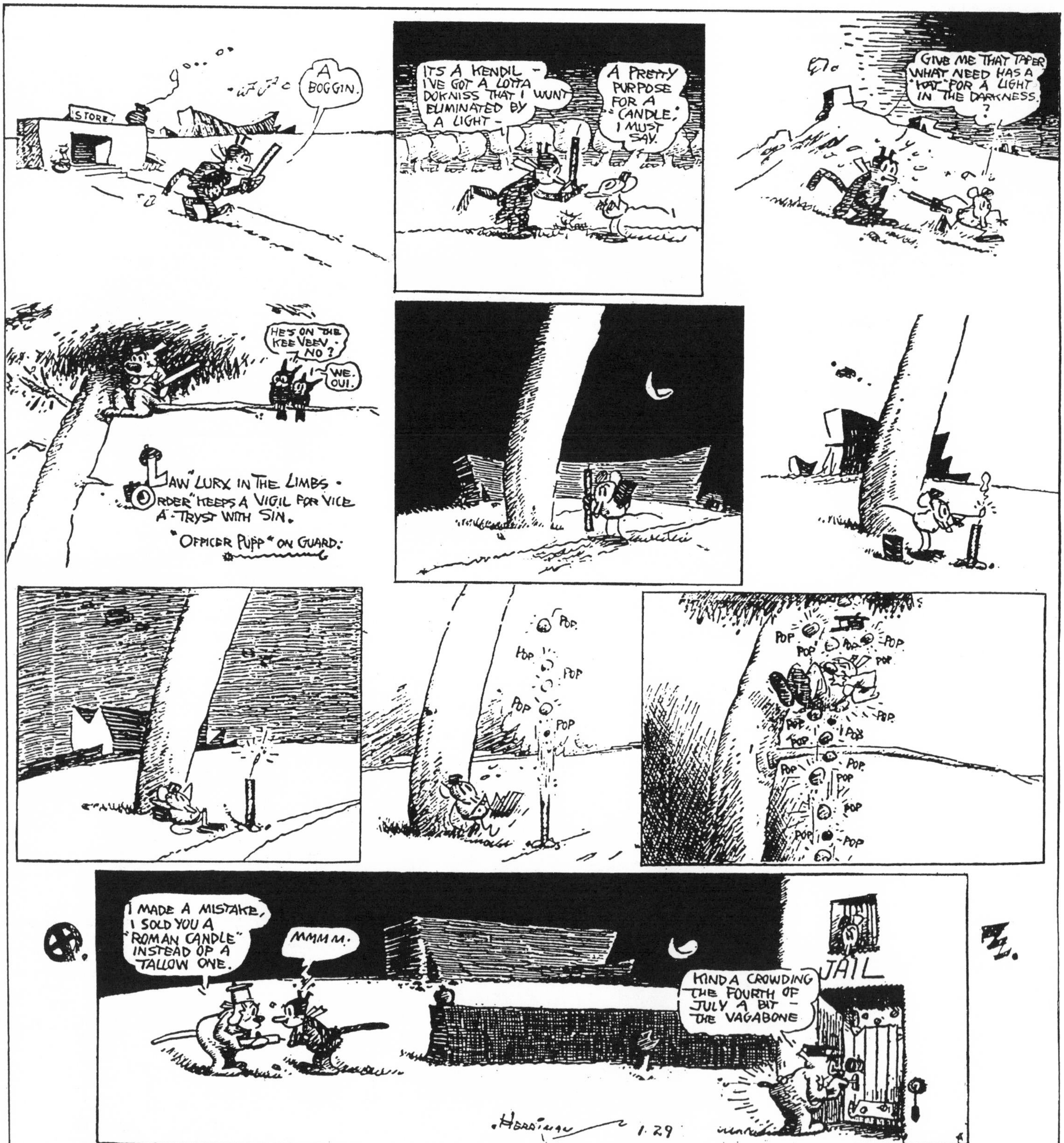
STORE
A BOGGIN.
ITS A KENDIL - I'VE GOT A LOTTA DOKNISS THAT I WUNT ELIMINATED BY A LIGHT -
A PRETTY PURPOSE FOR A CANDLE, I MUST SAY.
GIVE ME THAT TAPER WHAT NEED HAS A "KAT" FOR A LIGHT IN THE DARKNESS. ?
HE'S ON THE KEE VEEV, NO ?
WE. OUI.
"LAW" LURX IN THE LIMBS • "ORDER" KEEPS A VIGIL FOR VICE A-TRYST WITH SIN.
"OFFICER PUPP" ON GUARD.
POP. POP POP POP
POP POP POP POP POP POP POP POP POP POP
I MADE A MISTAKE, I SOLD YOU A "ROMAN CANDLE" INSTEAD OF A TALLOW ONE.
MMMM.
JAIL
KINDA CROWDING THE FOURTH OF JULY A BIT - THE VAGABONE
HERRIMAN 1.29

January 29th, 1933.

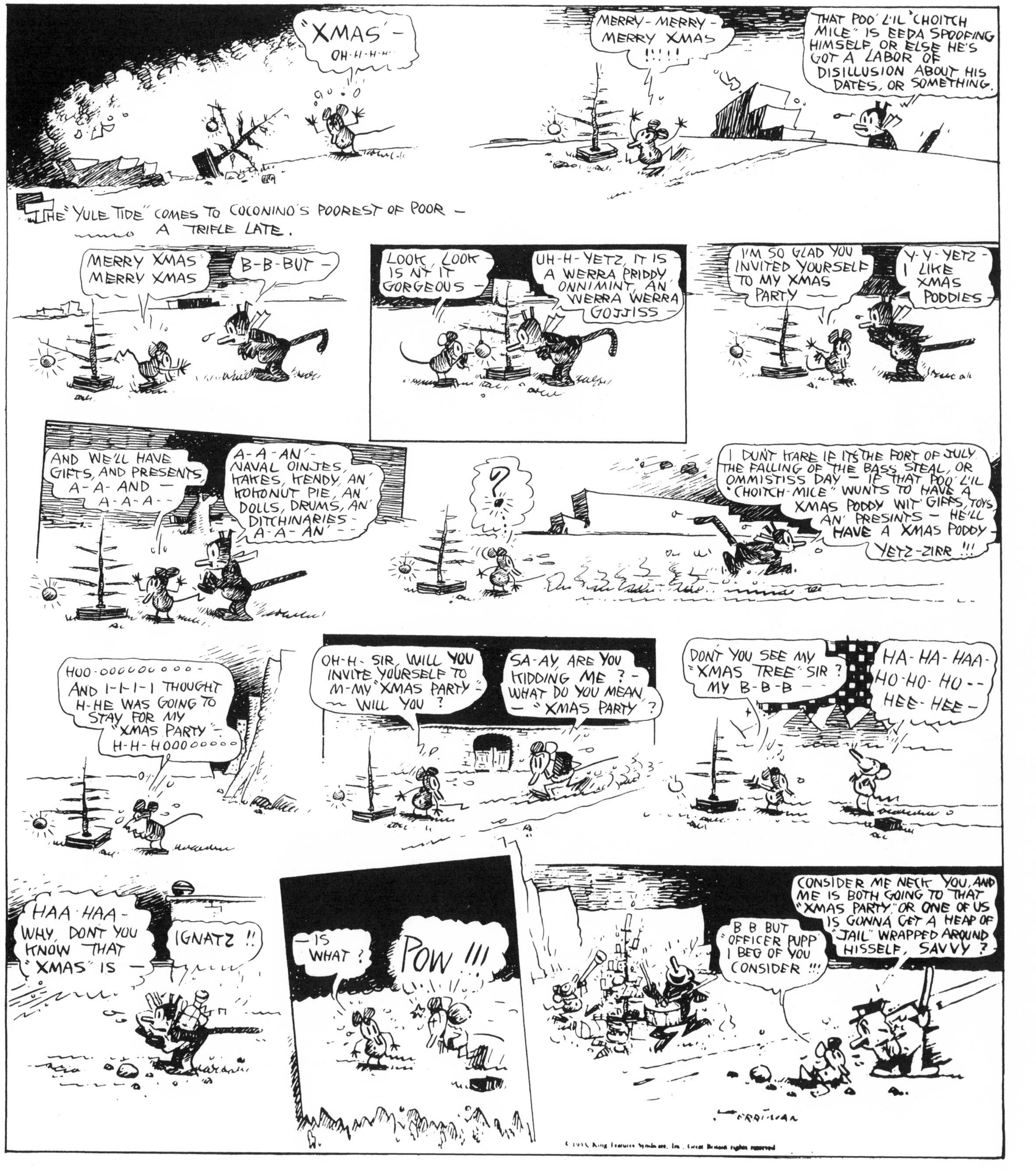
"XMAS" - OH-H-H-H
MERRY - MERRY - MERRY XMAS !!!!!
THAT POO' L'IL "CHOITCH MICE" IS EEDA SPOOFING HIMSELF OR ELSE HE'S GOT A LABOR OF DISILLUSION ABOUT HIS DATES, OR SOMETHING.
THE "YULE TIDE" COMES TO COCONINO'S POOREST OF POOR - A TRIFLE LATE.
MERRY XMAS MERRY XMAS
B-B-BUT -
LOOK, LOOK - IS N'T IT GORGEOUS -
UH-H- YETZ, IT IS A WERRA PRIDDY ONNIMINT, AN' WERRA WERRA GOJJISS -
I'M SO GLAD YOU INVITED YOURSELF TO MY XMAS PARTY -
Y-Y- YETZ - I LIKE XMAS PODDIES -
AND WE'LL HAVE GIFTS, AND PRESENTS, A-A- AND - A-A-A- -
A-A-AN' - NAVAL OINJES, KAKES, KENDY, AN' KOKONUT PIE, AN' DOLLS, DRUMS, AN' DITCHINARIES - A-A-AN' -
?
I DUN'T KARE IF IT'S THE FORT OF JULY, THE FALLING OF THE BASS STEAL, OR OMMISTISS DAY - IF THAT POO' L'IL "CHOITCH-MICE" WUNTS TO HAVE A XMAS PODDY WIT GIFFS, TOYS, AN' PRESINTS - HE'LL HAVE A XMAS PODDY - YETZ-ZIRR !!!
HOO-OOOOOOOOO - AND I-I-I-I THOUGHT H-HE WAS GOING TO STAY FOR MY "XMAS PARTY" - H-H-HOOOOOOOOO
OH-H- SIR, WILL YOU INVITE YOURSELF TO M-MY "XMAS PARTY" - WILL YOU ?
SA-AY, ARE YOU KIDDING ME ? - WHAT DO YOU MEAN - "XMAS PARTY" ?
DON'T YOU SEE MY "XMAS TREE" SIR ? MY B-B-B -
HA-HA-HAA - HO-HO-HO - - HEE-HEE -
HAA HAA - WHY, DON'T YOU KNOW THAT "XMAS" IS -
IGNATZ !!
- IS WHAT ?
POW !!!
B B BUT OFFICER PUPP I BEG OF YOU CONSIDER !!!
CONSIDER ME NECK YOU, AND ME IS BOTH GOING TO THAT "XMAS PARTY" OR ONE OF US IS GONNA GET A HEAP OF "JAIL" WRAPPED AROUND HISSELF, SAVVY ?

February 5th, 1933.

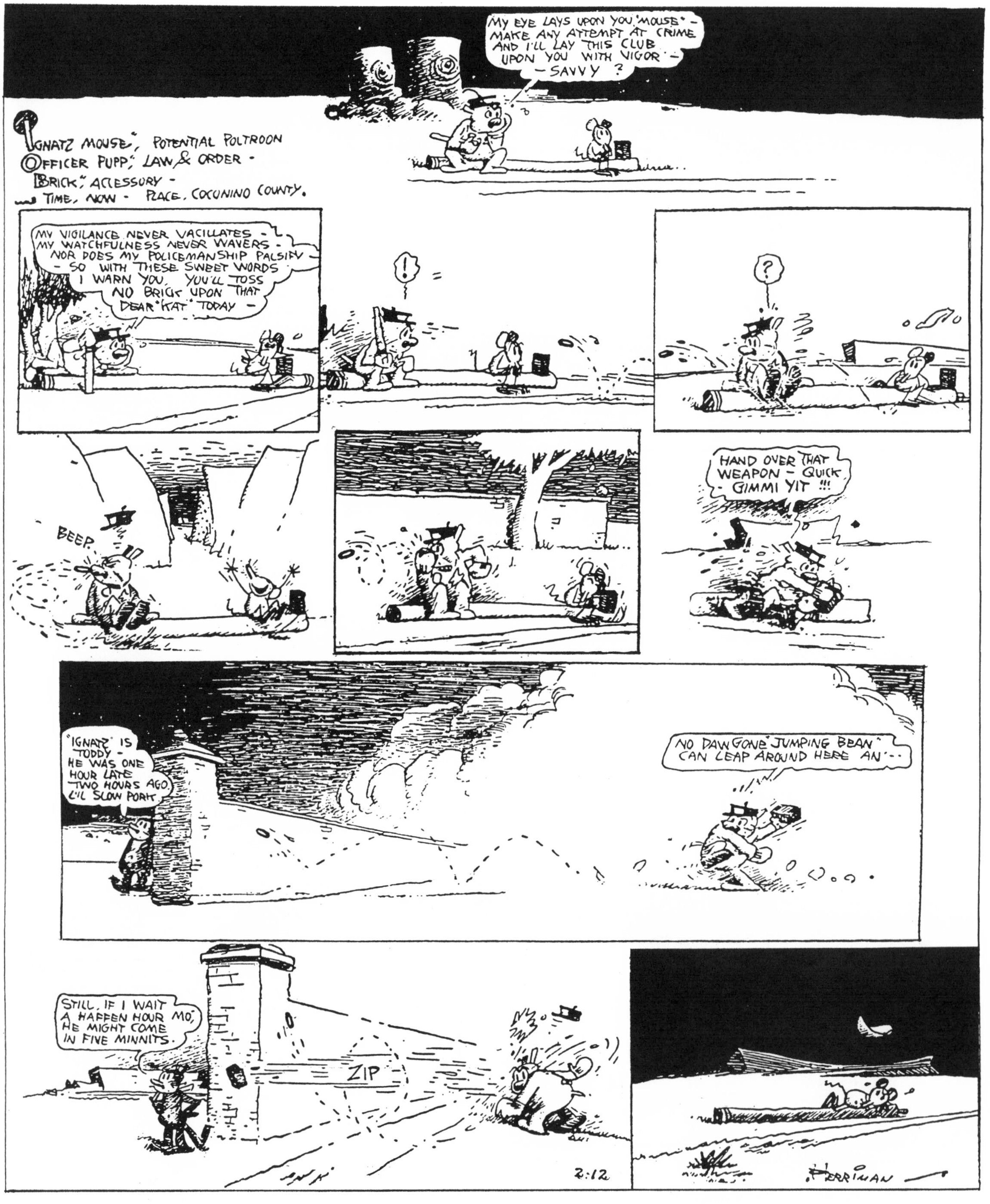
MY EYE LAYS UPON YOU, "MOUSE" - MAKE ANY ATTEMPT AT CRIME AND I'LL LAY THIS CLUB UPON YOU WITH VIGOR - - SAVVY ?
"IGNATZ MOUSE", POTENTIAL POLTROON
"OFFICER PUPP", LAW & ORDER -
"BRICK", ACCESSORY -
TIME, NOW - PLACE, COCONINO COUNTY.
MY VIGILANCE NEVER VACILLATES - MY WATCHFULNESS NEVER WAVERS - NOR DOES MY POLICEMANSHIP PALSIFY - SO WITH THESE SWEET WORDS I WARN YOU. YOU'LL TOSS NO BRICK UPON THAT DEAR "KAT" TODAY -
!
?
BEEP
HAND OVER THAT WEAPON - QUICK GIMMI YIT !!!
"IGNATZ" IS TODDY - HE WAS ONE HOUR LATE TWO HOURS AGO. LI'L SLOW POKE.
NO DAW GONE "JUMPING BEAN" CAN LEAP AROUND HERE AN' - -
STILL, IF I WAIT A HAFFEN HOUR MO', HE MIGHT COME IN FIVE MINNITS.
ZIP
2:12
HERRIMAN

February 12th, 1933.

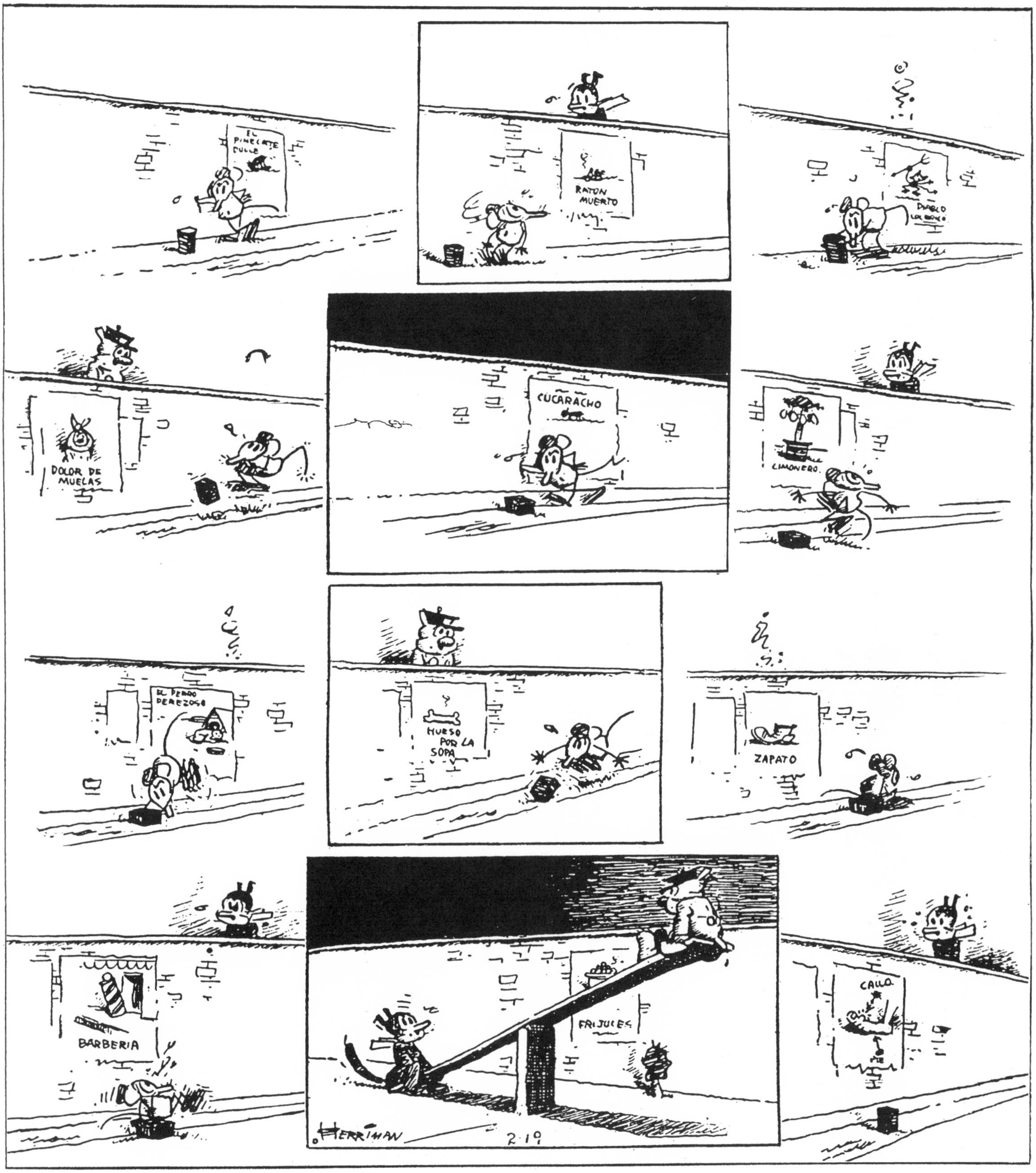
RATON MUERTO
DOLOR DE MUELAS
CUCARACHO
LIMONERO.
HUESO POR LA SOPA
ZAPATO
BARBERIA
FRIJOLES
CALLO
HERRIMAN
2-19

February 19th, 1933.

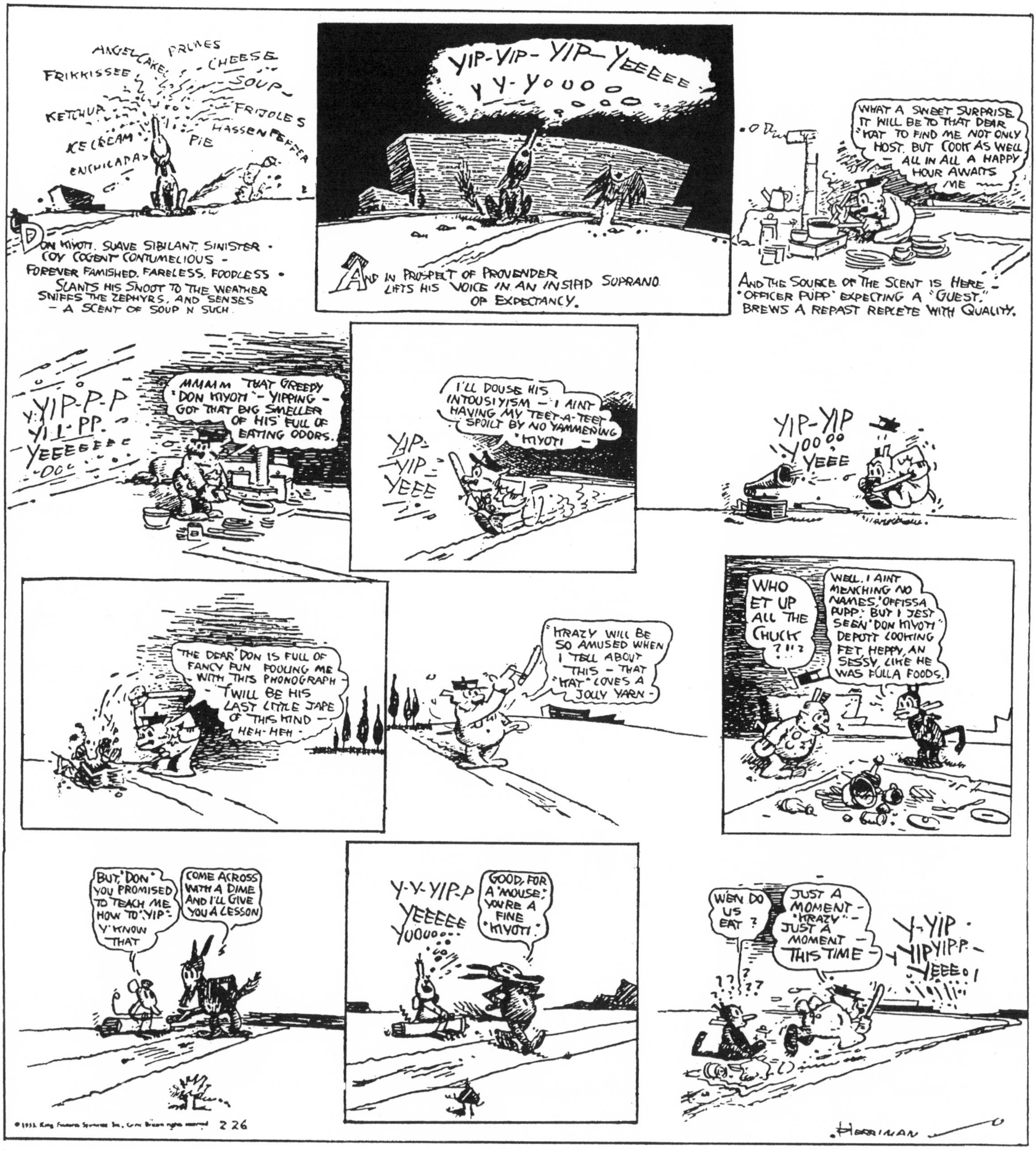
ANGEL CAKE
PRUNES
CHEESE
FRIKKISSEE
SOUP
KETCHUP
FRIJOLES
ICE CREAM
HASSENPFEFFER
PIE
ENCHILADAS
DON KIYOTI. SUAVE SIBILANT. SINISTER - COY COGENT CONTUMELIOUS - FOREVER FAMISHED. FARELESS. FOODLESS - SLANTS HIS SNOOT TO THE WEATHER SNIFFS THE ZEPHYRS, AND SENSES - A SCENT OF SOUP N SUCH.
YIP-YIP- YIP- YEEEEE Y Y- YOUOOO
AND IN PROSPECT OF PROVENDER LIFTS HIS VOICE IN AN INSIPID SOPRANO OF EXPECTANCY.
WHAT A SWEET SURPRISE IT WILL BE TO THAT DEAR 'KAT TO FIND ME NOT ONLY HOST, BUT COOK AS WELL - ALL IN ALL A HAPPY HOUR AWAITS ME
AND THE SOURCE OF THE SCENT IS HERE - "OFFICER PUPP" EXPECTING A "GUEST," BREWS A REPAST REPLETE WITH QUALITY.
Y-YIP-P-P YI-I-PP YEEEEEEE -OOO
MMMM THAT GREEDY 'DON KIYOTI' - YIPPING - GOT THAT BIG SMELLER OF HIS' FULL OF EATING ODORS.
YIP- YIP- YEEE
I'LL DOUSE HIS INTOUSIYISM - I AINT HAVING MY TEET-A-TEET SPOILT BY NO YAMMENING 'KIYOTI'
YIP-YIP YOOOO YEEE
THE DEAR 'DON' IS FULL OF FANCY FUN FOOLING ME WITH THIS PHONOGRAPH - 'TWILL BE HIS LAST LITTLE JAPE OF THIS KIND - HEH-HEH
KRAZY WILL BE SO AMUSED WHEN I TELL ABOUT THIS - THAT 'KAT' LOVES A JOLLY YARN -
WHO ET UP ALL THE CHUCK ?!!?
WELL, I AINT MENCHING NO NAMES, 'OFFISSA PUPP,' BUT I JEST SEEN 'DON KIYOTI' DEPOTT COOKING FET, HEPPY, AN SESSY, LIKE HE WAS FULLA FOODS.
BUT, 'DON' YOU PROMISED TO TEACH ME HOW TO 'YIP' Y'KNOW THAT
COME ACROSS WITH A DIME AND I'LL GIVE YOU A LESSON
Y-Y-YIP-P YEEEEE YOUOOO
GOOD, FOR A 'MOUSE,' YOU'RE A FINE 'KIYOTI.'
WEN DO US EAT ?
JUST A MOMENT - 'KRAZY' - JUST A MOMENT THIS TIME -
Y-YIP YIP YIP-P - YEEE
2 26
HERRIMAN

February 26th, 1933.

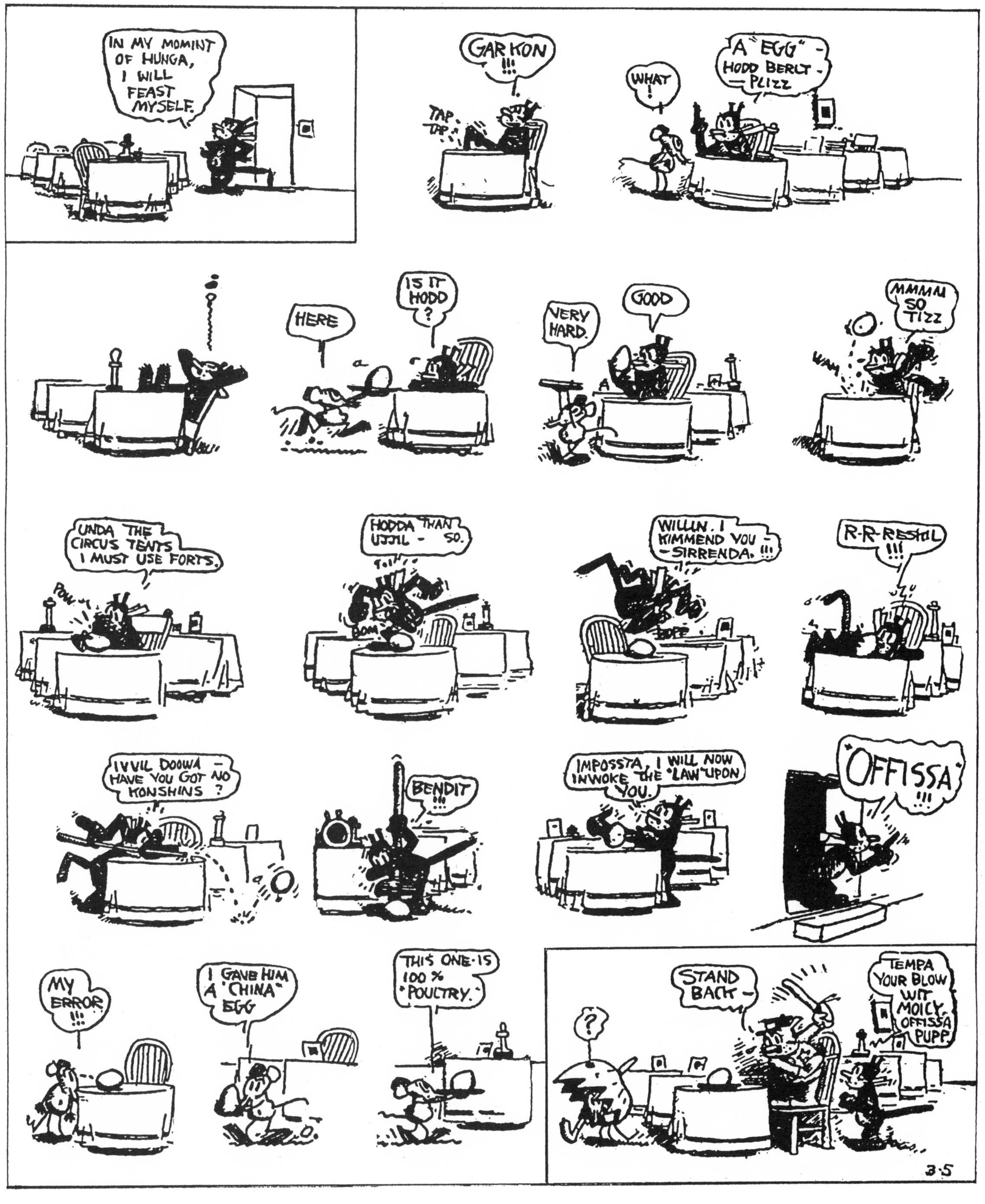
IN MY MOMINT OF HUNGA, I WILL FEAST MYSELF.
GAR KON !!!
TAP TAP
WHAT !
A "EGG" - HODD BERLT - PLIZZ
HERE
IS IT HODD ?
VERY HARD.
GOOD
MMMM SO TIZZ
UNDA THE CIRCUS TENTS I MUST USE FORTS.
POW
HODDA THAN UJJIL - SO.
BOM
WILLIN. I KIMMEND YOU - SIRRENDA. !!!
BOPP
R-R-RESTIL !!!
IVVIL DOOWA - HAVE YOU GOT NO KONSHINS ?
BENDIT !!!
IMPOSSTA, I WILL NOW INVOKE THE "LAW" UPON YOU.
"OFFISSA" !!!
MY ERROR !!!
I GAVE HIM A "CHINA" EGG
THIS ONE IS 100% "POULTRY."
?
STAND BACK -
TEMPA YOUR BLOW WIT MOICY. OFFISSA PUPP
3·5

March 5th, 1933.

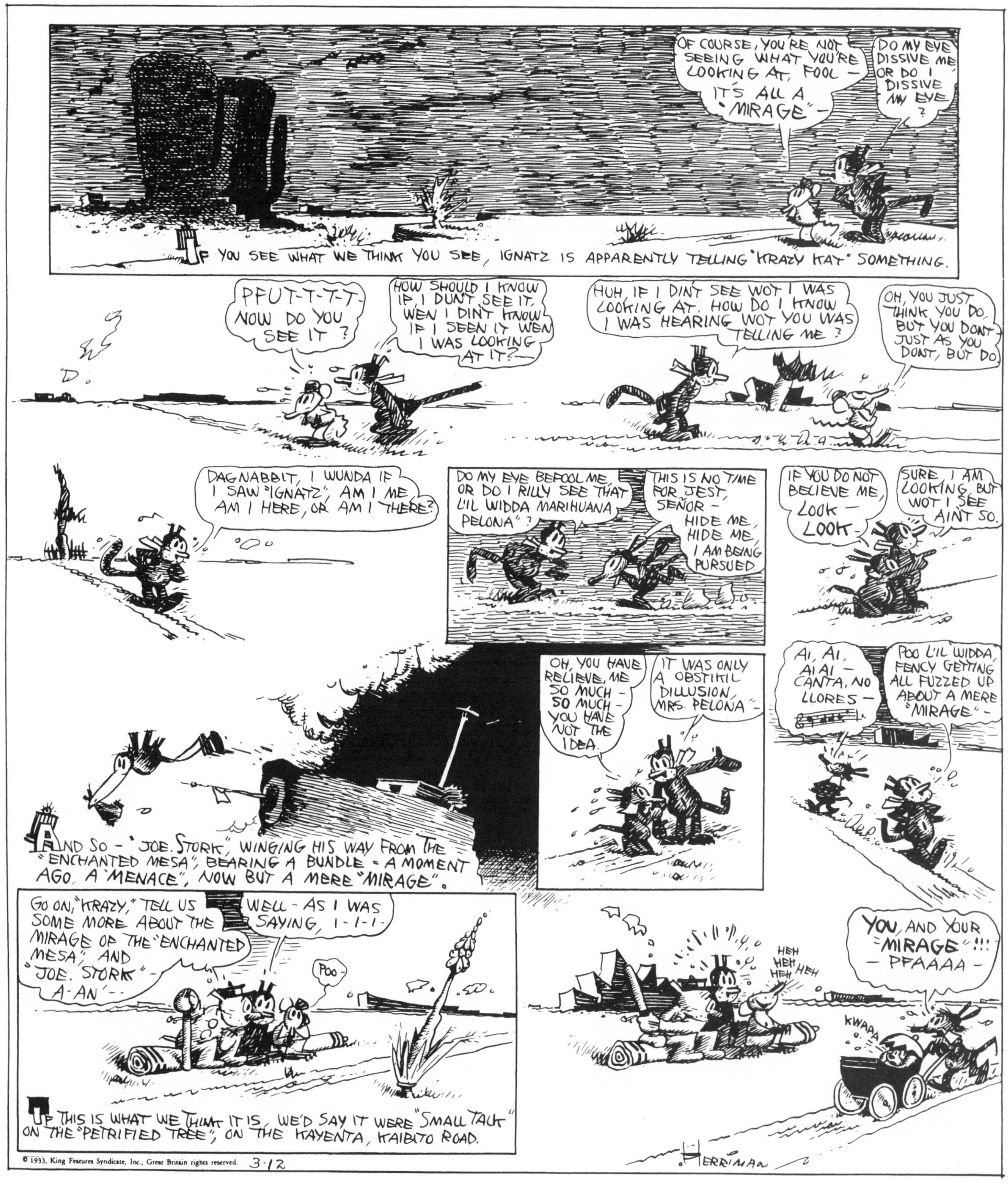
OF COURSE, YOU'RE NOT SEEING WHAT YOU'RE LOOKING AT, FOOL – IT'S ALL A "MIRAGE" –
DO MY EYE DISSIVE ME OR DO I DISSIVE MY EYE ?
IF YOU SEE WHAT WE THINK YOU SEE, IGNATZ IS APPARENTLY TELLING "KRAZY KAT" SOMETHING.
PFUT-T-T-T- NOW DO YOU SEE IT ?
HOW SHOULD I KNOW IF, I DUNT SEE IT, WEN I DIN'T KNOW IF I SEEN IT WEN I WAS LOOKING AT IT? –
HUH, IF I DIN'T SEE WOT I WAS LOOKING AT, HOW DO I KNOW I WAS HEARING WOT YOU WAS TELLING ME ?
OH, YOU JUST THINK YOU DO, BUT YOU DONT – JUST AS YOU DONT, BUT DO.
DAGNABBIT, I WUNDA IF I SAW "IGNATZ", AM I ME, AM I HERE, OR AM I THERE?
DO MY EYE BEFOOL ME, OR DO I RILLY SEE THAT L'IL WIDDA MARIHUANA PELONA" ?
THIS IS NO TIME FOR JEST, SEÑOR – HIDE ME, HIDE ME, I AM BEING PURSUED.
IF YOU DO NOT BELIEVE ME, LOOK LOOK –
SURE, I AM LOOKING, BUT WOT I SEE AINT SO.
AND SO – "JOE. STORK", WINGING HIS WAY FROM THE "ENCHANTED MESA", BEARING A BUNDLE – A MOMENT AGO, A "MENACE", NOW BUT A MERE "MIRAGE".
OH, YOU HAVE RELIEVE, ME SO MUCH – SO MUCH – YOU HAVE NOT THE IDEA.
IT WAS ONLY A OBSTIKIL DILLUSION, MRS. PELONA –
AI, AI, AI AI – CANTA, NO LLORES –
POO L'IL WIDDA, FENCY GETTING ALL FUZZED UP ABOUT A MERE "MIRAGE" –
GO ON, "KRAZY," TELL US SOME MORE ABOUT THE MIRAGE OF THE "ENCHANTED MESA", AND "JOE. STORK" – A-AN –
WELL – AS I WAS SAYING, I-I-I-
POO –
IF THIS IS WHAT WE THINK IT IS, WE'D SAY IT WERE "SMALL TALK" ON THE "PETRIFIED TREE", ON THE KAYENTA, KAIBITO ROAD.
HEH HEH HEH HEH
YOU, AND YOUR "MIRAGE" !!! – PFAAAAA –
KWAAA
© 1933, King Features Syndicate, Inc., Great Britain rights reserved.
3-12
HERRIMAN

March 12th, 1933.

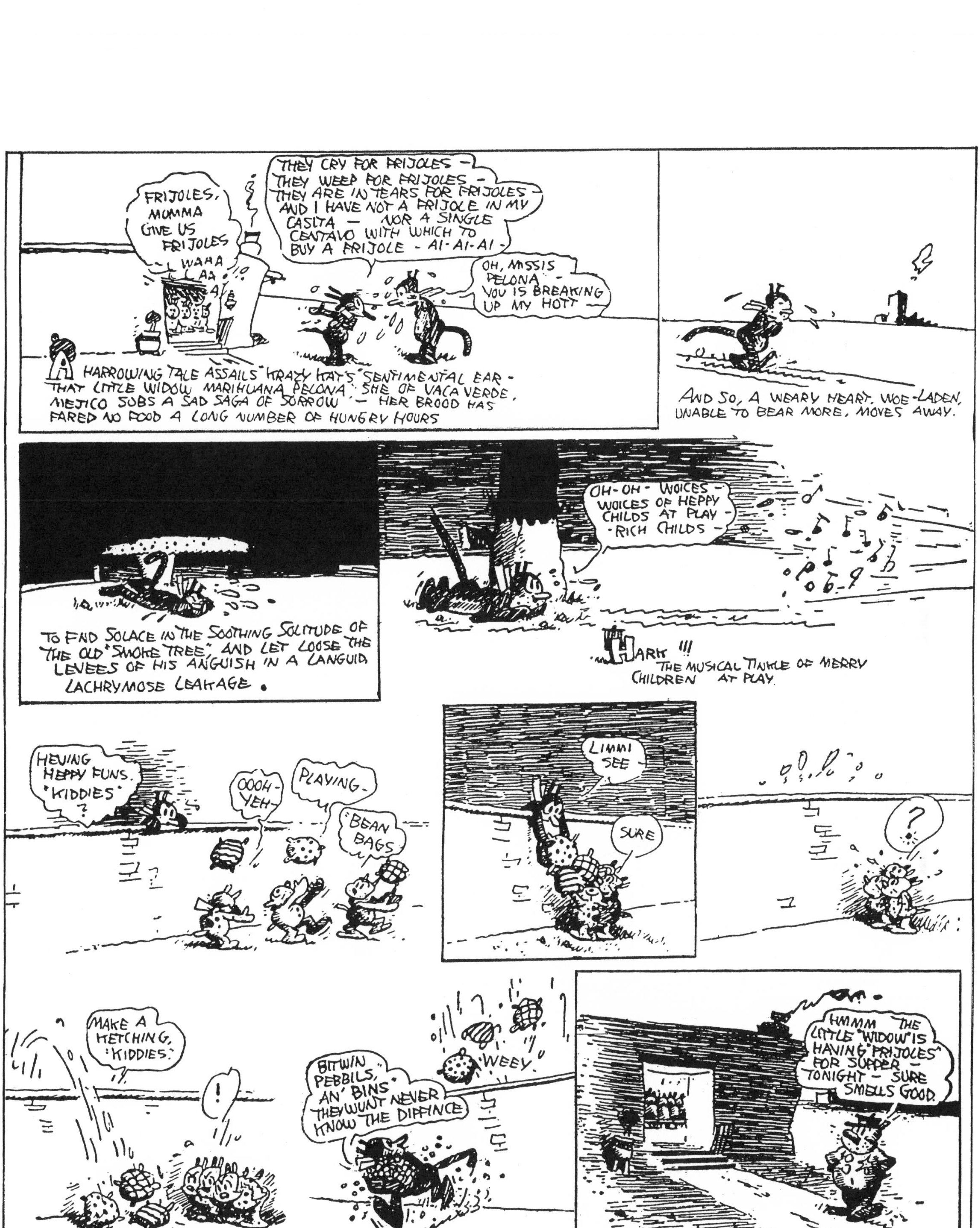
FRIJOLES, MOMMA GIVE US FRIJOLES
WAHA CAA AA A
THEY CRY FOR FRIJOLES - THEY WEEP FOR FRIJOLES - THEY ARE IN TEARS FOR FRIJOLES - AND I HAVE NOT A FRIJOLE IN MY CASITA - NOR A SINGLE CENTAVO WITH WHICH TO BUY A FRIJOLE - AI-AI-AI -
OH, MISSIS PELONA - YOU IS BREAKING UP MY HOTT
A HARROWING TALE ASSAILS KRAZY KAT'S SENTIMENTAL EAR - THAT LITTLE WIDOW MARIHUANA PELONA SHE OF VACA VERDE, MEJICO SOBS A SAD SAGA OF SORROW - HER BROOD HAS FARED NO FOOD A LONG NUMBER OF HUNGRY HOURS
AND SO, A WEARY HEART, WOE-LADEN, UNABLE TO BEAR MORE, MOVES AWAY.
TO FIND SOLACE IN THE SOOTHING SOLITUDE OF THE OLD "SMOKE TREE" AND LET LOOSE THE LEVEES OF HIS ANGUISH IN A LANGUID LACHRYMOSE LEAKAGE.
OH-OH - WOICES - WOICES OF HEPPY CHILDS AT PLAY - RICH CHILDS -
HARK !!! THE MUSICAL TINKLE OF MERRY CHILDREN AT PLAY.
HEVING HEPPY FUNS. "KIDDIES"?
OOOH-YEH
PLAYING -
BEAN BAGS
LIMMI SEE
SURE
?
MAKE A KETCHING, "KIDDIES"
!
BITWIN PEBBILS, AN' BINS THEY WUNT NEVER KNOW THE DIFFINCE
WEEY
HMMM THE LITTLE "WIDOW" IS HAVING "FRIJOLES" FOR SUPPER - TONIGHT - SURE SMELLS GOOD.
HERRIMAN 3-19

March 19th, 1933.

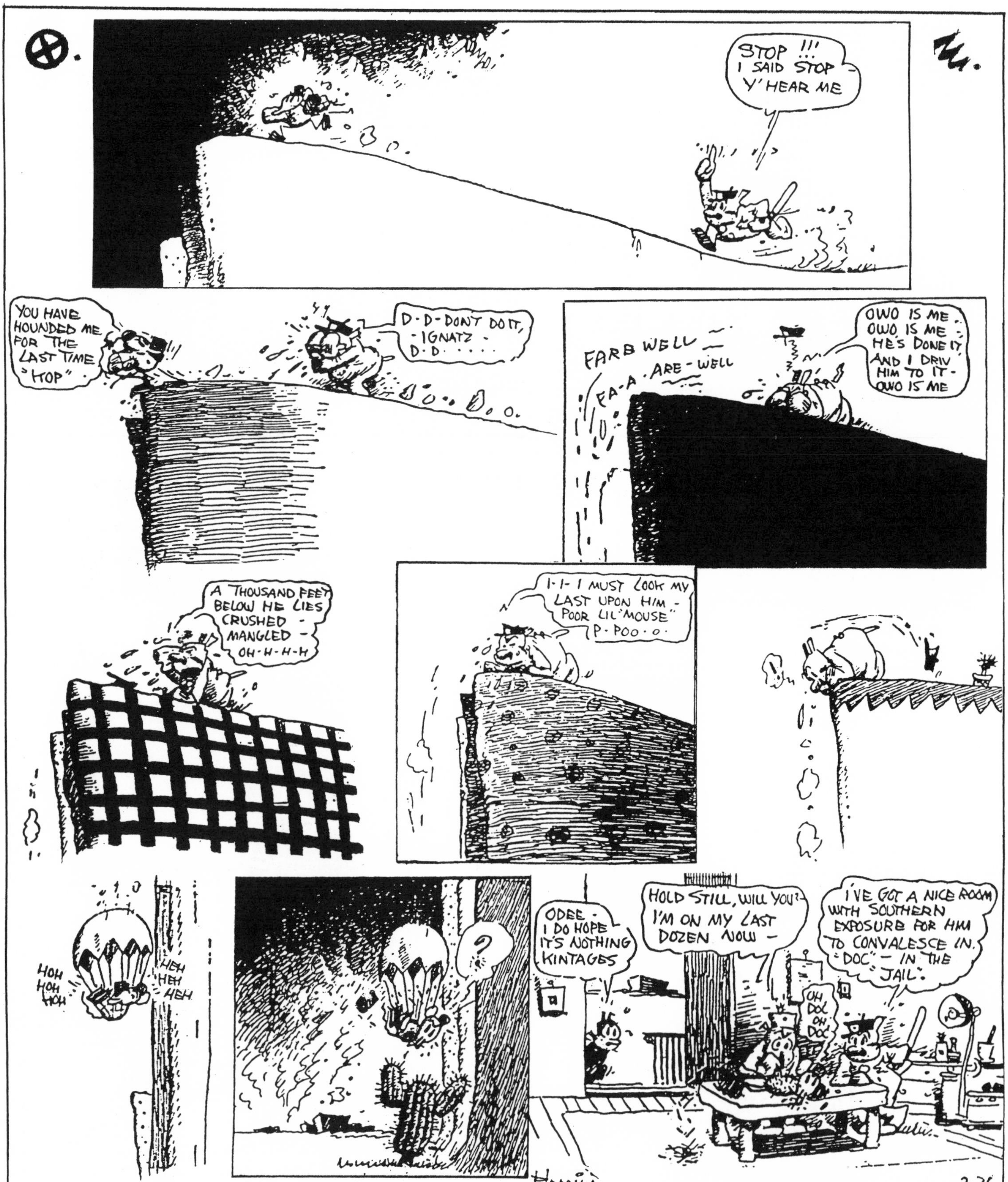
STOP !!!
I SAID STOP -
Y' HEAR ME
YOU HAVE HOUNDED ME FOR THE LAST TIME "HOP" -
D-D-DON'T DO IT, - IGNATZ - D-D . . . . .
FAREWELL —
FA-A-ARE-WELL
OWO IS ME - OWO IS ME - HE'S DONE IT AND I DRIV HIM TO IT - OWO IS ME
A THOUSAND FEET BELOW HE LIES CRUSHED - MANGLED - OH-H-H-H
I-I-I MUST LOOK MY LAST UPON HIM - POOR LIL' MOUSE" P-POO-O-
HOH HOH HOH
HEH HEH HEH
?
ODEE - I DO HOPE IT'S NOTHING KINTAGES
HOLD STILL, WILL YOU? I'M ON MY LAST DOZEN NOW -
OH DOC OH DOC
I'VE GOT A NICE ROOM WITH SOUTHERN EXPOSURE FOR HIM TO CONVALESCE IN, "DOC" - IN THE "JAIL".
HERRIMAN
3·26

March 26th, 1933.

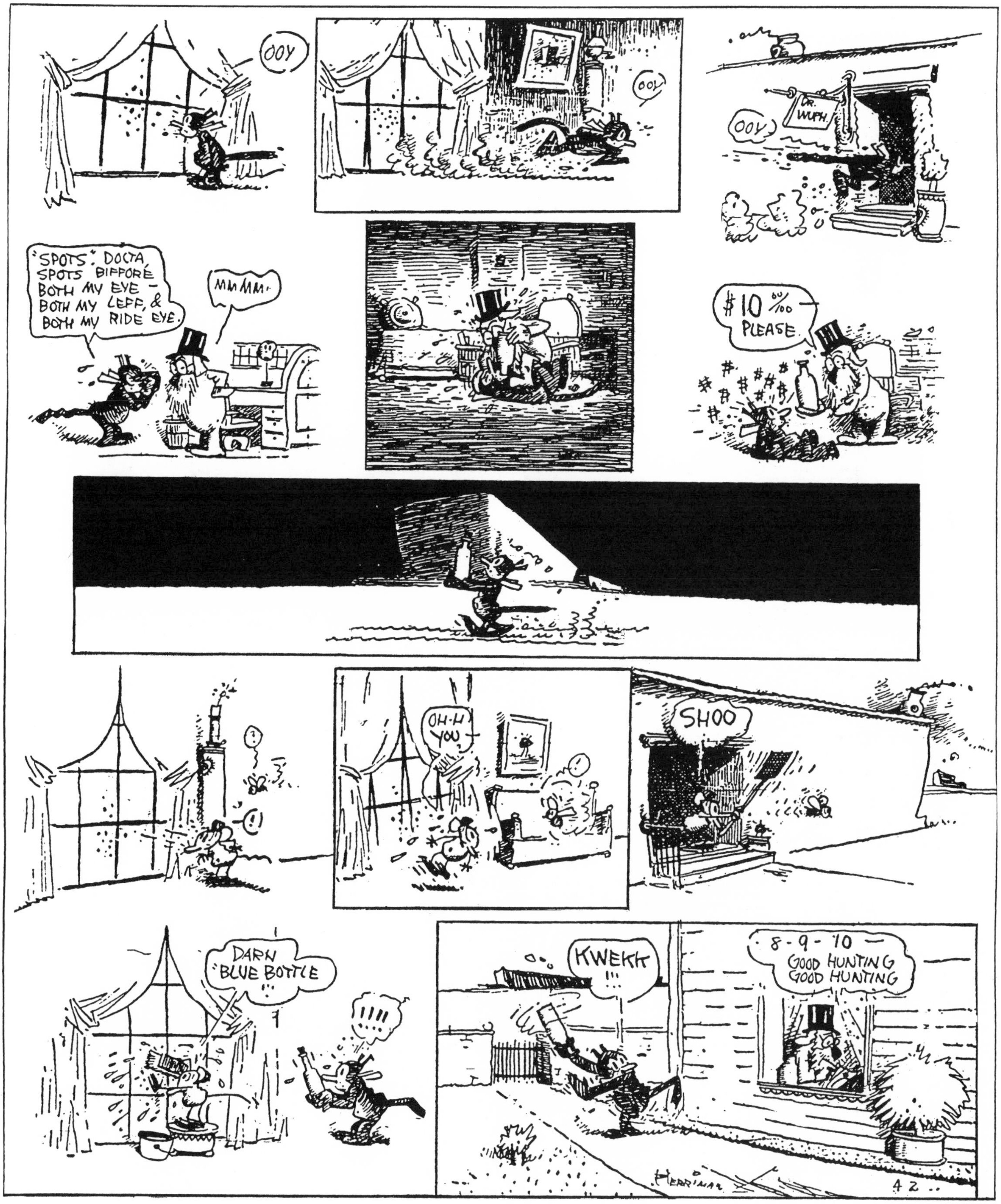
OOY
OOY
DR. WUPH
OOY
"SPOTS" DOCTA, SPOTS BIFFORE BOTH MY EYE — BOTH MY LEFF, & BOTH MY RIDE EYE.
MMMM
$10 00/100 PLEASE
OH-H YOU
SHOO
DARN BLUE BOTTLE
!!!!
KWEKK
8-9-10 GOOD HUNTING GOOD HUNTING
HERRIMAN
4 2

April 2nd, 1933.

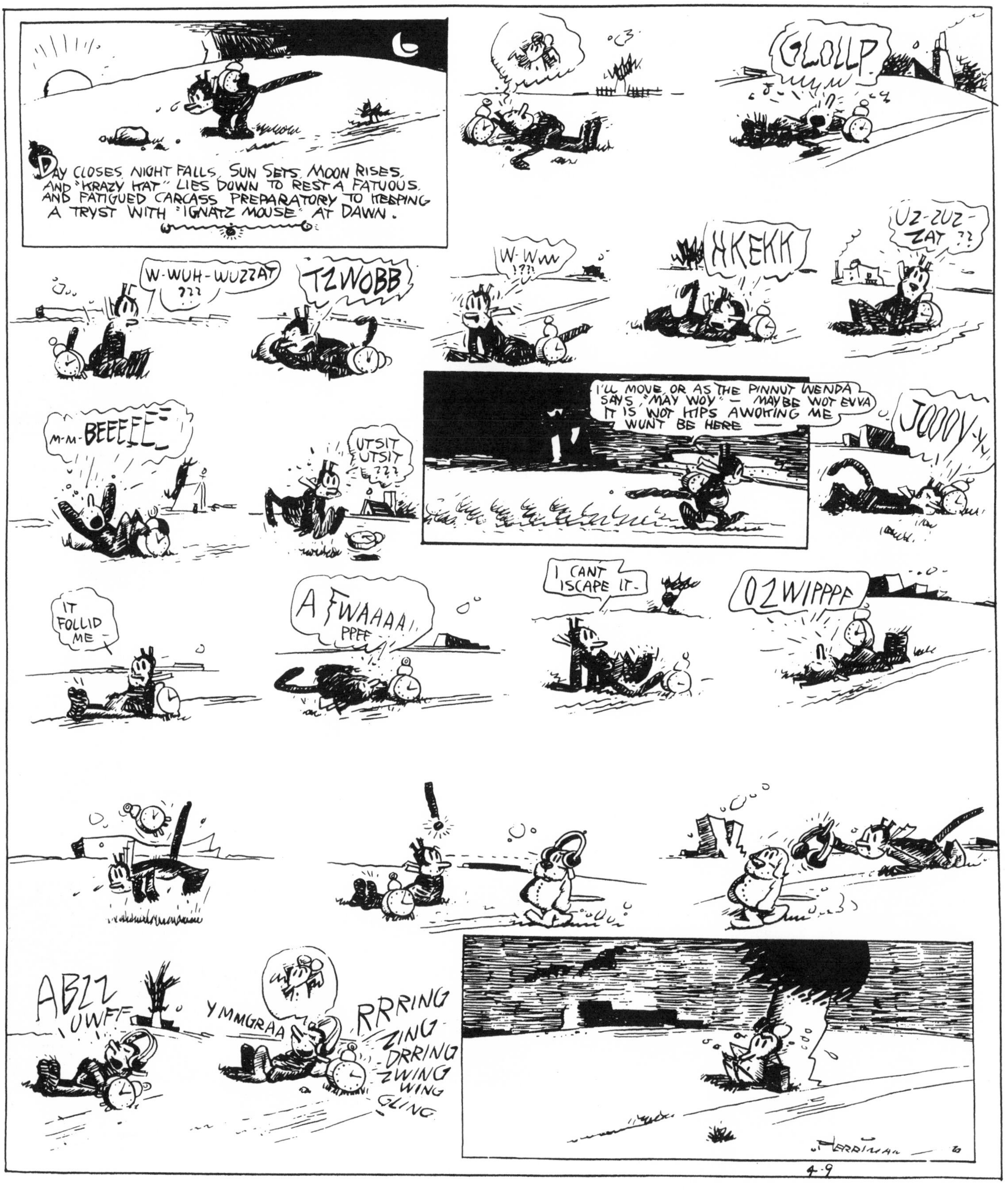
DAY CLOSES. NIGHT FALLS. SUN SETS. MOON RISES. AND "KRAZY KAT" LIES DOWN TO REST A FATUOUS AND FATIGUED CARCASS PREPARATORY TO KEEPING A TRYST WITH "IGNATZ MOUSE" AT DAWN.
GLOLLP
W-WUH-WUZZAT ???
TZWOBB
W-WW !???
HKEKK
UZ-ZUZ ZAT ??
M-M-BEEEEE
UTSIT UTSIT ???
I'LL MOVE OR AS THE PINNUT WENDA SAYS "MAY WOY" — MAYBE WOT EVVA IT IS WOT HIPS AWOKING ME WUNT BE HERE —
JOOOY-Y
IT FOLLID ME
A FWAAAA PPFF
I CANT ISCAPE IT.
OZWIPPPF
ABZZ UWFF
YMMGRAA
RRRING ZING DRRING ZWING WING GLING
HERRIMAN
4-9

April 9th, 1933.

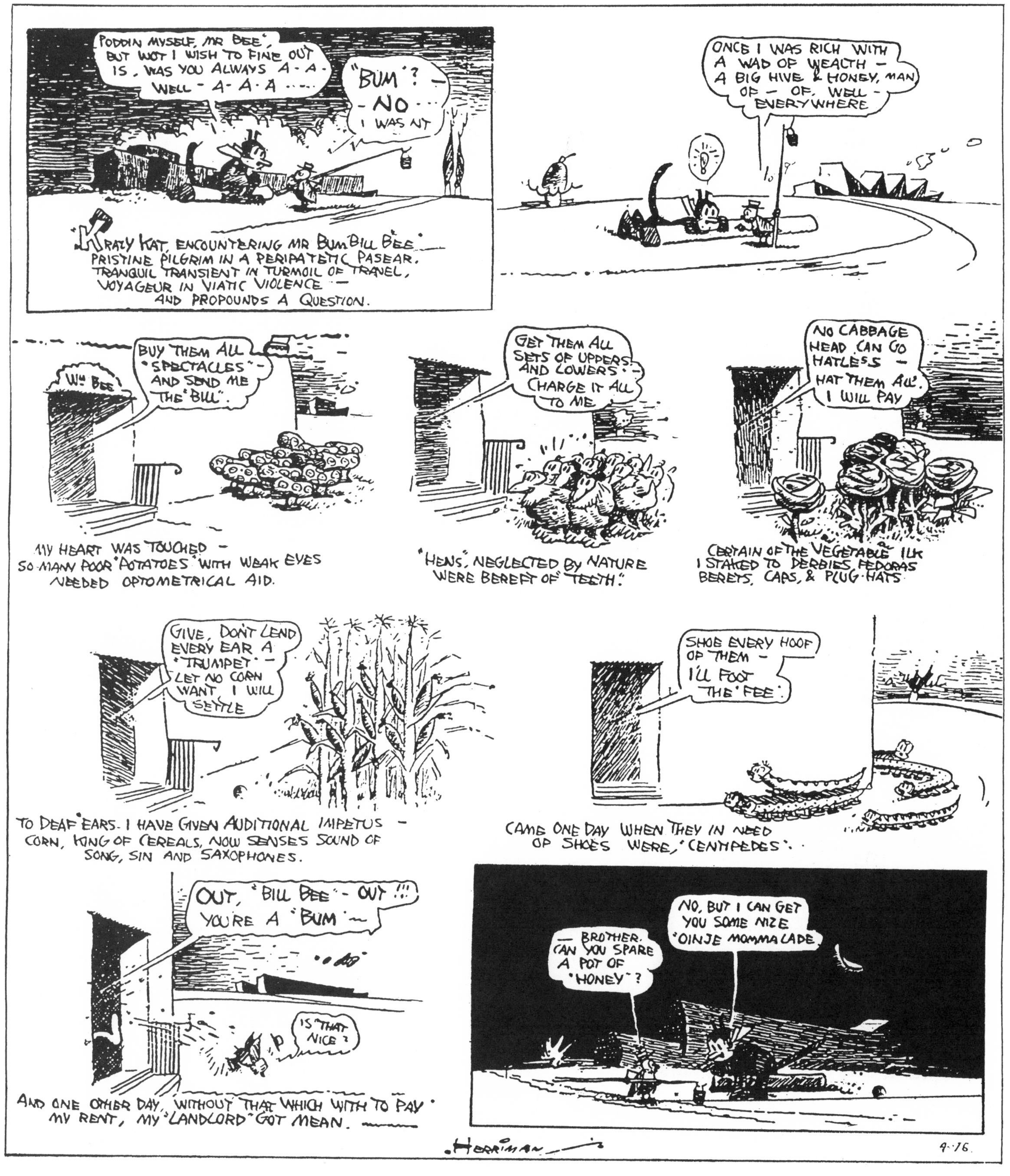
PODDIN MYSELF, MR BEE, BUT WOT I WISH TO FINE OUT IS, WAS YOU ALWAYS A-A WELL-A-A-A.....
"BUM"? - NO - I WAS N'T
"KRAZY KAT, ENCOUNTERING MR BUM BILL BEE" PRISTINE PILGRIM IN A PERIPATETIC PASEAR. TRANQUIL TRANSIENT IN TURMOIL OF TRAVEL, VOYAGEUR IN VIATIC VIOLENCE - AND PROPOUNDS A QUESTION.
ONCE I WAS RICH WITH A WAD OF WEALTH - A BIG HIVE & HONEY, MAN OF - OF, WELL - EVERYWHERE
BUY THEM ALL "SPECTACLES" - AND SEND ME THE "BILL".
W. BEE
MY HEART WAS TOUCHED - SO MANY POOR "POTATOES" WITH WEAK EYES NEEDED OPTOMETRICAL AID.
GET THEM ALL SETS OF UPPERS AND LOWERS - CHARGE IT ALL TO ME
"HENS", NEGLECTED BY NATURE WERE BEREFT OF "TEETH".
NO CABBAGE HEAD CAN GO HATLESS - HAT THEM ALL. I WILL PAY
CERTAIN OF THE VEGETABLE ILK I STAKED TO DERBIES, FEDORAS BERETS, CAPS, & PLUG HATS
GIVE, DON'T LEND EVERY EAR A "TRUMPET" - LET NO CORN WANT, I WILL SETTLE
TO DEAF "EARS" I HAVE GIVEN AUDITIONAL IMPETUS - CORN, KING OF CEREALS, NOW SENSES SOUND OF SONG, SIN AND SAXOPHONES.
SHOE EVERY HOOF OF THEM - I'LL FOOT THE "FEE".
CAME ONE DAY WHEN THEY IN NEED OF SHOES WERE, "CENTIPEDES".
OUT, "BILL BEE" - OUT!!! YOU'RE A "BUM"
IS "THAT" NICE?
AND ONE OTHER DAY, WITHOUT THAT WHICH WITH TO PAY MY RENT, MY "LANDLORD" GOT MEAN.
- BROTHER. CAN YOU SPARE A POT OF "HONEY"?
NO, BUT I CAN GET YOU SOME NIZE "OINJE MOMMA LADE"
HERRIMAN
4-16.

April 16th, 1933.

YEASK -
WESK -
NOTT -
SOTT - I YEMMA LONE.
AH-H- A MOMENT OF ECSTASY -
FRIVOLENCE AND FANTASIA THE GAMUT OF EMOTION
WILD ABANDON
FRAUGHT WITH UNLEASHED ENTHUSIASM
AQUIVER WITH THE THRALLDOM OF RAPTURE
MADDENED WITH THE UNTAMED TRANSPORT OF RHYTHMIC ELATION -
WHAT'S GOING ON HERE ?
SH-H-H-H- Y-Y- YOU WAGABONE - SHHHH!!!
BUSTING OUT WITH AUTHORITY AGAIN - HEH ?
OH, YAAH- AND SINCE WHEN HAS A LOW-LIFE LIKE YOU GOT THE RIGHT TO MINGLE IN THE PRESENCE OF VIBRATILE POESY? - AND NOW
AM I NOT WANTED HERE "OFFICER PUPP"
NOW I HOPE I CAN FINISH MY "FIT" IN PRIVATE
!
HO HO HO HO
JAIL.
HERRIMAN 4-23

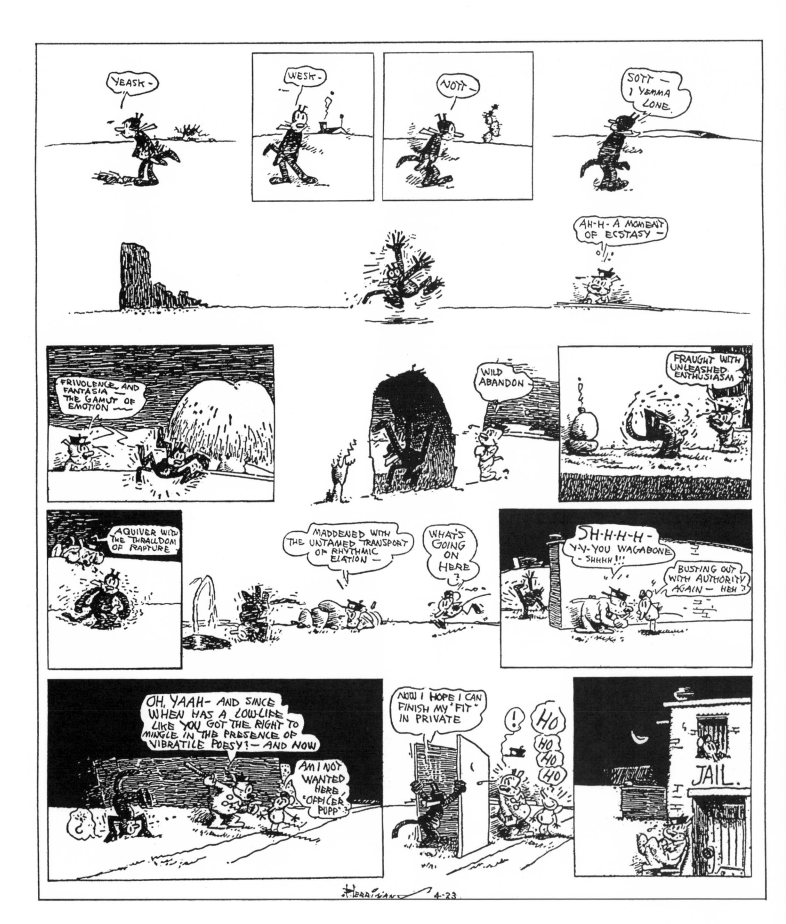

April 23rd, 1933.

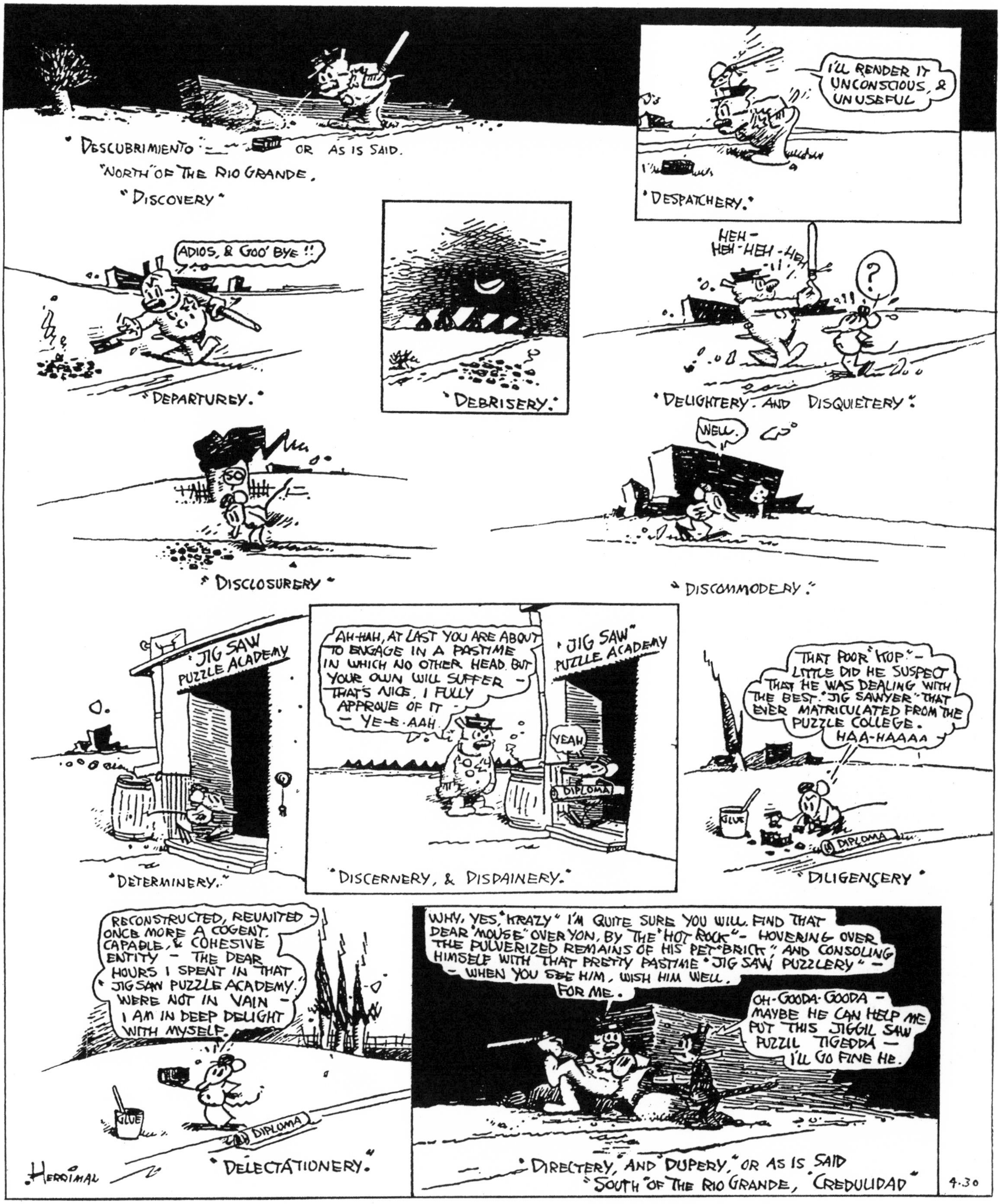

"DESCUBRIMIENTO" — OR AS IS SAID, "NORTH" OF THE RIO GRANDE, "DISCOVERY"
I'LL RENDER IT UNCONSCIOUS, & UNUSEFUL
"DESPATCHERY."
ADIOS, & GOO' BYE !!
"DEPARTUREY."
"DEBRISERY."
HEH-HEH-HEH-HEH
?
"DELIGHTERY" AND "DISQUIETERY"
"DISCLOSUREY"
WELL.
"DISCOMMODERY."
"JIG SAW" PUZZLE ACADEMY
"DETERMINERY."
AH-HAH, AT LAST YOU ARE ABOUT TO ENGAGE IN A PASTIME IN WHICH NO OTHER HEAD BUT YOUR OWN WILL SUFFER — THAT'S NICE. I FULLY APPROVE OF IT — YE-E-AAH.
YEAH
DIPLOMA
"DISCERNERY, & DISDAINERY."
THAT POOR "KOP" — LITTLE DID HE SUSPECT THAT HE WAS DEALING WITH THE BEST "JIG SAWYER" THAT EVER MATRICULATED FROM THE PUZZLE COLLEGE. HAA-HAAAA
GLUE
"DILIGENCERY"
RECONSTRUCTED, REUNITED ONCE MORE A COGENT, CAPABLE, & COHESIVE ENTITY — THE DEAR HOURS I SPENT IN THAT "JIG SAW PUZZLE ACADEMY" WERE NOT IN VAIN — I AM IN DEEP DELIGHT WITH MYSELF.
"DELECTATIONERY."
HERRIMAN
WHY, YES, "KRAZY" I'M QUITE SURE YOU WILL FIND THAT DEAR "MOUSE" OVER YON, BY THE "HOT ROCK" — HOVERING OVER THE PULVERIZED REMAINS OF HIS PET "BRICK" AND CONSOLING HIMSELF WITH THAT PRETTY PASTIME "JIG SAW PUZZLERY" — — WHEN YOU SEE HIM, WISH HIM WELL FOR ME.
OH-GOODA-GOODA — MAYBE HE CAN HELP ME PUT THIS JIGGIL SAW PUZZIL TIGEDDA — I'LL GO FINE HE.
"DIRECTERY" AND "DUPERY," OR AS IS SAID "SOUTH" OF THE RIO GRANDE, "CREDULIDAD"
4.30

April 30th, 1933.

IT OFFERS SHELTER IT GIVES UMBRAGE, AND WITH IT ALL, IT IS EASY TO FIND.
DZIL-LITZIN, KNOWN TO THE KOSMOPOLITE OF KAYENTA, KAIBITO, & KOKONINO AS "BLACK MOUNTAIN" LOOKS DOWN UPON "MUSHROOM ROCK", AND "IGNATZ MOUSE" ALSO LOOKS UPON IT WITH KOGENT, AND KOHESIVE KONTEMPLATION
NOW TO PLEASE MYSELF WITH A "TRYST" WITH THAT "KAT" —
I'M SO GLAD YOU CAME BY MRS KWAKK-WAKK - I WONDER WOULD YOU FAVOR ME BY GIVING THIS NOTE TO "KRAZY KAT"?
IT WOULD GIVE ME A NICE JOY TO RENDER YOU SUCH A SERVICE MR MOUSE
LET COME THE NIGHT, AND BEN THE MOON - - I WILL ANNOINT THAT KAT'S BROW WITH A BONNIE BRICK
MITT ME AT THE "MUSHAROON" HE SAID - MITT ME AT THE "MUSHAROON" WITCH MUSHAROON"
BUT WITH THE NIGHT A MILLION MUSHROOMS, MINIONS OF THE MOON, RISE TO FEAST IN FLORID FUNGUSHOOD
SOMETIMES SOMETIMES HE FETCHES A "JOKE" TOO FUR - MAKES ME SO DOWN MEDD - HIM, AN' HIS "MUSHAROON" PFAAAAAAA
THE MOON EBBS, WANES, AND WAXES WEAK, AND —— SINKS,
PFUI !!!
HUH, HE IS HERE - I THOUGHT MRS. KWAKK WAKK WAS JUST GABBING
UPS THE "SUN", AND A MYRIAD MUSHROOMS FADE, AND A "MOUSE" MEDITATES
UPON THE { FRETFUL FICKLENESS OF FORTUNE, AND - THE FATUOUS FUMBLES OF FATE.
5.7.

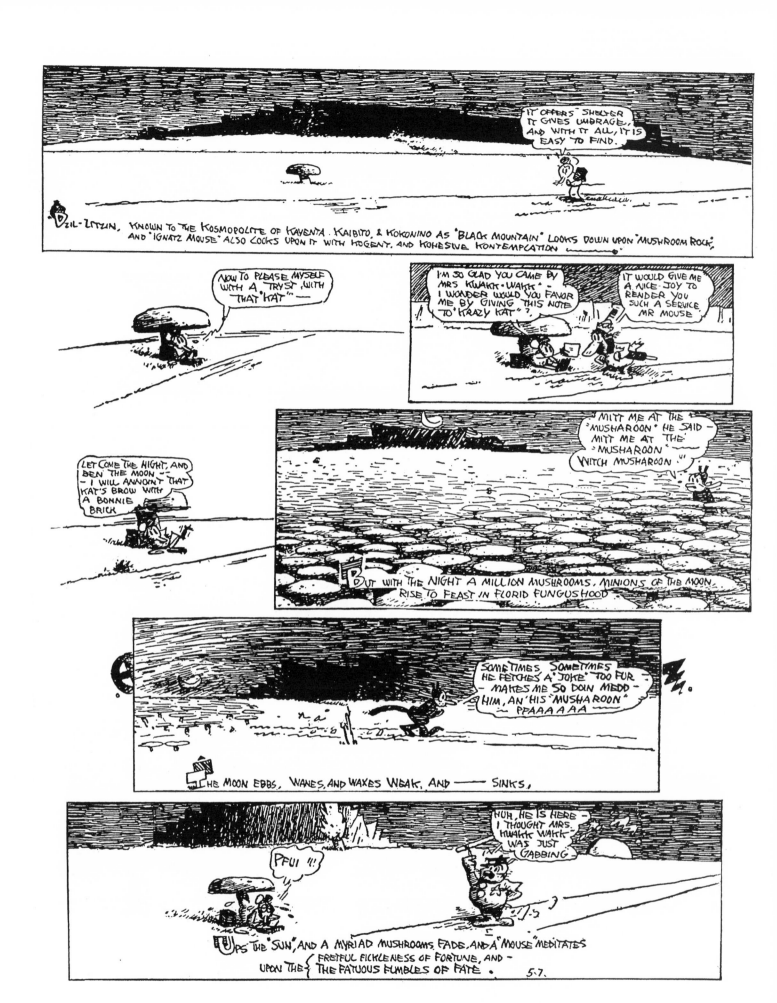

May 7th, 1933.

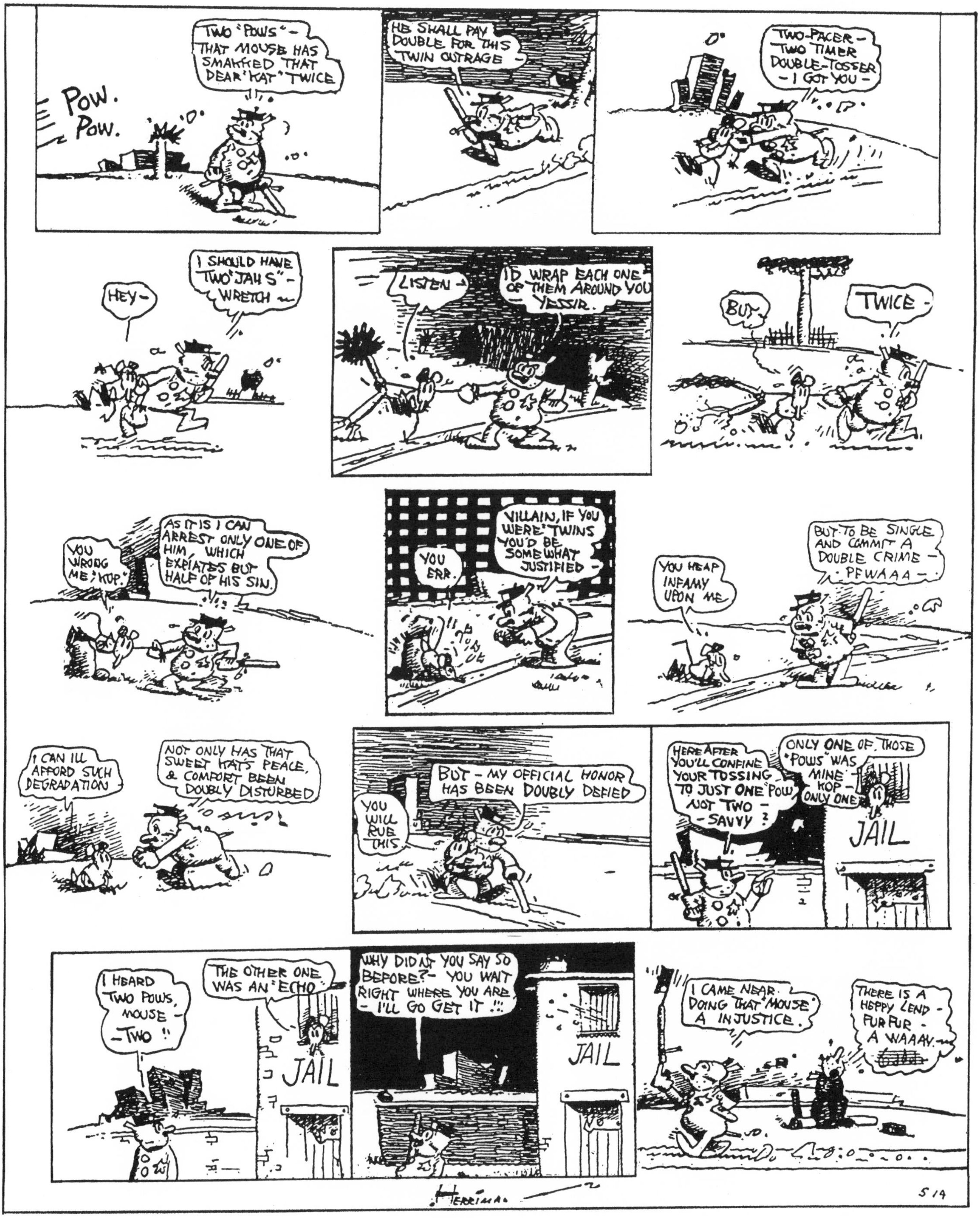

POW.
POW.
TWO "POWS" - THAT MOUSE HAS SMAKKED THAT DEAR "KAT" TWICE
HE SHALL PAY DOUBLE FOR THIS TWIN OUTRAGE -
TWO-FACER - TWO TIMER DOUBLE-TOSSER - I GOT YOU -
HEY -
I SHOULD HAVE TWO "JAHS" - WRETCH -
LISTEN -
I'D WRAP EACH ONE OF THEM AROUND YOU YESSIR.
BUT -
TWICE -
YOU WRONG ME, "KOP."
AS IT IS I CAN ARREST ONLY ONE OF HIM, WHICH EXPIATES BUT HALF OF HIS SIN.
YOU ERR.
VILLAIN, IF YOU WERE TWINS YOU'D BE SOMEWHAT JUSTIFIED -
YOU HEAP INFAMY UPON ME
BUT TO BE SINGLE AND COMMIT A DOUBLE CRIME - PFWAAA -
I CAN ILL AFFORD SUCH DEGRADATION
NOT ONLY HAS THAT SWEET HAT'S PEACE, & COMFORT BEEN DOUBLY DISTURBED
YOU WILL RUE THIS.
BUT - MY OFFICIAL HONOR HAS BEEN DOUBLY DEFIED
HERE AFTER YOU'LL CONFINE YOUR TOSSING TO JUST ONE POW NOT TWO - SAVVY ?
ONLY ONE OF THOSE "POWS" WAS MINE - KOP - ONLY ONE.
JAIL
I HEARD TWO POWS, MOUSE - TWO !!
THE OTHER ONE WAS AN "ECHO"
JAIL
WHY DIDN'T YOU SAY SO BEFORE? - YOU WAIT RIGHT WHERE YOU ARE - I'LL GO GET IT !!!
JAIL
I CAME NEAR DOING THAT "MOUSE" A INJUSTICE.
THERE IS A HEPPY LEND - FUR FUR - A WAAAY.
HERRIMAN
5 14

May 14th, 1933.

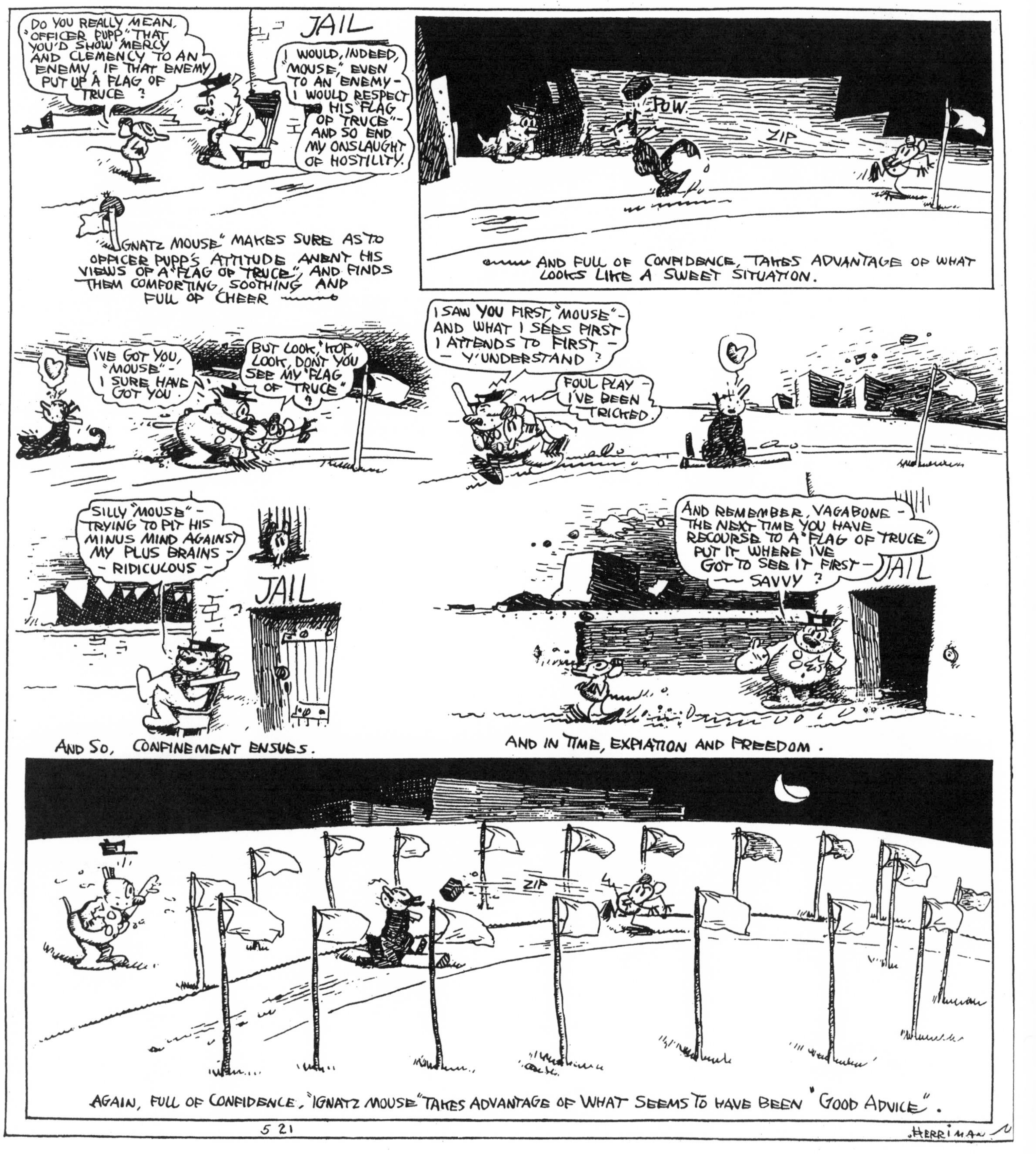
DO YOU REALLY MEAN, "OFFICER PUPP," THAT YOU'D SHOW MERCY AND CLEMENCY TO AN ENEMY, IF THAT ENEMY PUT UP A FLAG OF TRUCE ?
JAIL
I WOULD, INDEED, "MOUSE," EVEN TO AN ENEMY - I WOULD RESPECT HIS "FLAG OF TRUCE" - AND SO END MY ONSLAUGHT OF HOSTILITY.
"IGNATZ MOUSE" MAKES SURE AS TO OFFICER PUPP'S ATTITUDE ANENT HIS VIEWS OF A "FLAG OF TRUCE", AND FINDS THEM COMFORTING, SOOTHING AND FULL OF CHEER
POW
ZIP
AND FULL OF CONFIDENCE, TAKES ADVANTAGE OF WHAT LOOKS LIKE A SWEET SITUATION.
I'VE GOT YOU, "MOUSE" - I SURE HAVE GOT YOU.
BUT LOOK, "KOP" LOOK, DON'T YOU SEE MY "FLAG OF TRUCE" ?
I SAW YOU FIRST, "MOUSE" - AND WHAT I SEES FIRST I ATTENDS TO FIRST - - Y'UNDERSTAND ?
FOUL PLAY - I'VE BEEN TRICKED.
SILLY "MOUSE" - TRYING TO PIT HIS MINUS MIND AGAINST MY PLUS BRAINS - - RIDICULOUS -
JAIL
AND SO, CONFINEMENT ENSUES.
AND REMEMBER, VAGABONE - THE NEXT TIME YOU HAVE RECOURSE TO A "FLAG OF TRUCE" PUT IT WHERE I'VE GOT TO SEE IT FIRST - - SAVVY ?
JAIL
AND IN TIME, EXPIATION AND FREEDOM.
ZIP
AGAIN, FULL OF CONFIDENCE, "IGNATZ MOUSE" TAKES ADVANTAGE OF WHAT SEEMS TO HAVE BEEN "GOOD ADVICE".
5 21
HERRIMAN

May 21st, 1933.

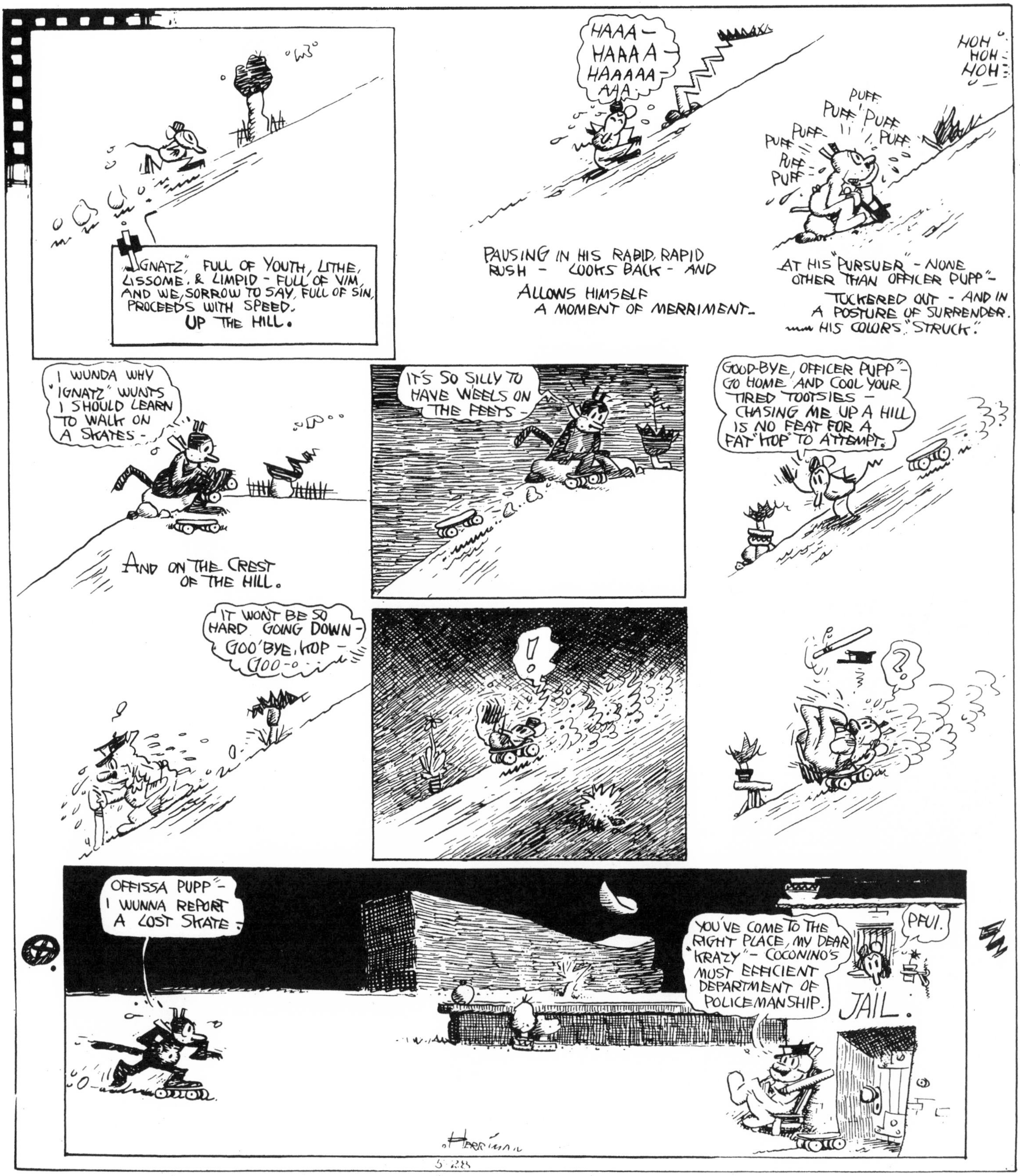
"IGNATZ", FULL OF YOUTH, LITHE, LISSOME, & LIMPID - FULL OF VIM, AND WE, SORROW TO SAY, FULL OF SIN, PROCEEDS WITH SPEED. UP THE HILL.
HAAA - HAAAA - HAAAAA - AAA
PAUSING IN HIS RABID, RAPID RUSH - LOOKS BACK - AND ALLOWS HIMSELF A MOMENT OF MERRIMENT -
HOH HOH HOH
PUFF PUFF PUFF PUFF PUFF PUFF PUFF PUFF
AT HIS "PURSUER" - NONE OTHER THAN OFFICER PUPP - TUCKERED OUT - AND IN A POSTURE OF SURRENDER. HIS COLORS "STRUCK."
I WUNDA WHY "IGNATZ" WUNTS I SHOULD LEARN TO WALK ON A SKATES -
AND ON THE CREST OF THE HILL.
IT'S SO SILLY TO HAVE WEELS ON THE FEETS -
GOOD-BYE, OFFICER PUPP - GO HOME AND COOL YOUR TIRED TOOTSIES - CHASING ME UP A HILL IS NO FEAT FOR A FAT "KOP" TO ATTEMPT.
IT WON'T BE SO HARD GOING DOWN - GOO'BYE, KOP - GOO-O
!
?
OFFISSA PUPP - I WUNNA REPORT A LOST SKATE -
YOU'VE COME TO THE RIGHT PLACE, MY DEAR "KRAZY" - COCONINO'S MUST EFFICIENT DEPARTMENT OF POLICEMANSHIP.
PFUI.
JAIL.
Herriman
5 28

May 28th, 1933.

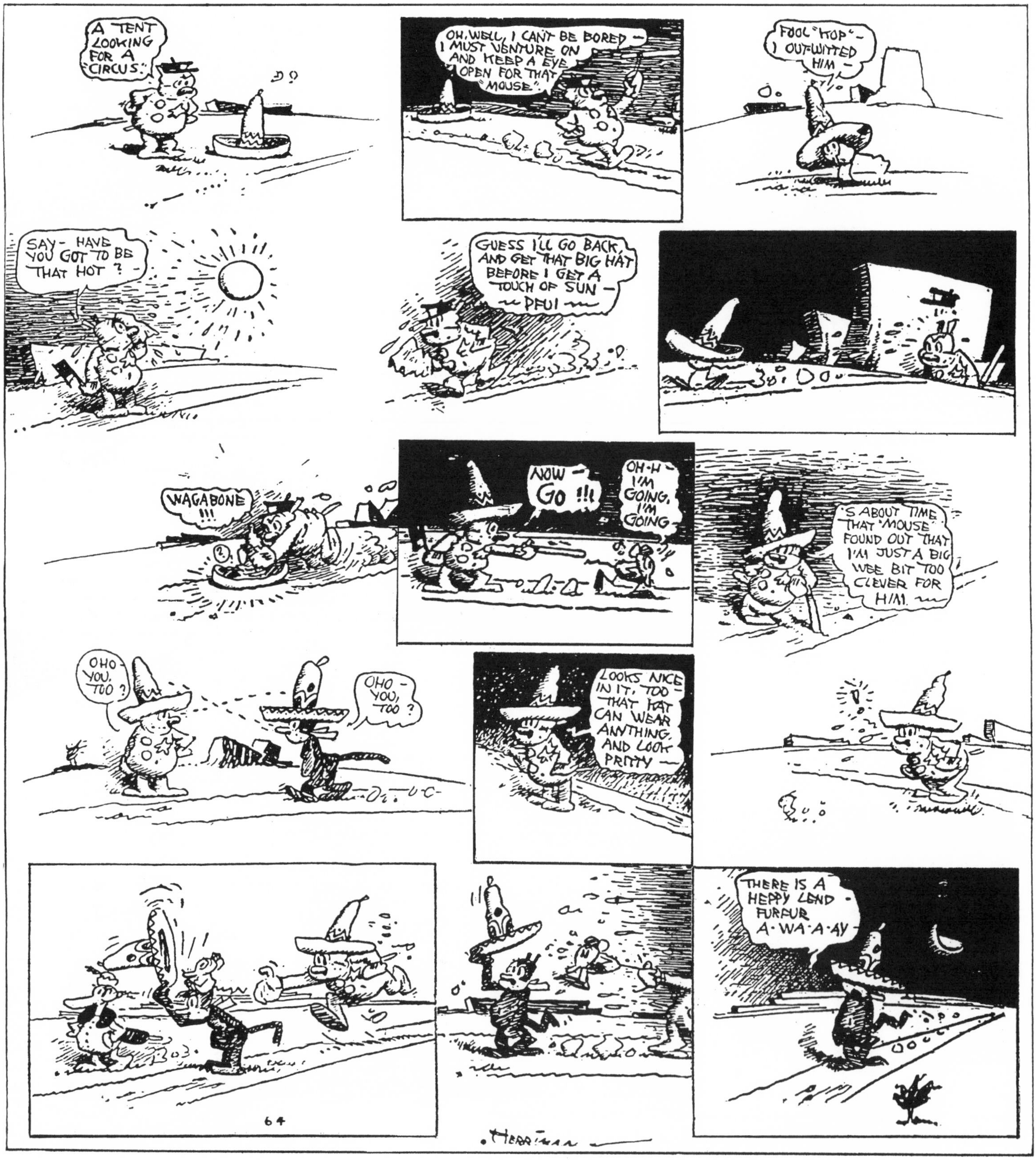
A TENT LOOKING FOR A "CIRCUS".
OH, WELL, I CAN'T BE BORED — I MUST VENTURE ON AND KEEP A EYE OPEN FOR THAT "MOUSE".
FOOL "KOP" — I OUT-WITTED HIM —
SAY — HAVE YOU GOT TO BE THAT HOT ?
GUESS I'LL GO BACK AND GET THAT BIG HAT BEFORE I GET A TOUCH OF SUN —
PFUI
WAGABONE !!!
NOW — GO !!!
OH-H I'M GOING, I'M GOING —
'S ABOUT TIME THAT 'MOUSE' FOUND OUT THAT I'M JUST A BIG WEE BIT TOO CLEVER FOR HIM.
OHO YOU, TOO ?
OHO — YOU, TOO ?
LOOKS NICE IN IT, TOO — THAT KAT CAN WEAR ANYTHING AND LOOK PRITTY —
THERE IS A HEPPY LEND FURFUR A-WA-A-AY —
64
HERRIMAN

June 4th, 1933.

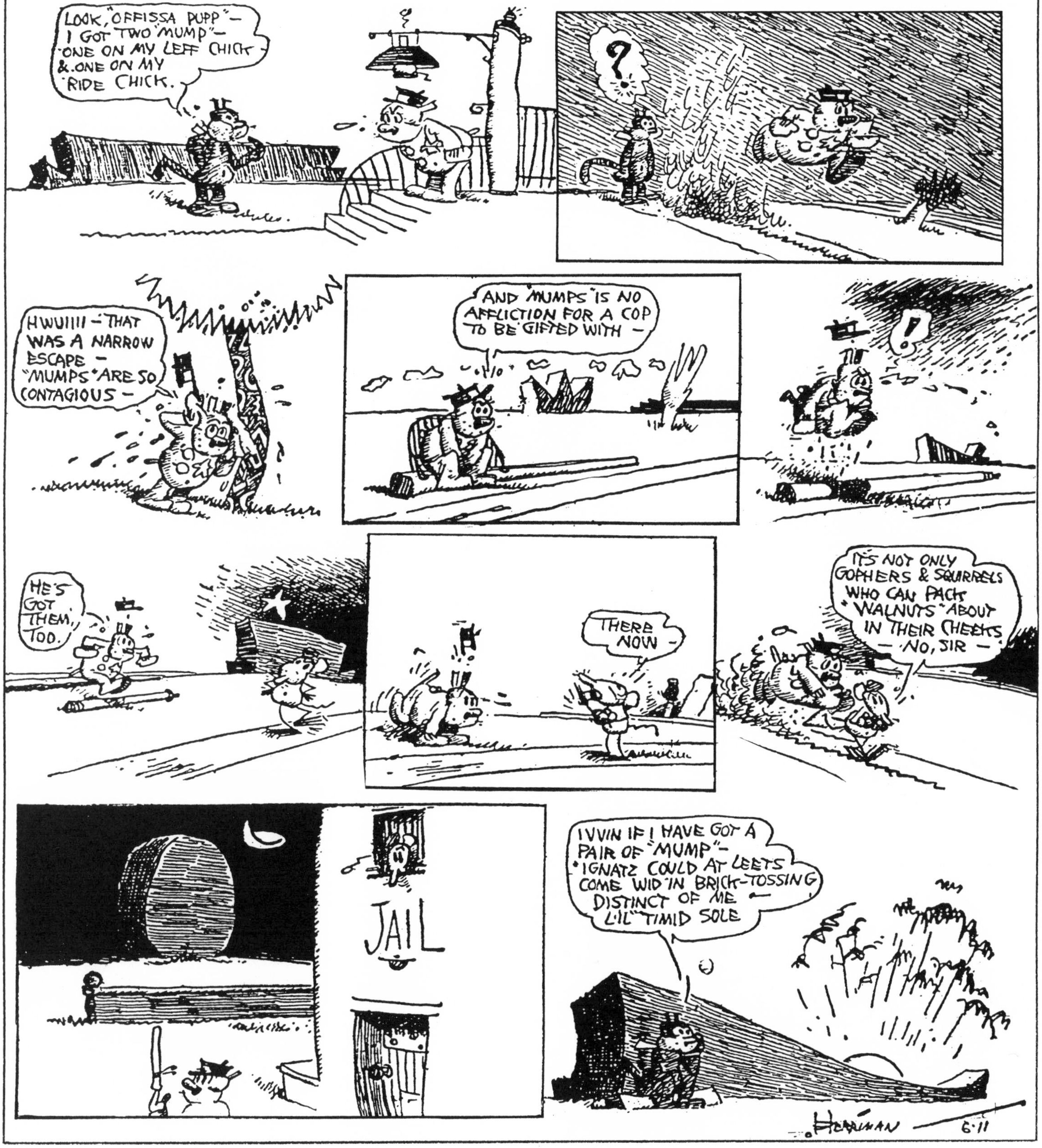
LOOK, "OFFISSA PUPP" – I GOT TWO "MUMP" – ONE ON MY LEFF CHICK &. ONE ON MY RIDE CHICK.
?
HWUIIII – THAT WAS A NARROW ESCAPE – "MUMPS" ARE SO CONTAGIOUS –
AND "MUMPS" IS NO AFFLICTION FOR A COP TO BE GIFTED WITH –
!
HE'S GOT THEM, TOO.
THERE NOW –
IT'S NOT ONLY GOPHERS & SQUIRRELS WHO CAN PACK "WALNUTS" ABOUT IN THEIR CHEEKS – NO, SIR –
JAIL
IVVIN IF I HAVE GOT A PAIR OF "MUMP" – IGNATZ COULD AT LEETS COME WID'IN BRICK-TOSSING DISTINCT OF ME – L'IL' TIMID SOLE
HERRIMAN 6·11

June 11th, 1933.

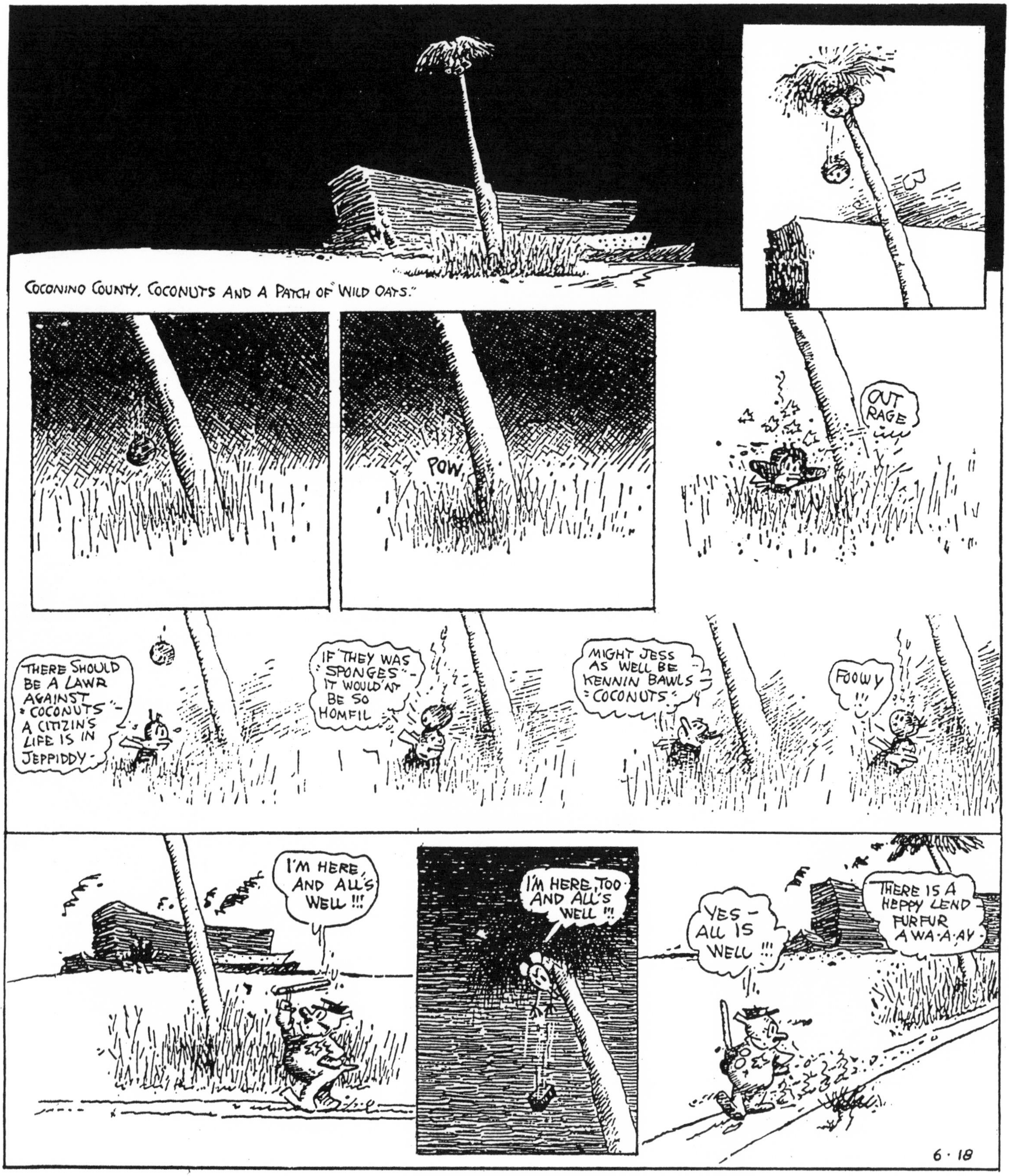
COCONINO COUNTY, COCONUTS AND A PATCH OF "WILD OATS."
POW
OUT RAGE
THERE SHOULD BE A LAWR AGAINST COCONUTS - A CITIZIN'S LIFE IS IN JEPPIDDY -
IF THEY WAS SPONGES IT WOULD'N BE SO HOMFIL
MIGHT JESS AS WELL BE KENNIN BAWLS COCONUTS
FOOWY !!!
I'M HERE, AND ALL'S WELL !!!
I'M HERE, TOO AND ALL'S WELL !!!
YES - ALL IS WELL !!!
THERE IS A HEPPY LEND FURFUR A WA-A-AY
6 · 18

June 18th, 1933.

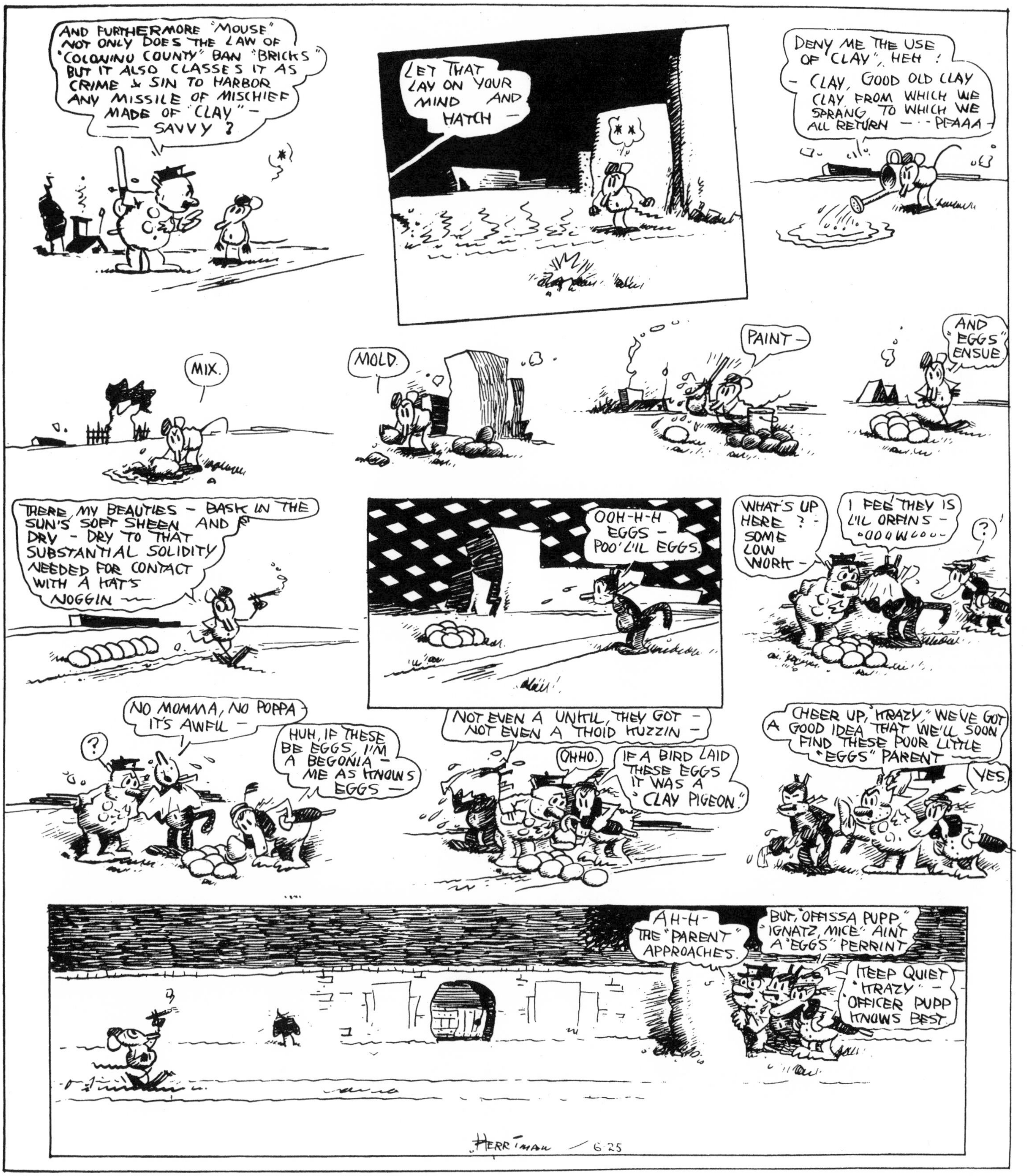
AND FURTHERMORE "MOUSE" NOT ONLY DOES THE LAW OF "COCONINO COUNTY" BAN "BRICKS" BUT IT ALSO CLASSES IT AS CRIME & SIN TO HARBOR ANY MISSILE OF MISCHIEF MADE OF "CLAY" — SAVVY ?
LET THAT LAY ON YOUR MIND AND HATCH —
DENY ME THE USE OF "CLAY", HEH ! — CLAY, GOOD OLD CLAY CLAY, FROM WHICH WE SPRANG, TO WHICH WE ALL RETURN — PFAAA —
MIX.
MOLD.
PAINT —
AND "EGGS" ENSUE
THERE, MY BEAUTIES — BASK IN THE SUN'S SOFT SHEEN AND DRY — DRY TO THAT SUBSTANTIAL SOLIDITY NEEDED FOR CONTACT WITH A KAT'S NOGGIN —
OOH-H-H EGGS — POO' L'IL EGGS.
WHAT'S UP HERE ? — SOME LOW WORK —
I FEE' THEY IS LI'L ORFINS — OOOW
?
?
NO MOMMA, NO POPPA — IT'S AWFUL —
HUH, IF THESE BE EGGS, I'M A BEGONIA — ME AS KNOWS EGGS —
NOT EVEN A UNKIL, THEY GOT — NOT EVEN A THOID KUZZIN —
OHHO.
IF A BIRD LAID THESE EGGS IT WAS A "CLAY PIGEON."
CHEER UP, "KRAZY," WE'VE GOT A GOOD IDEA THAT WE'LL SOON FIND THESE POOR LITTLE "EGGS" PARENT
YES.
AH-H- THE "PARENT" APPROACHES.
BUT, "OFFISSA PUPP" IGNATZ, MICE AIN'T A "EGGS" PERRINT
KEEP QUIET "KRAZY" — "OFFICER PUPP" KNOWS BEST.
HERRIMAN — 6.25

June 25th, 1933.

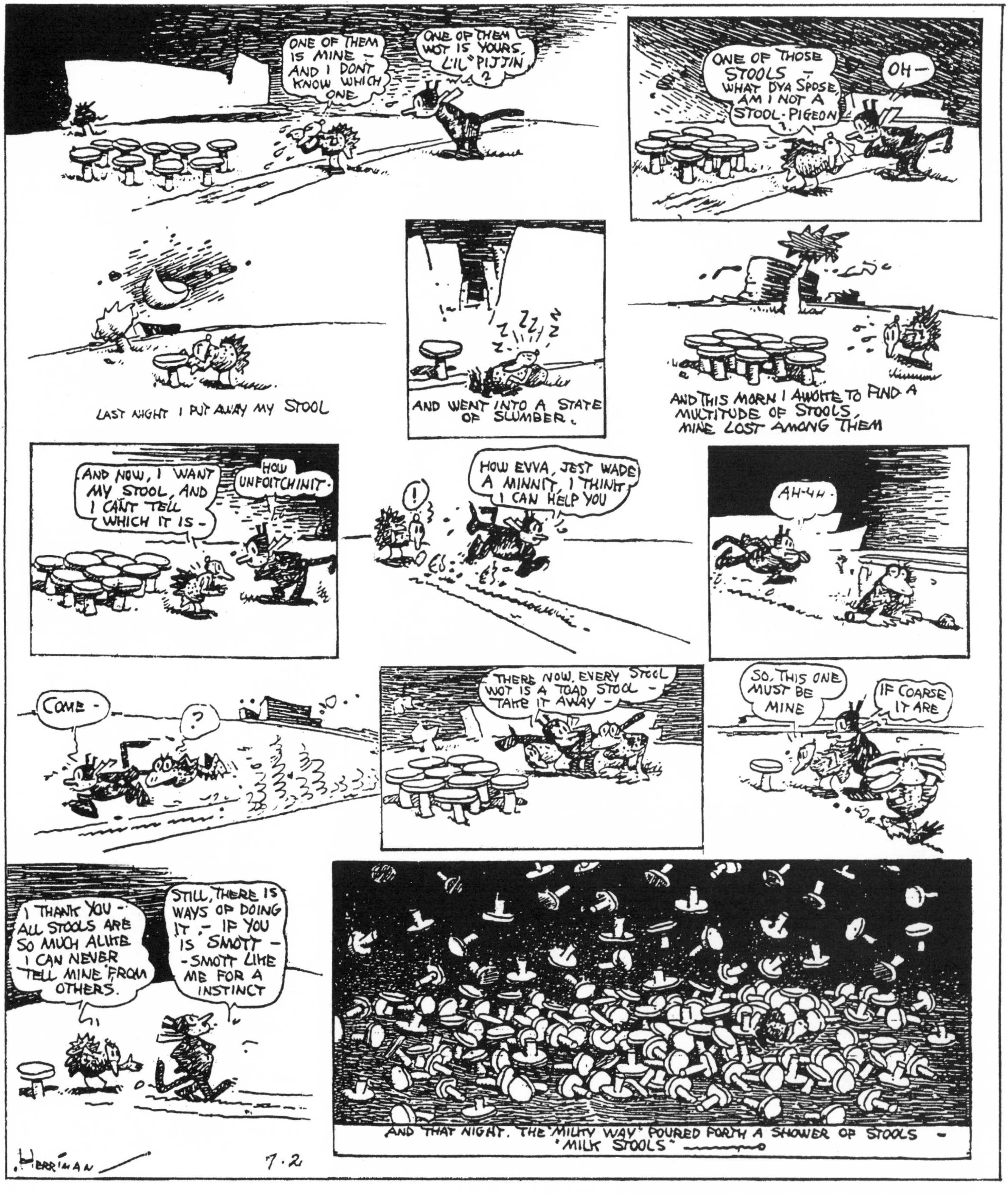

ONE OF THEM IS MINE - AND I DONT KNOW WHICH ONE
ONE OF THEM WOT IS YOURS, L'IL "PIJJIN" ?
ONE OF THOSE STOOLS - WHAT DYA SPOSE, AM I NOT A STOOL-PIGEON ?
OH-
LAST NIGHT I PUT AWAY MY STOOL
AND WENT INTO A STATE OF SLUMBER.
AND THIS MORN I AWOKE TO FIND A MULTITUDE OF STOOLS, MINE LOST AMONG THEM
AND NOW, I WANT MY STOOL, AND I CANT TELL WHICH IT IS -
HOW UNFOITCHINIT -
!
HOW EVVA, JEST WADE A MINNIT, I THINK I CAN HELP YOU
AH-AH
COME -
?
THERE NOW, EVERY STOOL WOT IS A TOAD STOOL - TAKE IT AWAY -
SO, THIS ONE MUST BE MINE
IF COARSE IT ARE
I THANK YOU - ALL STOOLS ARE SO MUCH ALIKE I CAN NEVER TELL MINE FROM OTHERS.
STILL, THERE IS WAYS OF DOING IT - IF YOU IS SMOTT - - SMOTT LIKE ME FOR A INSTINCT
AND THAT NIGHT, THE "MILKY WAY" POURED FORTH A SHOWER OF STOOLS - "MILK STOOLS"
HERRIMAN
7.2

July 2nd, 1933.

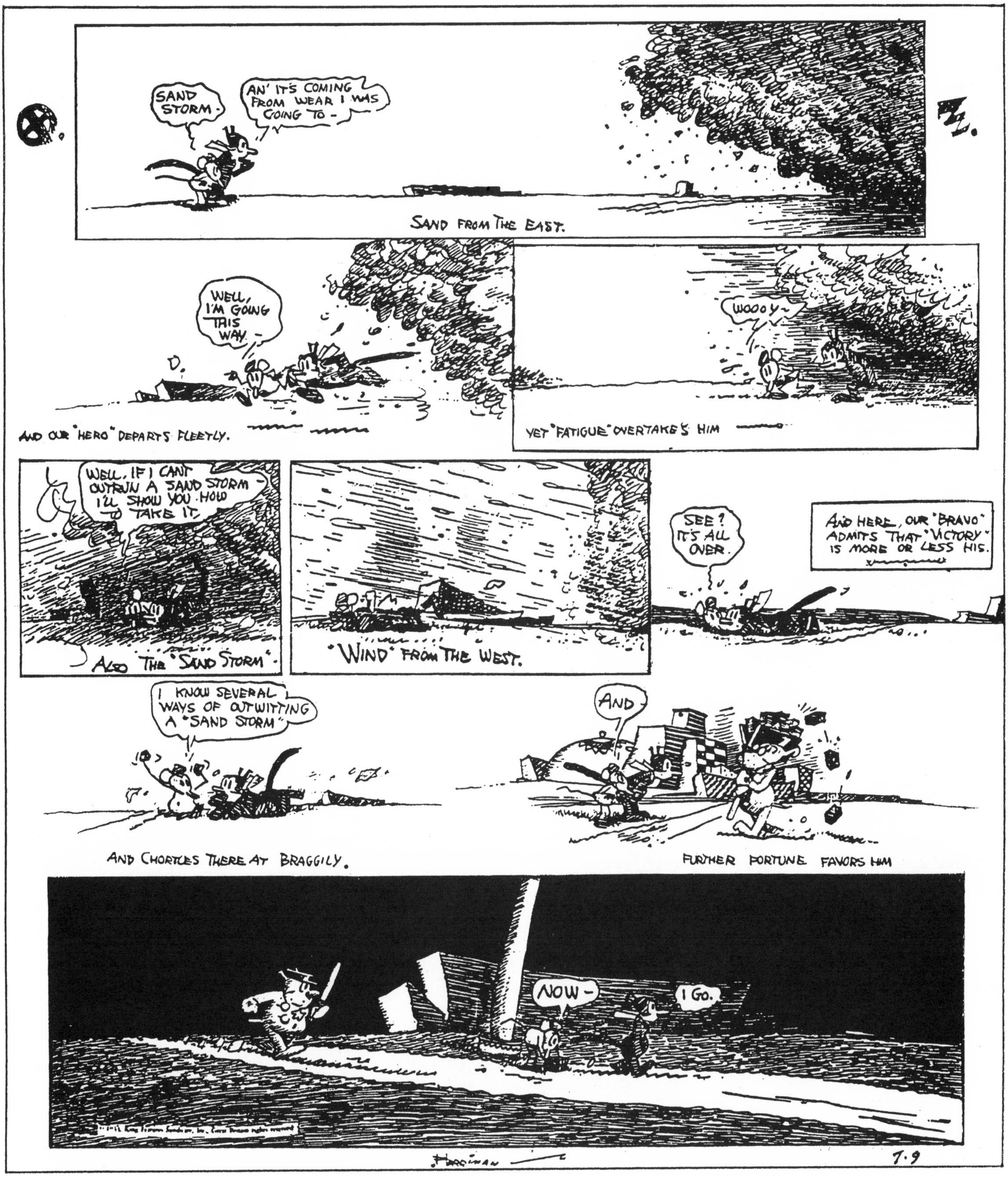
SAND STORM -
AN' IT'S COMING FROM WEAR I WAS GOING TO -
SAND FROM THE EAST.
WELL, I'M GOING THIS WAY.
AND OUR "HERO" DEPARTS FLEETLY.
WOOOY-
YET "FATIGUE" OVERTAKES HIM
WELL, IF I CAN'T OUTRUN A SAND STORM I'LL SHOW YOU HOW TO TAKE IT.
ALSO THE "SAND STORM".
"WIND" FROM THE WEST.
SEE? IT'S ALL OVER.
AND HERE, OUR "BRAVO" ADMITS THAT "VICTORY" IS MORE OR LESS HIS.
I KNOW SEVERAL WAYS OF OUTWITTING A "SAND STORM"
AND CHORTLES THERE AT BRAGGILY.
AND
FURTHER FORTUNE FAVORS HIM
NOW-
I GO.
HERRIMAN
7·9

July 9th, 1933.

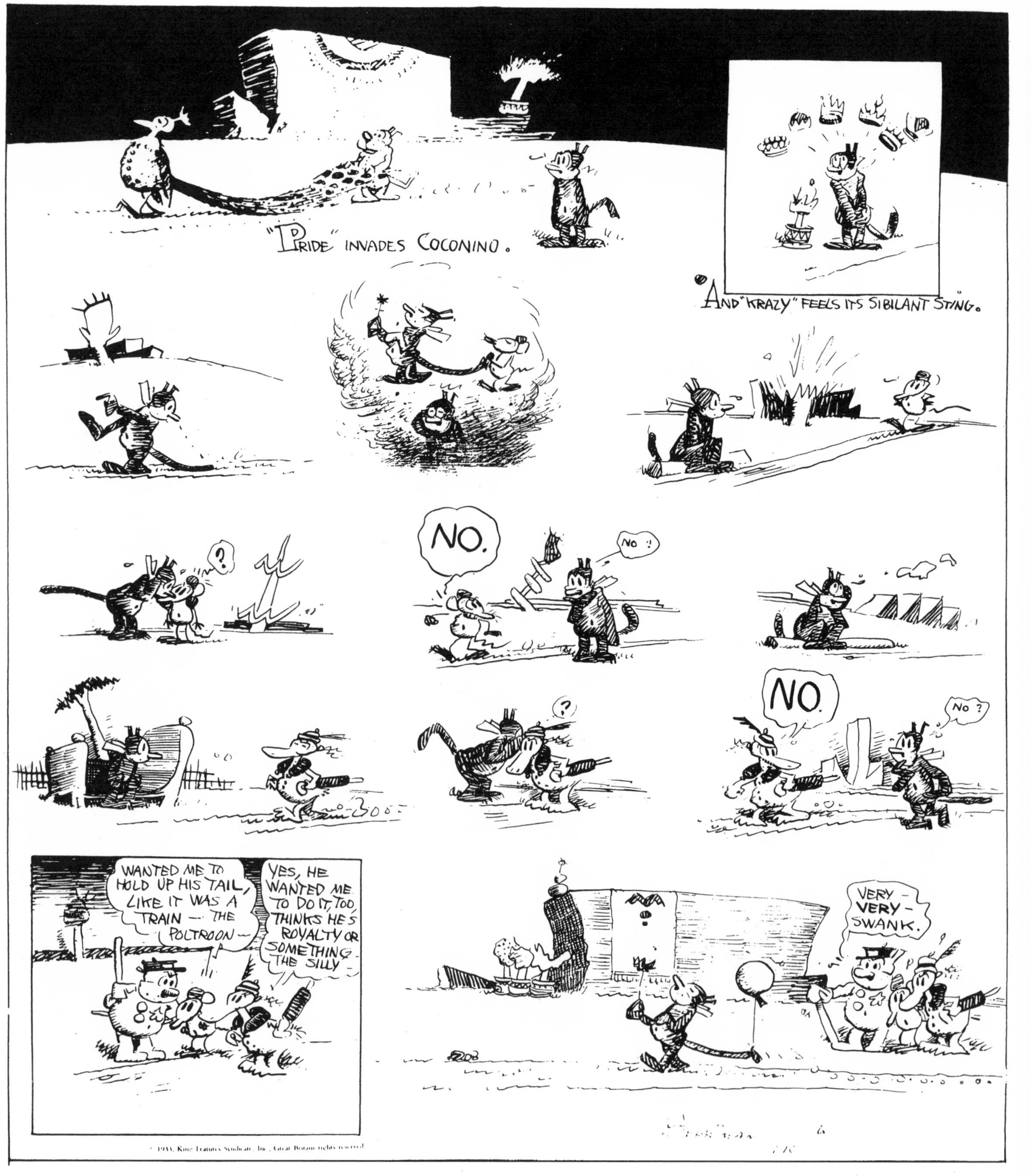
"PRIDE" INVADES COCONINO.
AND "KRAZY" FEELS ITS SIBILANT STING.
NO.
NO ?
NO.
NO ?
WANTED ME TO HOLD UP HIS TAIL, LIKE IT WAS A TRAIN — THE POLTROON —
YES, HE WANTED ME TO DO IT, TOO, THINKS HE'S ROYALTY OR SOMETHING THE SILLY
VERY — VERY — SWANK.

July 16th, 1933.

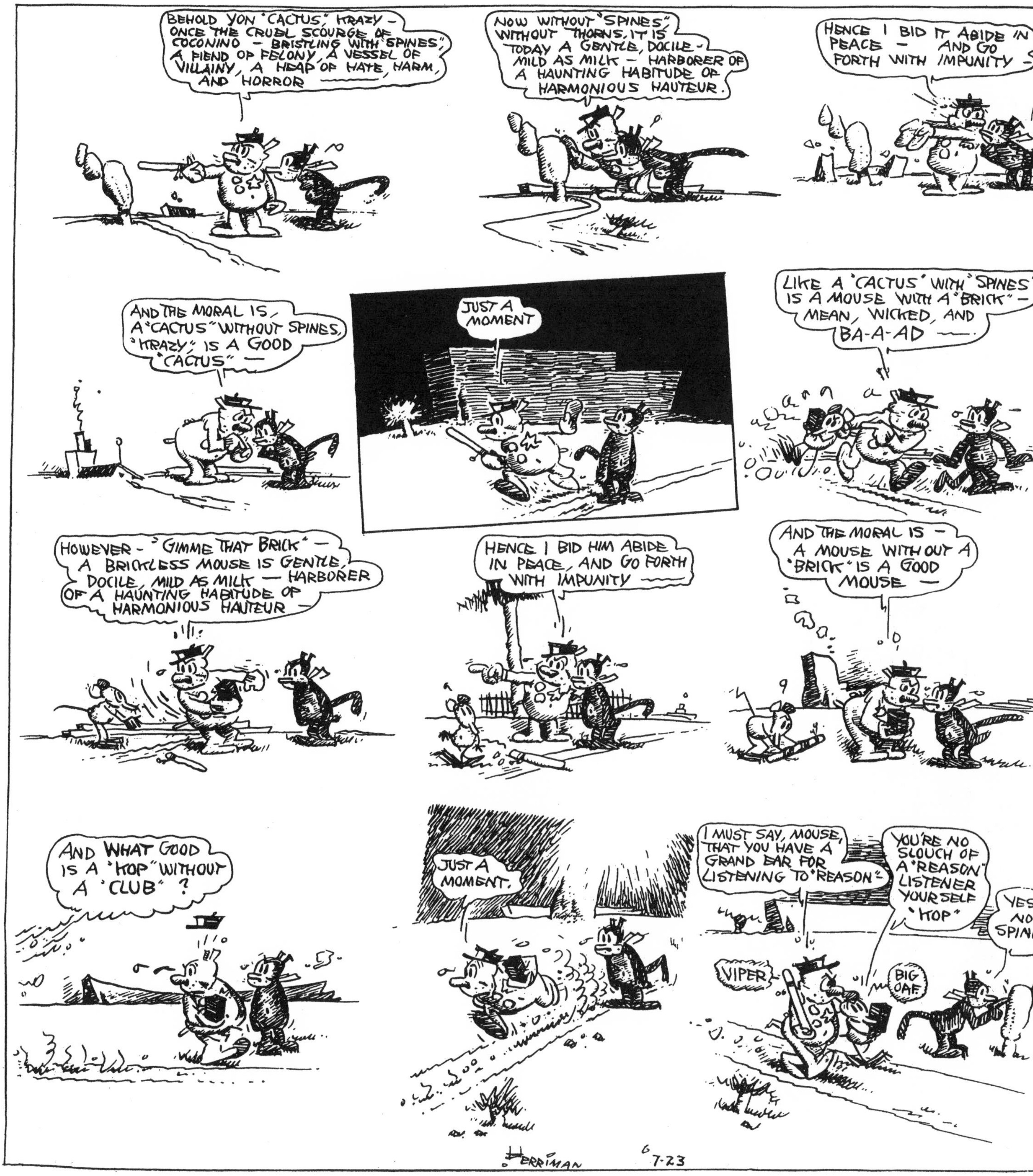
BEHOLD YON "CACTUS," KRAZY - ONCE THE CRUEL SCOURGE OF COCONINO - BRISTLING WITH "SPINES," A FIEND OF FELONY, A VESSEL OF VILLAINY, A HEAP OF HATE, HARM, AND HORROR
NOW WITHOUT "SPINES" WITHOUT THORNS, IT IS TODAY A GENTLE, DOCILE - MILD AS MILK - HARBORER OF A HAUNTING HABITUDE OF HARMONIOUS HAUTEUR.
HENCE I BID IT ABIDE IN PEACE - AND GO FORTH WITH IMPUNITY -
AND THE MORAL IS, A "CACTUS" WITHOUT SPINES, "KRAZY," IS A GOOD "CACTUS" -
JUST A MOMENT
LIKE A "CACTUS" WITH "SPINES" IS A MOUSE WITH A "BRICK" - MEAN, WICKED, AND BA-A-AD
HOWEVER - "GIMME THAT BRICK" - A BRICKLESS MOUSE IS GENTLE, DOCILE, MILD AS MILK - HARBORER OF A HAUNTING HABITUDE OF HARMONIOUS HAUTEUR -
HENCE I BID HIM ABIDE IN PEACE, AND GO FORTH WITH IMPUNITY
AND THE MORAL IS - A MOUSE WITHOUT A "BRICK" IS A GOOD MOUSE -
AND WHAT GOOD IS A "KOP" WITHOUT A "CLUB"?
JUST A MOMENT.
I MUST SAY, MOUSE, THAT YOU HAVE A GRAND EAR FOR LISTENING TO "REASON"
YOU'RE NO SLOUCH OF A "REASON" LISTENER YOURSELF "KOP"
YES NO SPINES
VIPER
BIG OAF
HERRIMAN
7-23

July 23rd, 1933.

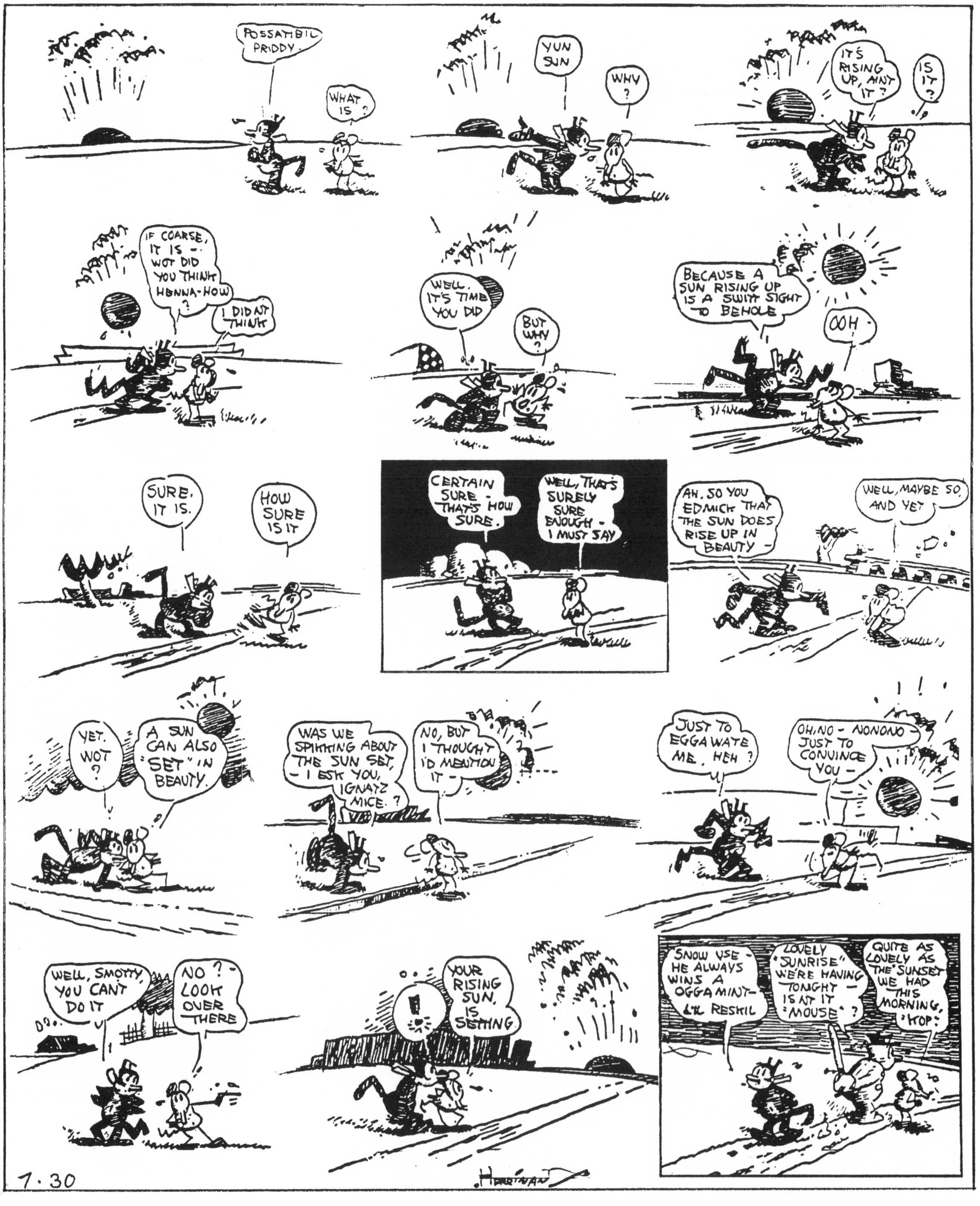
POSSAHBIL PRIDDY.
WHAT IS ?
YUN SUN
WHY ?
IT'S RISING UP, AIN'T IT ?
IS IT ?
IF COARSE, IT IS - WOT DID YOU THINK HENNA-HOW ?
I DIDN'T THINK
WELL, IT'S TIME YOU DID
BUT WHY ?
BECAUSE A SUN RISING UP IS A SWITT SIGHT TO BEHOLE
OOH
SURE, IT IS.
HOW SURE IS IT
CERTAIN SURE - THAT'S HOW SURE.
WELL, THAT'S SURELY SURE ENOUGH - I MUST SAY
AH, SO YOU EDMICK THAT THE SUN DOES RISE UP IN BEAUTY -
WELL, MAYBE SO, AND YET
YET, WOT ?
A SUN CAN ALSO "SET" IN BEAUTY.
WAS WE SPIKKING ABOUT THE SUN SET, - I ESK YOU, IGNATZ MICE ?
NO, BUT I THOUGHT I'D MENTION IT -
JUST TO EGGAWATE ME, HEH ?
OH, NO - NONONO - JUST TO CONVINCE YOU -
WELL, SMOTTY, YOU CAN'T DO IT
NO ? - LOOK OVER THERE
!
YOUR RISING SUN, IS SETTING.
SNOW USE - HE ALWAYS WINS A OGGAMINT - L'IL RESKIL
LOVELY "SUNRISE" WE'RE HAVING TONGHT - IS N'T IT "MOUSE" ?
QUITE AS LOVELY AS THE "SUNSET" WE HAD THIS MORNING, "KOP".
7·30
HERRIMAN

July 30th, 1933.

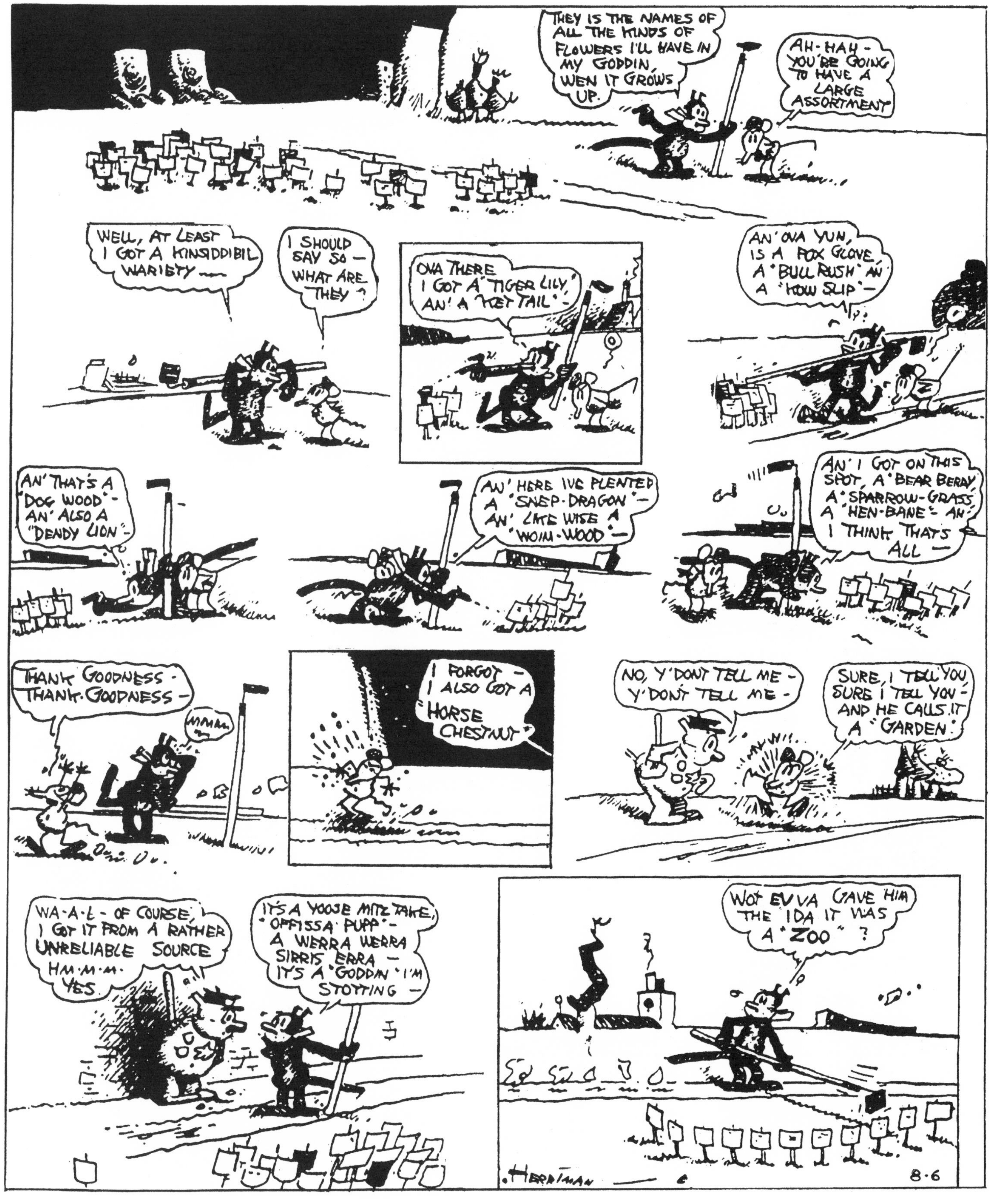
THEY IS THE NAMES OF ALL THE KINDS OF FLOWERS I'LL HAVE IN MY GODDIN, WEN IT GROWS UP.
AH-HAH - YOU'RE GOING TO HAVE A LARGE ASSORTMENT
WELL, AT LEAST I GOT A KINSIDDIBIL WARIETY —
I SHOULD SAY SO — WHAT ARE THEY ?
OVA THERE I GOT A "TIGER LILY" AN' A "KET TAIL" -
AN' OVA YUN, IS A "FOX GLOVE" A "BULL RUSH" AN' A "KOW SLIP" —
AN' THAT'S A "DOG WOOD" - AN' ALSO A "DENDY LION" -
AN' HERE IVE PLENTED A "SNEP-DRAGON" - AN' LIKE WISE A "WOIM-WOOD" -
AN' I GOT ON THIS SPOT, A "BEAR BERRY" A "SPARROW-GRASS" A "HEN-BANE" - AN' I THINK THAT'S ALL —
THANK GOODNESS - THANK GOODNESS -
I FORGOT - I ALSO GOT A "HORSE CHESTNUT"
NO, Y'DON'T TELL ME - Y'DON'T TELL ME -
SURE, I TELL YOU, SURE I TELL YOU - AND HE CALLS IT A "GARDEN".
WA-A-L - OF COURSE, I GOT IT FROM A RATHER UNRELIABLE SOURCE HM-M-M. YES.
IT'S A YOOJE MITE TAKE, "OFFISSA PUPP" - A WERRA WERRA SIRRIS ERRA - IT'S A "GODDIN" I'M STOTTING -
WOT EVVA GAVE HIM THE IDA IT WAS A "ZOO" ?
HERRIMAN
8-6

August 6th, 1933.

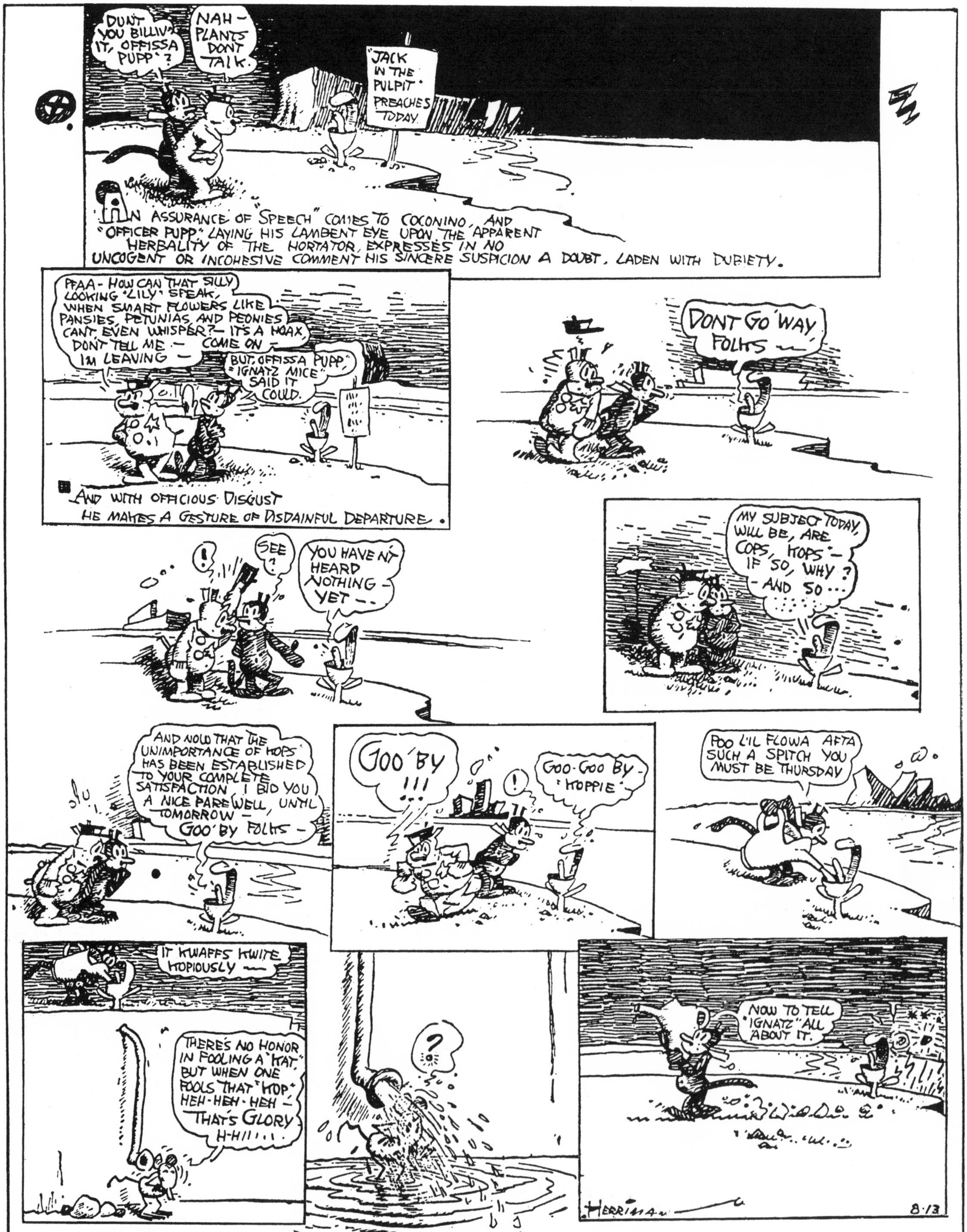
DUNT YOU BILLIV' IT, OFFISSA PUPP ?
NAH - PLANTS DONT TALK.
JACK IN THE PULPIT PREACHES TODAY
AN ASSURANCE OF "SPEECH" COMES TO COCONINO, AND "OFFICER PUPP" LAYING HIS LAMBENT EYE UPON THE APPARENT HERBALITY OF THE HORTATOR, EXPRESSES IN NO UNCOGENT OR INCOHESIVE COMMENT HIS SINCERE SUSPICION A DOUBT, LADEN WITH DUBIETY.
PFAA - HOW CAN THAT SILLY LOOKING "LILY" SPEAK, WHEN SMART FLOWERS LIKE PANSIES, PETUNIAS, AND PEONIES CANT EVEN WHISPER? - ITS A HOAX DONT TELL ME - COME ON - IM LEAVING -
BUT, OFFISSA PUPP, "IGNATZ MICE" SAID IT COULD.
AND WITH OFFICIOUS DISGUST HE MAKES A GESTURE OF DISDAINFUL DEPARTURE.
DONT GO 'WAY FOLKS --
!
SEE ?
YOU HAVEN'T HEARD NOTHING YET --
MY SUBJECT TODAY, WILL BE, ARE COPS, KOPS - IF SO, WHY ? - AND SO ...
AND NOW THAT THE UNIMPORTANCE OF KOPS HAS BEEN ESTABLISHED TO YOUR COMPLETE SATISFACTION I BID YOU A NICE FAREWELL, UNTIL TOMORROW - GOO'BY FOLKS -
GOO'BY !!!
!
GOO-GOO BY - "KOPPIE"
POO L'IL FLOWA AFTA SUCH A SPITCH YOU MUST BE THURSDAY
IT KWAFFS KWITE KOPIOUSLY ---
THERE'S NO HONOR IN FOOLING A "KAT" BUT WHEN ONE FOOLS THAT "KOP" HEH-HEH-HEH - THAT'S GLORY H-H!!...
?
NOW TO TELL "IGNATZ" ALL ABOUT IT.
HERRIMAN
8.13

August 13th, 1933.

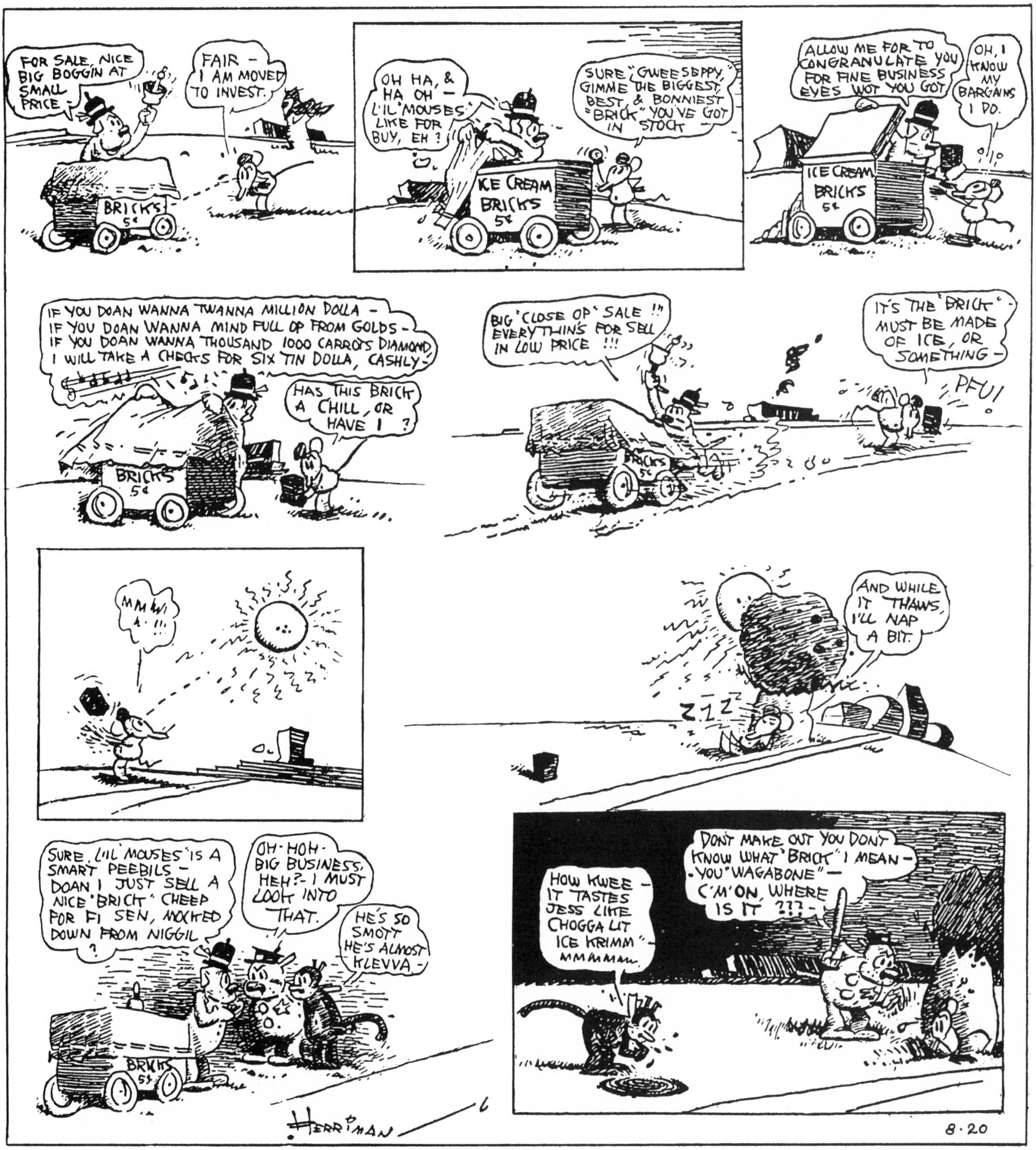

FOR SALE, NICE BIG BOGGIN AT SMALL PRICE -
FAIR - I AM MOVED TO INVEST.
OH HA, & HA OH - L'IL MOUSES LIKE FOR BUY, EH ?
SURE "GWEESEPPY" GIMME THE BIGGEST, BEST, & BONNIEST "BRICK" YOU'VE GOT IN STOCK
ICE CREAM BRICKS 5¢
ALLOW ME FOR TO CONGRANULATE YOU FOR FINE BUSINESS EYES WOT YOU GOT
OH, I KNOW MY BARGAINS I DO.
ICE CREAM BRICKS 5¢
IF YOU DOAN WANNA TWANNA MILLION DOLLA - IF YOU DOAN WANNA MIND FULL OP FROM GOLDS - IF YOU DOAN WANNA THOUSAND 1000 CARROTS DIAMOND I WILL TAKE A CHECKS FOR SIX TIN DOLLA, CASHLY -
HAS THIS BRICK A CHILL, OR HAVE I ?
BRICKS 5¢
BIG "CLOSE OP" SALE !! EVERYTHINS FOR SELL IN LOW PRICE !!!
IT'S THE "BRICK" - MUST BE MADE OF ICE, OR SOMETHING -
PFU!
MMM A !!!
AND WHILE IT THAWS, I'LL NAP A BIT.
ZZZ
SURE, L'IL MOUSES IS A SMART PEEBILS - DOAN I JUST SELL A NICE "BRICK" CHEEP FOR FI SEN, MOCKED DOWN FROM NIGGIL ?
OH - HOH - BIG BUSINESS, HEH? - I MUST LOOK INTO THAT.
HE'S SO SMOTT HE'S ALMOST KLEVVA -
HOW KWEE - IT TASTES JESS LIKE CHOGGA LIT ICE KRIMM - MMMMM
DON'T MAKE OUT YOU DON'T KNOW WHAT "BRICK" I MEAN - YOU "WAGABONE" - C'M'ON, WHERE IS IT ??? -
HERRIMAN
8·20

August 20th, 1933.

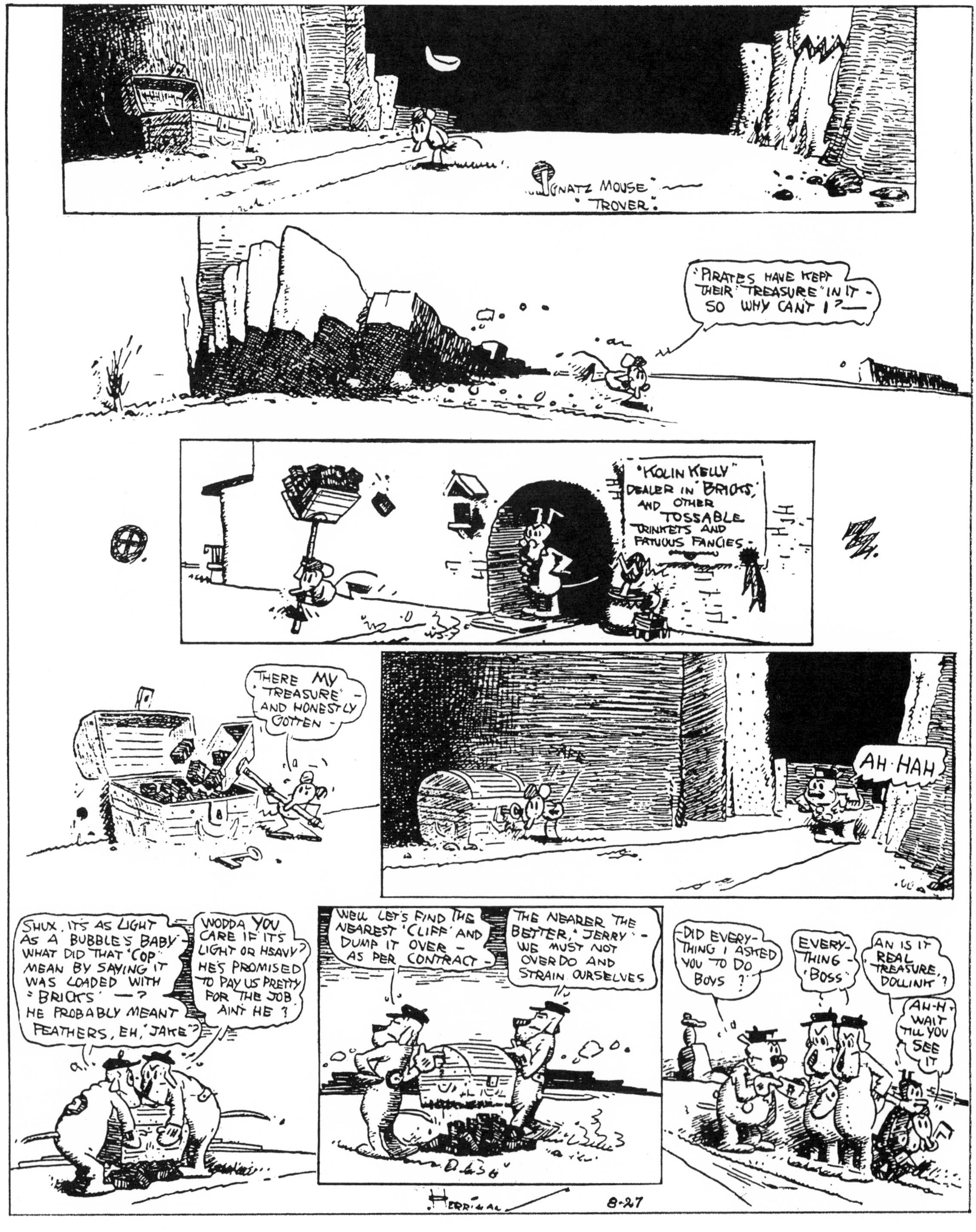
"IGNATZ MOUSE" "TROVER"
"PIRATES HAVE KEPT THEIR "TREASURE" IN IT - SO WHY CAN'T I?
"KOLIN KELLY" DEALER IN "BRICKS," AND OTHER TOSSABLE TRINKETS AND FATUOUS FANCIES
THERE MY "TREASURE" - AND HONESTLY GOTTEN -
AH HAH
SHUX, IT'S AS LIGHT AS A BUBBLE'S BABY - WHAT DID THAT 'COP' MEAN BY SAYING IT WAS LOADED WITH "BRICKS" —? HE PROBABLY MEANT FEATHERS, EH, "JAKE"?
WODDA YOU CARE IF IT'S LIGHT OR HEAVY? HE'S PROMISED TO PAY US PRETTY FOR THE JOB AIN'T HE?
WELL LET'S FIND THE NEAREST 'CLIFF' AND DUMP IT OVER - AS PER CONTRACT -
THE NEARER THE BETTER, "JERRY" - WE MUST NOT OVERDO AND STRAIN OURSELVES
DID EVERY-THING I ASKED YOU TO DO BOYS?
EVERY-THING - 'BOSS'
AN IS IT REAL TREASURE, DOLLINK?
AH-H WAIT TILL YOU SEE IT
HERRIMAN
8-27

August 27th, 1933.

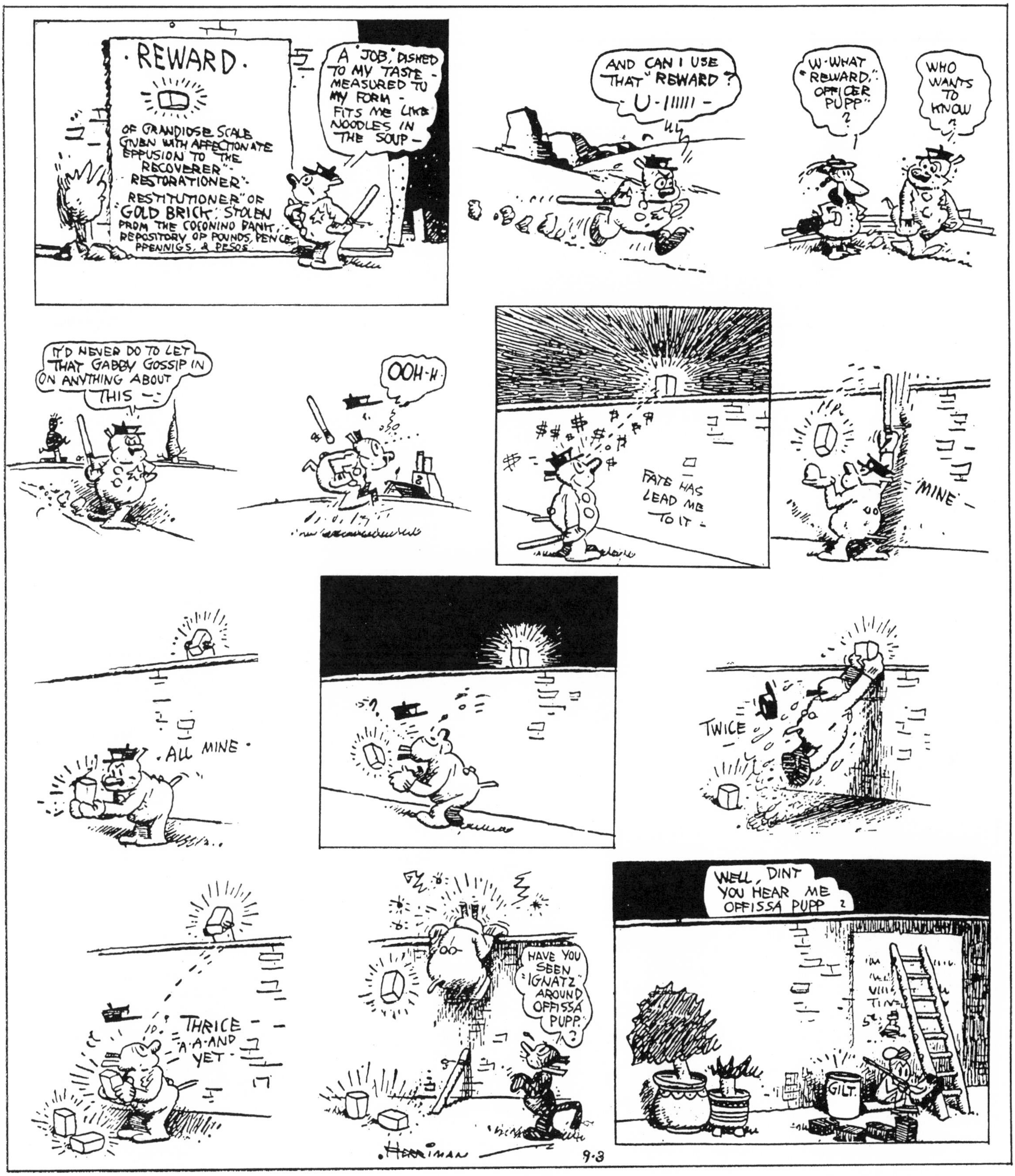

REWARD
OF GRANDIOSE SCALE GIVEN WITH AFFECTIONATE EFFUSION TO THE "RECOVERER" - "RESTORATIONER" - "RESTITUTIONER" OF GOLD BRICK: STOLEN FROM THE COCONINO BANK, REPOSITORY OF POUNDS, PENCE, PFENNIGS, & PESOS
A "JOB" DISHED TO MY TASTE - MEASURED TO MY FORM - FITS ME LIKE NOODLES IN THE SOUP -
AND CAN I USE THAT "REWARD"? - U-IIIIII -
W-WHAT "REWARD," OFFICER PUPP?
WHO WANTS TO KNOW?
IT'D NEVER DO TO LET THAT GABBY GOSSIP IN ON ANYTHING ABOUT THIS
OOH-H
FATE HAS LEAD ME TO IT -
MINE
ALL MINE
TWICE
THRICE A-A-AND YET
HAVE YOU SEEN "IGNATZ" AROUND OFFISSA PUPP?
WELL, DINT YOU HEAR ME OFFISSA PUPP?
GILT
HERRIMAN 9-3

September 3rd, 1933.

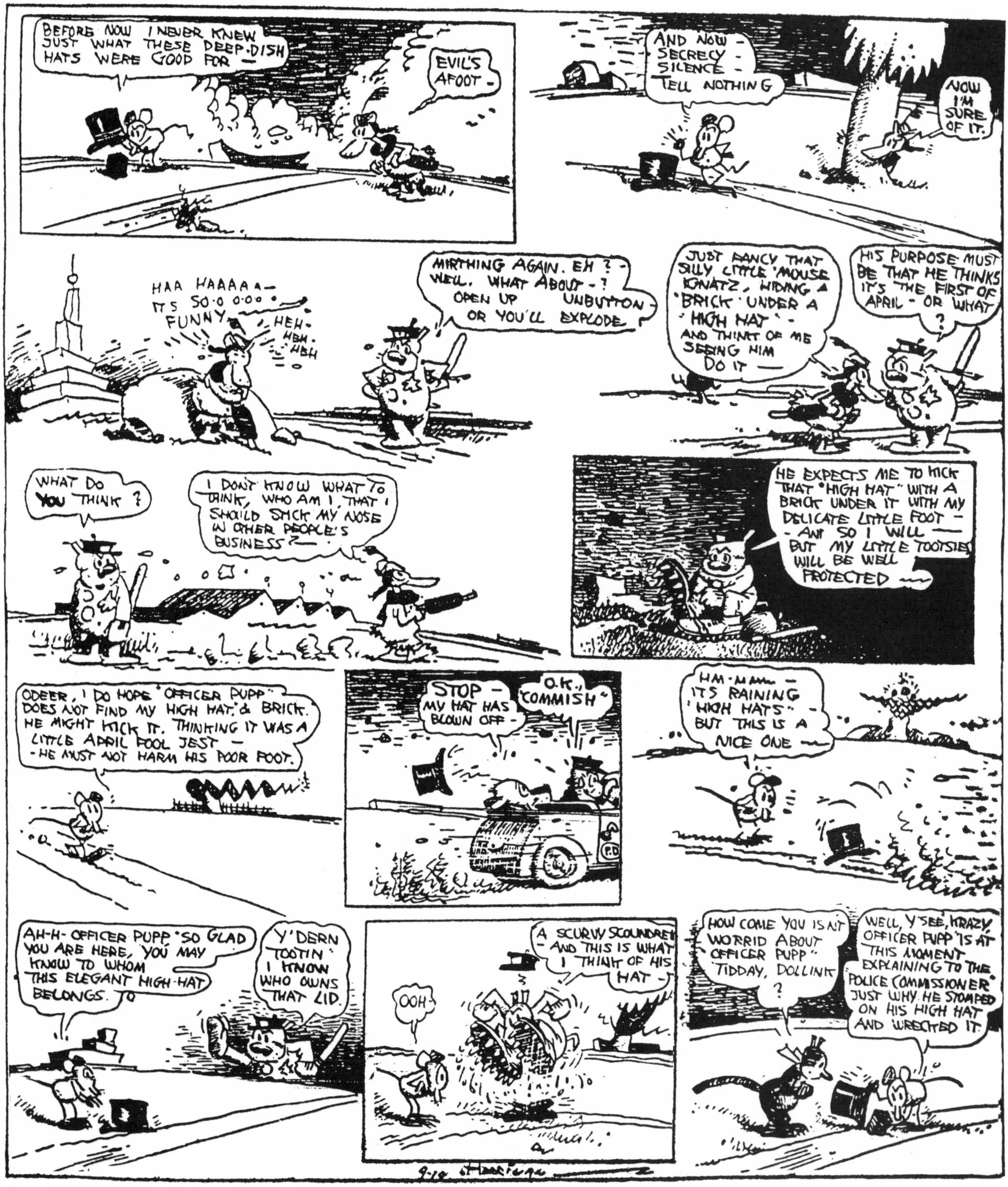

BEFORE NOW I NEVER KNEW JUST WHAT THESE DEEP-DISH HATS WERE GOOD FOR —
EVIL'S AFOOT —
AND NOW - SECRECY - SILENCE - TELL NOTHING
NOW I'M SURE OF IT.
HAA HAAAAA — IT'S SO-O-O-O-O FUNNY —
HEH - HEH - HEH
MIRTHING AGAIN. EH ? — WELL, WHAT ABOUT — ? OPEN UP UNBUTTON — OR YOU'LL EXPLODE
JUST FANCY THAT SILLY LITTLE MOUSE IGNATZ, HIDING A "BRICK" UNDER A "HIGH HAT" — AND THINK OF ME SEEING HIM DO IT —
HIS PURPOSE MUST BE THAT HE THINKS IT'S THE FIRST OF APRIL — OR WHAT ?
WHAT DO YOU THINK ?
I DON'T KNOW WHAT TO THINK, WHO AM I, THAT I SHOULD STICK MY NOSE IN OTHER PEOPLE'S BUSINESS ? —
HE EXPECTS ME TO KICK THAT "HIGH HAT" WITH A BRICK UNDER IT WITH MY DELICATE LITTLE FOOT — AN' SO I WILL — BUT MY LITTLE TOOTSIES WILL BE WELL PROTECTED —
ODEER, I DO HOPE "OFFICER PUPP" DOES NOT FIND MY HIGH HAT, & BRICK. HE MIGHT KICK IT. THINKING IT WAS A LITTLE APRIL FOOL JEST — HE MUST NOT HARM HIS POOR FOOT.
STOP — MY HAT HAS BLOWN OFF —
O.K., "COMMISH"
HM-MMM — IT'S RAINING "HIGH HATS" — BUT THIS IS A NICE ONE —
AH-H- OFFICER PUPP SO GLAD YOU ARE HERE, YOU MAY KNOW TO WHOM THIS ELEGANT HIGH-HAT BELONGS.
Y'DERN TOOTIN' I KNOW WHO OWNS THAT LID.
OOH —
A SCURVY SCOUNDREL — AND THIS IS WHAT I THINK OF HIS HAT —
HOW COME YOU IS N'T WORRID ABOUT "OFFICER PUPP" TIDDAY, DOLLINK ?
WELL, Y'SEE, KRAZY, "OFFICER PUPP" IS AT THIS MOMENT EXPLAINING TO THE "POLICE COMMISSIONER" JUST WHY HE STOMPED ON HIS HIGH HAT AND WRECKED IT.

September 10th, 1933.

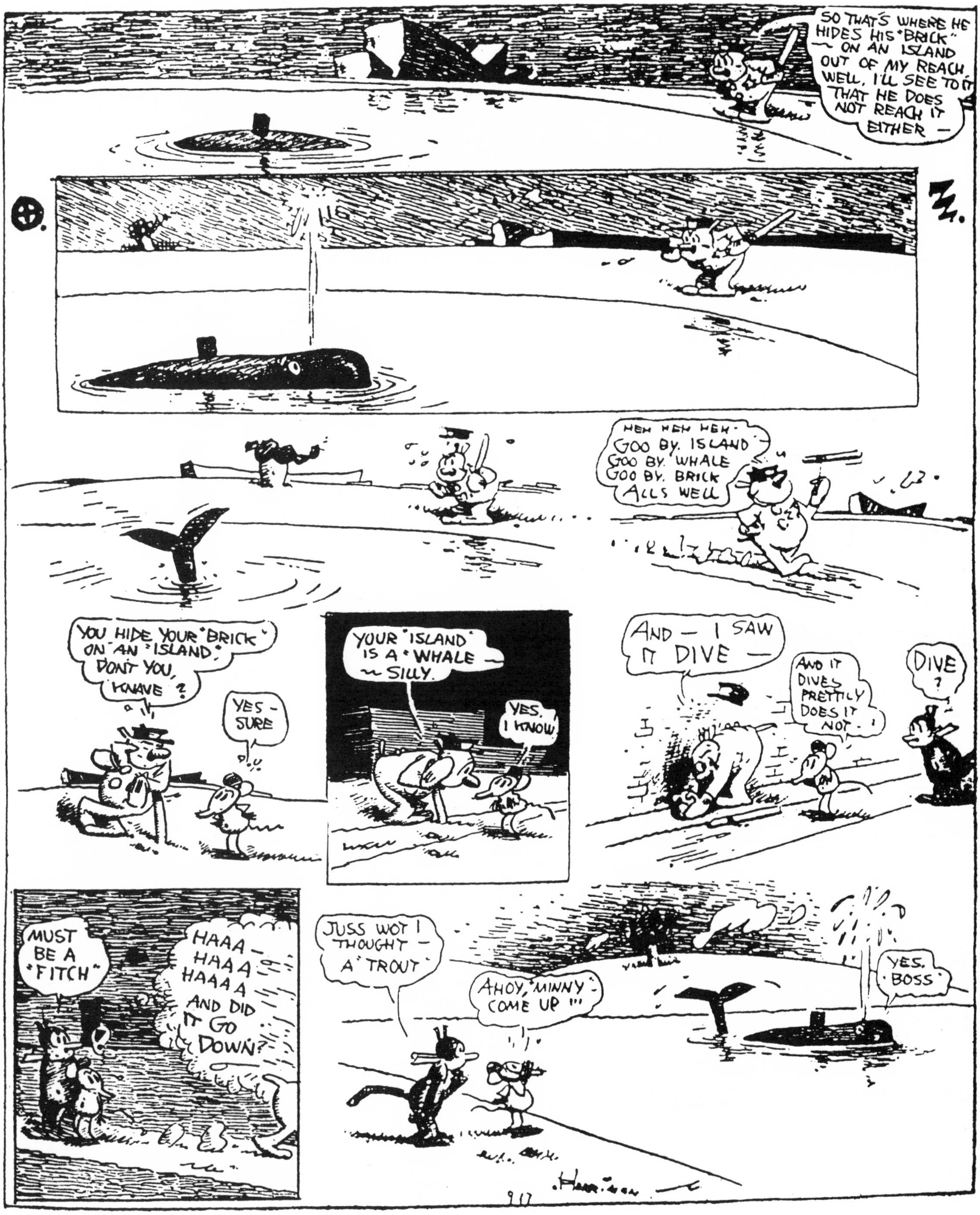
SO THAT'S WHERE HE HIDES HIS "BRICK" ~ ON AN ISLAND OUT OF MY REACH. WELL, I'LL SEE TO IT THAT HE DOES NOT REACH IT EITHER -
HEH HEH HEH. GOO BY. ISLAND GOO BY. WHALE GOO BY. BRICK ALLS WELL
YOU HIDE YOUR "BRICK" ON AN "ISLAND" DONT YOU, KNAVE ?
YES - SURE
YOUR "ISLAND" IS A "WHALE" ~ SILLY.
YES, I KNOW
AND - I SAW IT DIVE -
AND IT DIVES PRETTILY DOES IT NOT
DIVE ?
MUST BE A "FITCH"
HAAA - HAAA A HAAA A AND DID IT GO DOWN?
JUSS WOT I THOUGHT - A "TROUT"
AHOY, "MINNY" COME UP !!"
YES, BOSS

September 17th, 1933.

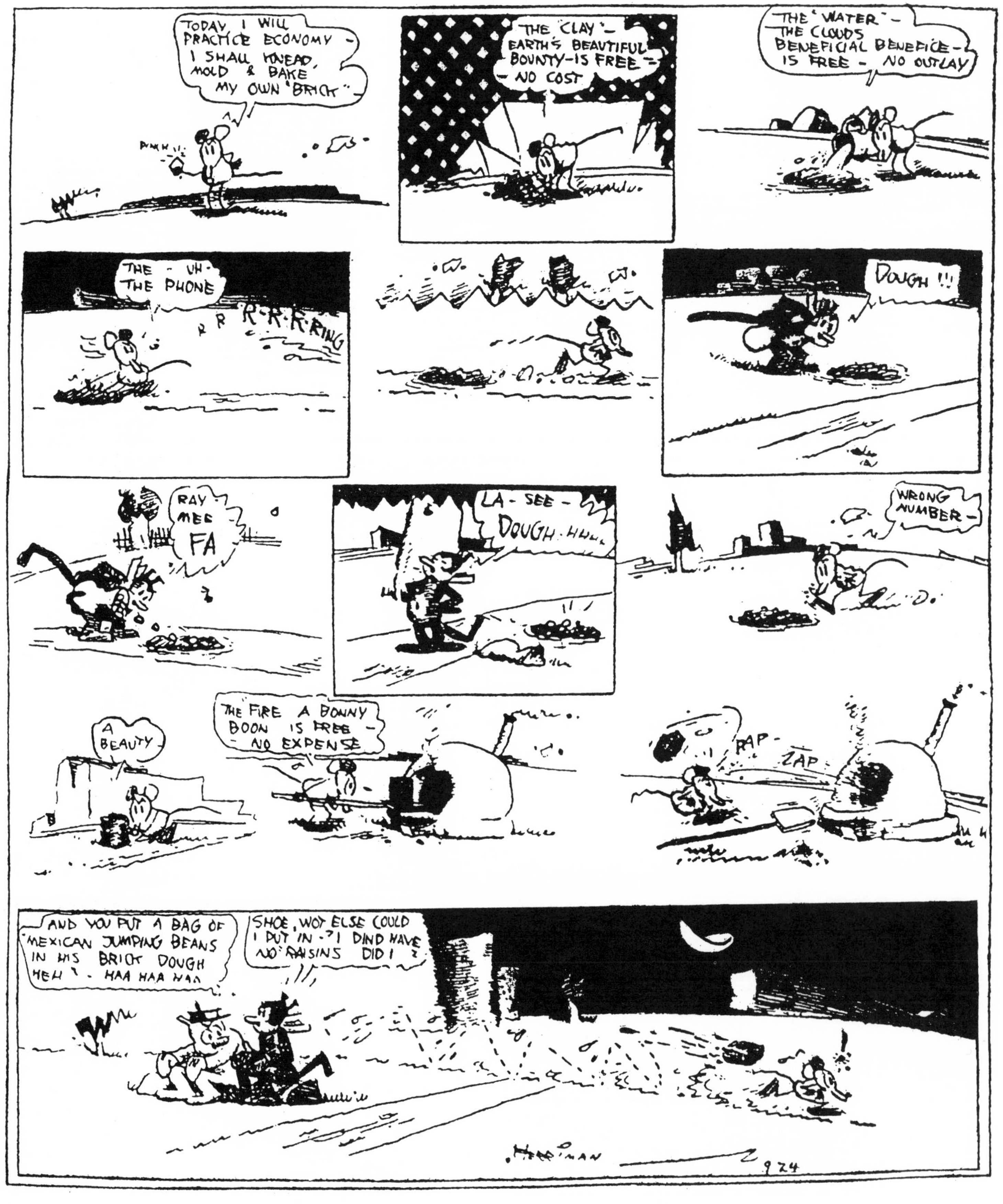
TODAY, I WILL PRACTICE ECONOMY - I SHALL KNEAD, MOLD & BAKE MY OWN "BRICK" -
THE "CLAY" - EARTH'S BEAUTIFUL BOUNTY - IS FREE - NO COST
THE "WATER" - THE CLOUDS BENEFICIAL BENEFICE - IS FREE - NO OUTLAY
THE - UH - THE PHONE
R R R-R-R-RING
DOUGH !!!
RAY MEE FA
LA - SEE - DOUGH
WRONG NUMBER -
A BEAUTY -
THE FIRE A BONNY BOON IS FREE - NO EXPENSE
RAP -
ZAP
AND YOU PUT A BAG OF MEXICAN JUMPING BEANS IN HIS BRICK DOUGH HEH - HAA HAA HAA
SHOE, WOT ELSE COULD I PUT IN - ? I DIND HAVE NO RAISINS DID I ?
HERRIMAN
9 24

September 24th, 1933.

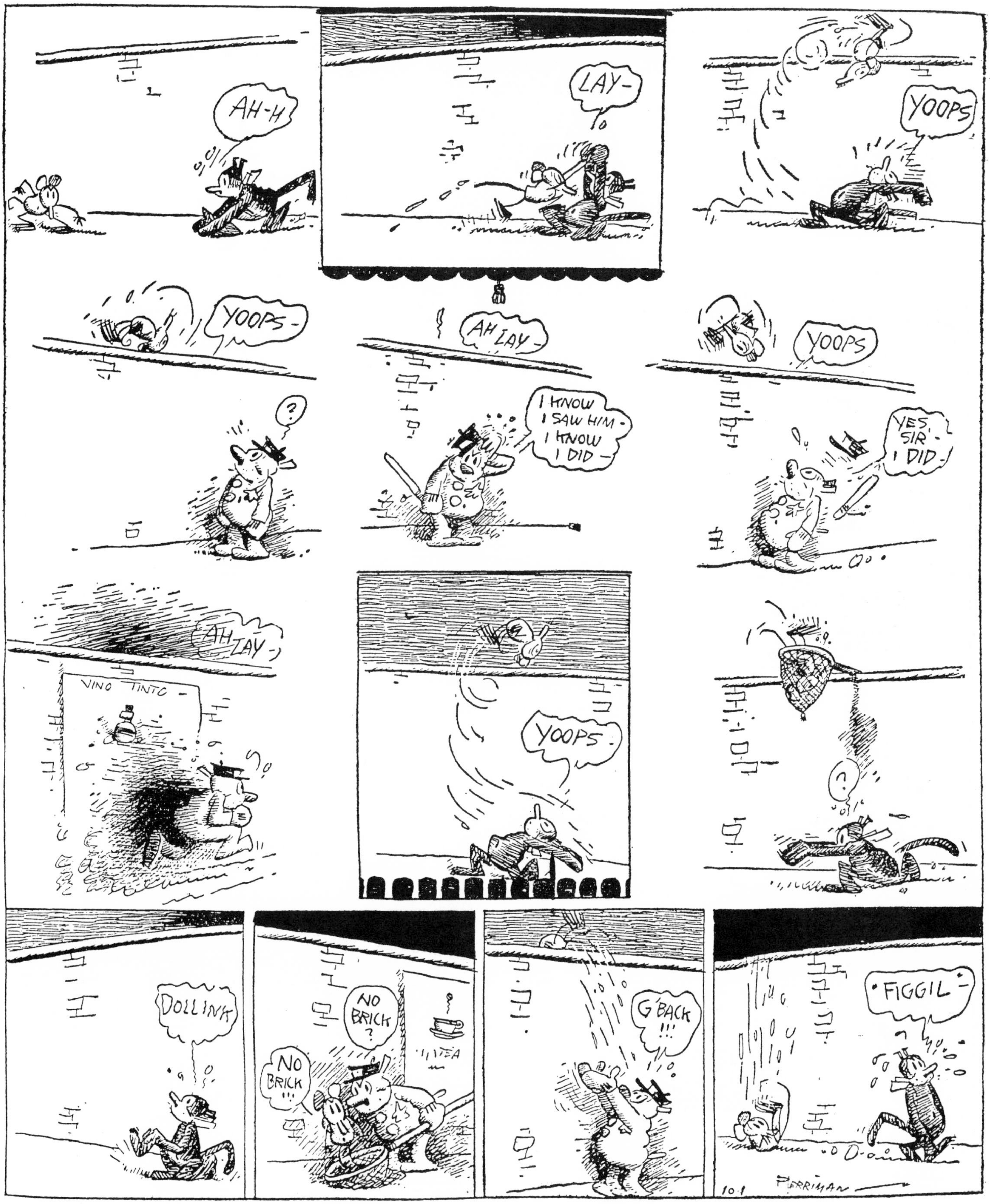
AH-H
LAY-
YOOPS
YOOPS-
?
AH LAY-
I KNOW I SAW HIM- I KNOW I DID-
YOOPS
YES, SIR- I DID-
AH LAY-
VINO TINTO
YOOPS
?
DOLLINK
NO BRICK ?
NO BRICK !!!
TEA
G'BACK !!!
FIGGIL
10-1
HERRIMAN

October 1st, 1933.

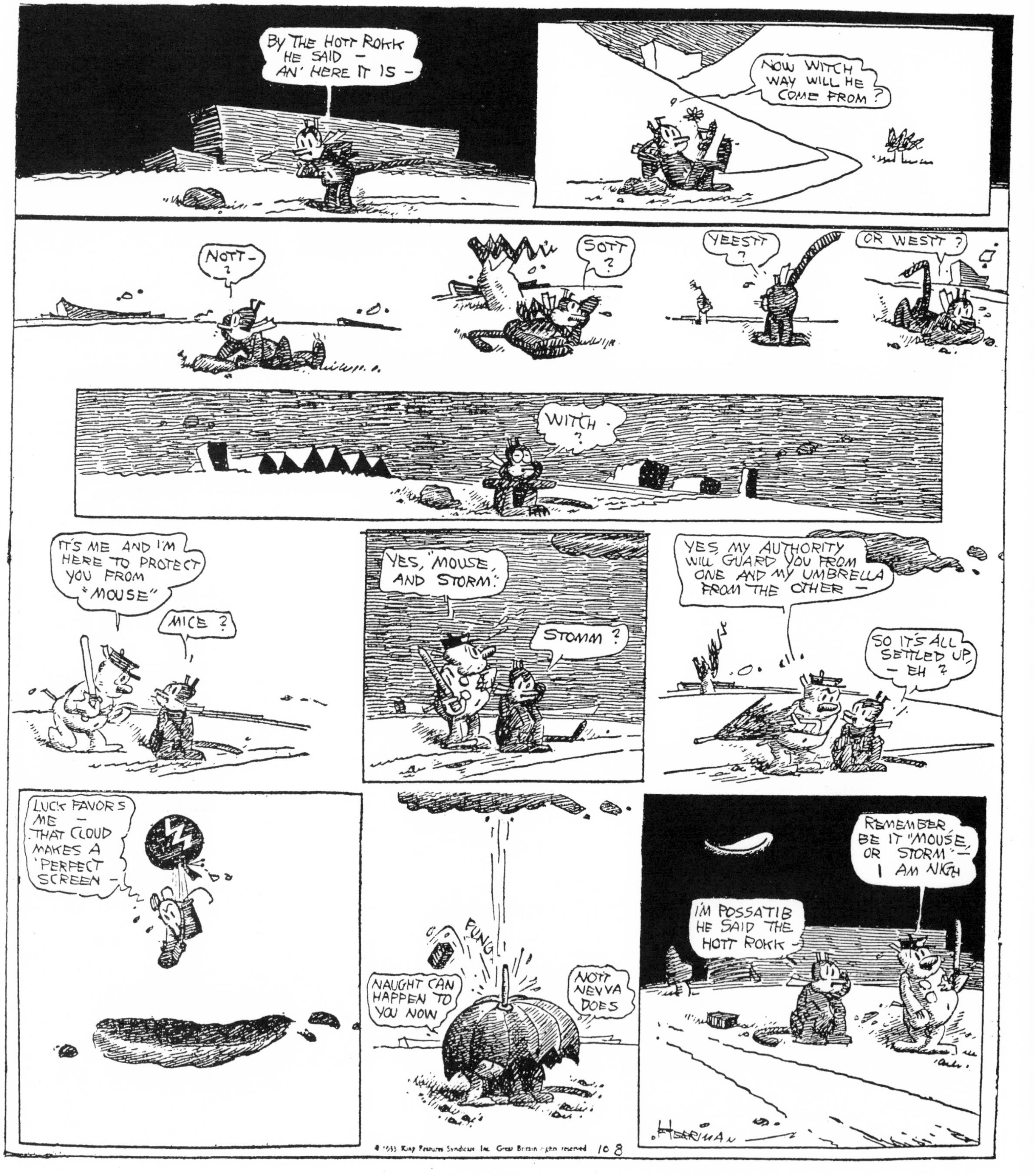
BY THE HOTT ROKK HE SAID – AN' HERE IT IS –
NOW WITCH WAY WILL HE COME FROM ?
NOTT – ?
SOTT ?
YEESTT ?
OR WESTT ?
WITCH – ?
IT'S ME AND I'M HERE TO PROTECT YOU FROM "MOUSE"
MICE ?
YES, "MOUSE, AND STORM."
STOMM ?
YES MY AUTHORITY WILL GUARD YOU FROM ONE AND MY UMBRELLA FROM THE OTHER –
SO IT'S ALL SETTLED UP, – EH ?
LUCK FAVORS ME – THAT CLOUD MAKES A PERFECT SCREEN –
PUNG
NAUGHT CAN HAPPEN TO YOU NOW
NOTT NEVVA DOES
REMEMBER, BE IT "MOUSE, OR STORM" – I AM NIGH
I'M POSSATIB HE SAID THE HOTT ROKK –
HERRIMAN

October 8th, 1933.

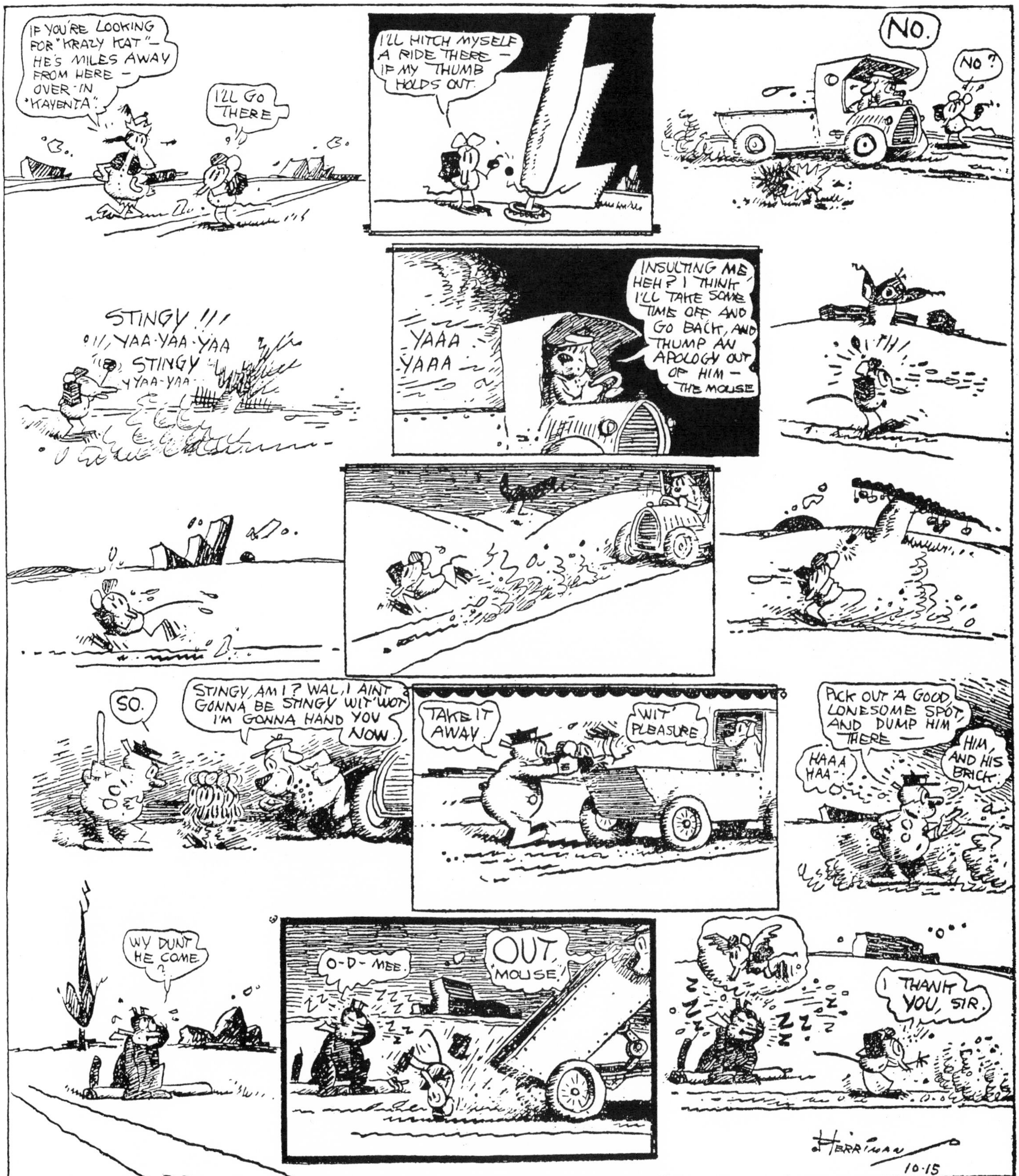

IF YOU'RE LOOKING FOR "KRAZY KAT" — HE'S MILES AWAY FROM HERE — OVER IN "KAYENTA".
I'LL GO THERE
I'LL HITCH MYSELF A RIDE THERE — IF MY THUMB HOLDS OUT.
NO.
NO?
STINGY !!! YAA-YAA-YAA STINGY YYAA-YAA
YAAA YAAA
INSULTING ME, HEH? I THINK I'LL TAKE SOME TIME OFF AND GO BACK, AND THUMP AN APOLOGY OUT OF HIM — THE MOUSE
SO.
STINGY, AM I? WAL, I AINT GONNA BE STINGY WIT WOT I'M GONNA HAND YOU NOW.
TAKE IT AWAY.
WIT' PLEASURE
PICK OUT A GOOD, LONESOME SPOT AND DUMP HIM THERE —
HAAA HAA
HIM, AND HIS BRICK.
WY DUNT HE COME?
O-D-MEE.
OUT, MOUSE!
I THANK YOU, SIR.
HERRIMAN
10-15

October 15th, 1933.

YOUR FACE HAS TOOK ON A GREAT LOOK OF EXUBERANT EXPRESSAGE, "KRAZY" - FOO IT WA?
AN' WELL SHOULD MY FACE BE HEPPY WIT JOY - FOR TIMORRA MORNING AT DARN I MIT "IGNATZ MICE" BY THE OLE SMOKE TREE.
JUST HE, JUST ME, AN' JUST US.
IT'S A SECRET.
OH, SURE, SURE -
SOME HOW OR OTHER I SEEM TO FEEL THAT I AM GOING TO SPEND THE NIGHT BY THE OLD "SMOKE TREE" - AND SO, IN ALL PROBABILITIES, I WILL BE THERE AT DAWN - WIDE-EYED, ALERT - AWAKE -
YOU HERE?
IN PERSON, "MOUSE" - AND HERE I'LL BE TILL "DAWN"
SHUX, THIS CAN'T BE - HOW DID HE FIND OUT - I MUST DO SOMETHING ABOUT IT.
HE'LL BE WEARY WITH WORRY - WELL, I'LL TAKE ON A LI'L NAP FOR MY SELF - UNTIL DAWN
HE'S SMART - I'M SMARTER -
HUH, STILL DARK, "STARS" & MOON" STILL OUT — WILL THAT DARN DAWN" NEVER COME? — OWELL, ANOTHER NAP -
"LOVE" CAME TO ME IN A SPRING TIME TO STAY BUT A DAY IN MY HOTT - HE LINGGID A WIKK, A MONTH AN' A YEAR - AN' HE'LL NEVVA NO MO WILL DEPOTT.
JAIL
"HIGH NOON"!?? GET OUT, S'PITCH DARK
REMOVE THEM SMOKIES," AND YOU'LL CHANGE YOUR MIND -
HERRIMAN
10-22

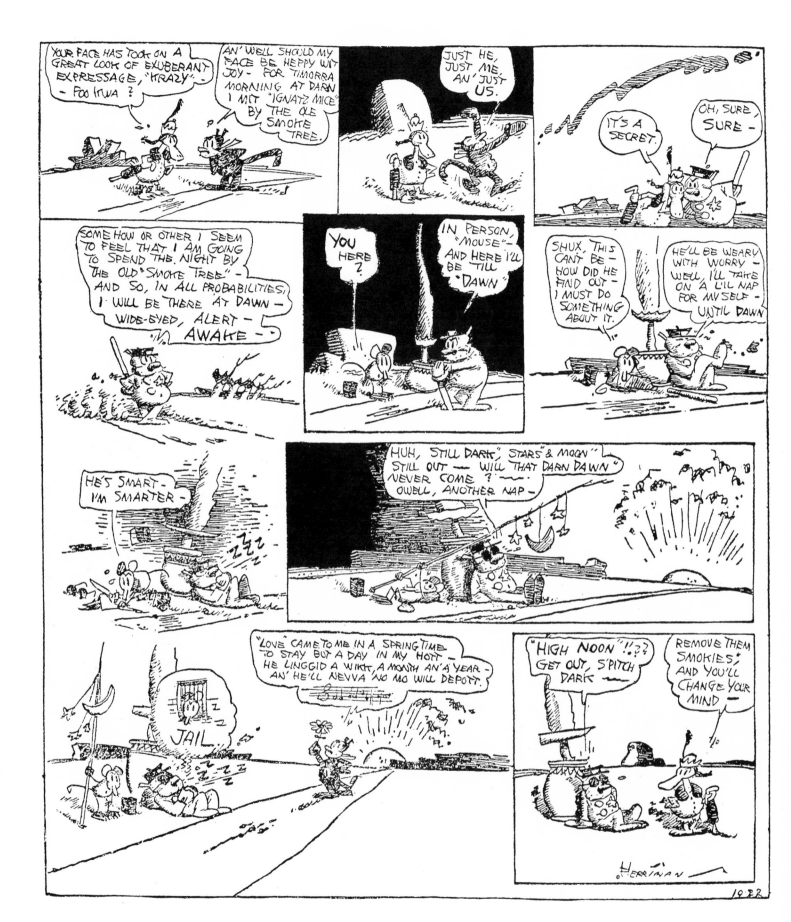

October 22nd, 1933.

DON'T TELL ME YOU'RE NOT GUILTY, MOUSE, YOU'VE GOT GUILT WRITTEN ALL OVER YOUR UGLY MUSH, YOUR MUG SPELLS IT LIKE A DICTIONARY —
BUT, OFFICER PUPP, I GIVE YOU MY WORD AS A "MOUSE" — I'M AS FREE OF EVIL INTENT AS A GLASS EYE AT A KEYHOLE.
AND, WHO CAN SUBSTANTIATE YOUR CLAIM, VERMIN ? WHO ???
ALAS — I HAVE NO WITNESS — ONLY MY WORD — MY GOOD WORD —
AND I HAVE ONLY MY SUSPICION, MY GOOD SUSPICION — AND MY GOOD SUSPICION IS BETTER THAN YOUR GOOD WORD, — SAVVY ?
OH-H- OFFICER — OFFICER PUPP — HOW YOU WRONG ME — ME, AN UNGUILTY PERSON —
COME, MY SUSPICION IS GOOD ENOUGH TO JAIL YOU — COME —
NO-NO-NO — NOH-H-H —
ONE MOMENT — ONE-MO-MENT — OFFICER PUPP — ONE MOMENT !!!!
WELL ?
SPARE THAT "MOUSE" — SPARE HIM — HE IS INNOCENT — HE IS ALL THAT HE CLAIMS — — I KNOW !!!
ARE YOU A WITNESS OF HIS "INNOCENCE" ?
WITH MY OWN EYE, AYE, WITH BOTH MY OWN EYES, I SAW HIS INNOCENCE.
GO, YOU ARE FREE, THE WORD OF THIS BIRDLIKE STRANGER HAS SAVED YOU — GO !!!
I'M SO GLAD I WAS AN INSTRUMENT OF JUSTICE
WELL, I GUESS I, TOO, WILL GO !!!
JUST A MOMENT WHO ARE YOU ?
I AM A "LYRE BIRD" SIR. THE BEST "LYRE BIRD" FROM FIBBA-FIBBA, JAVA —
OH — YOU ARE HEH ?
HEY, "MOUSE"
CALLING HIS L'IL PLAYING MATE — HOW KUTE —
HERRIMAN
10 29
© 1933, King Features Syndicate, Inc. Great Britain rights reserved

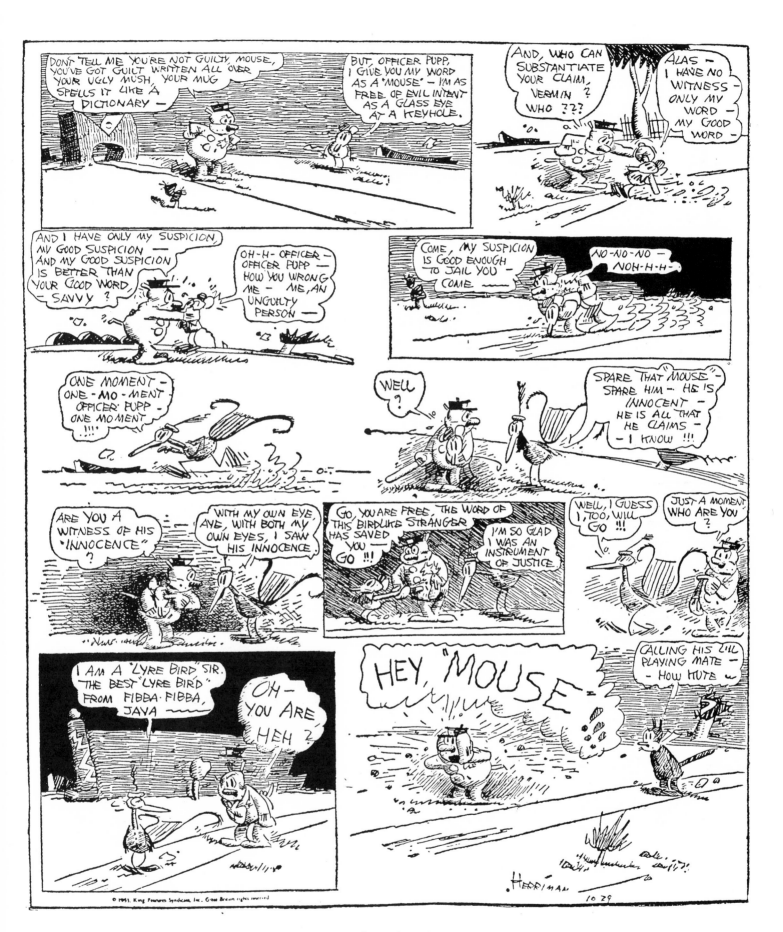

October 29th, 1933.

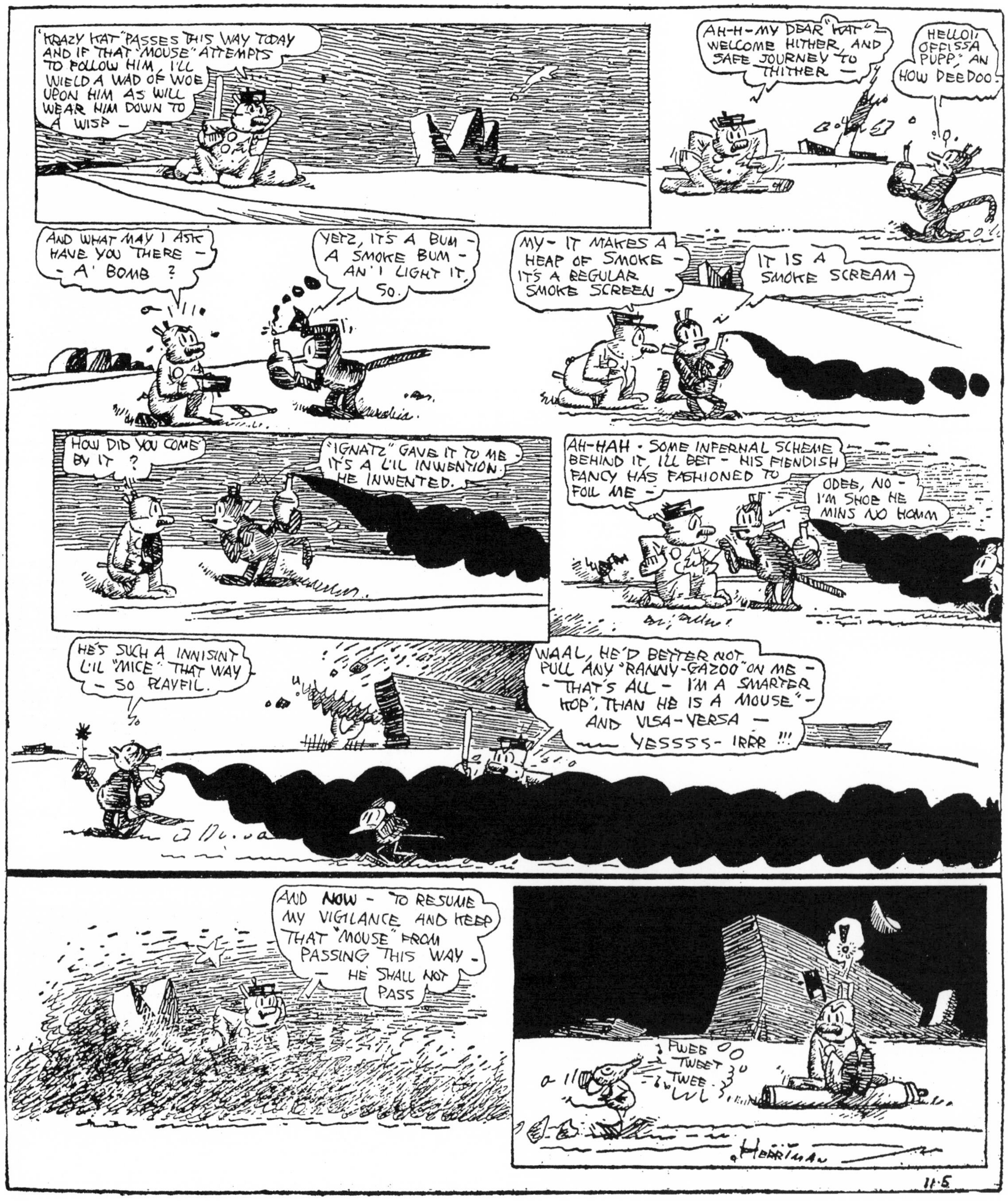
"KRAZY KAT" PASSES THIS WAY TODAY AND IF THAT "MOUSE" ATTEMPTS TO FOLLOW HIM, I'LL WIELD A WAD OF WOE UPON HIM AS WILL WEAR HIM DOWN TO A WISP –
AH-H – MY DEAR "KAT" – WELCOME HITHER, AND SAFE JOURNEY TO THITHER –
HELLO!! OFFISSA PUPP," AN HOW DEE DOO.
AND WHAT MAY I ASK HAVE YOU THERE – – A' BOMB ?
YETZ, IT'S A BUM – A SMOKE BUM – AN' I LIGHT IT, SO.
MY – IT MAKES A HEAP OF SMOKE – IT'S A REGULAR SMOKE SCREEN –
IT IS A SMOKE SCREAM –
HOW DID YOU COME BY IT ?
"IGNATZ" GAVE IT TO ME IT'S A L'IL INWENTION HE INWENTED.
AH-HAH – SOME INFERNAL SCHEME BEHIND IT, I'LL BET – HIS FIENDISH FANCY HAS FASHIONED TO FOIL ME –
ODEE, NO – I'M SHOE HE MINS NO HOMM
HE'S SUCH A INNISINT L'IL "MICE" THAT WAY – SO PLAYFIL.
WAAL, HE'D BETTER NOT PULL ANY "RANNY-GAZOO" ON ME – – THAT'S ALL – I'M A SMARTER "KOP", THAN HE IS A MOUSE" – AND VLSA-VERSA – —— YESSSS – IRRR !!!
AND NOW – TO RESUME MY VIGILANCE AND KEEP THAT "MOUSE" FROM PASSING THIS WAY – – HE SHALL NOT PASS
FWEE TWEET TWEE
HERRIMAN
11-5

November 5th, 1933.

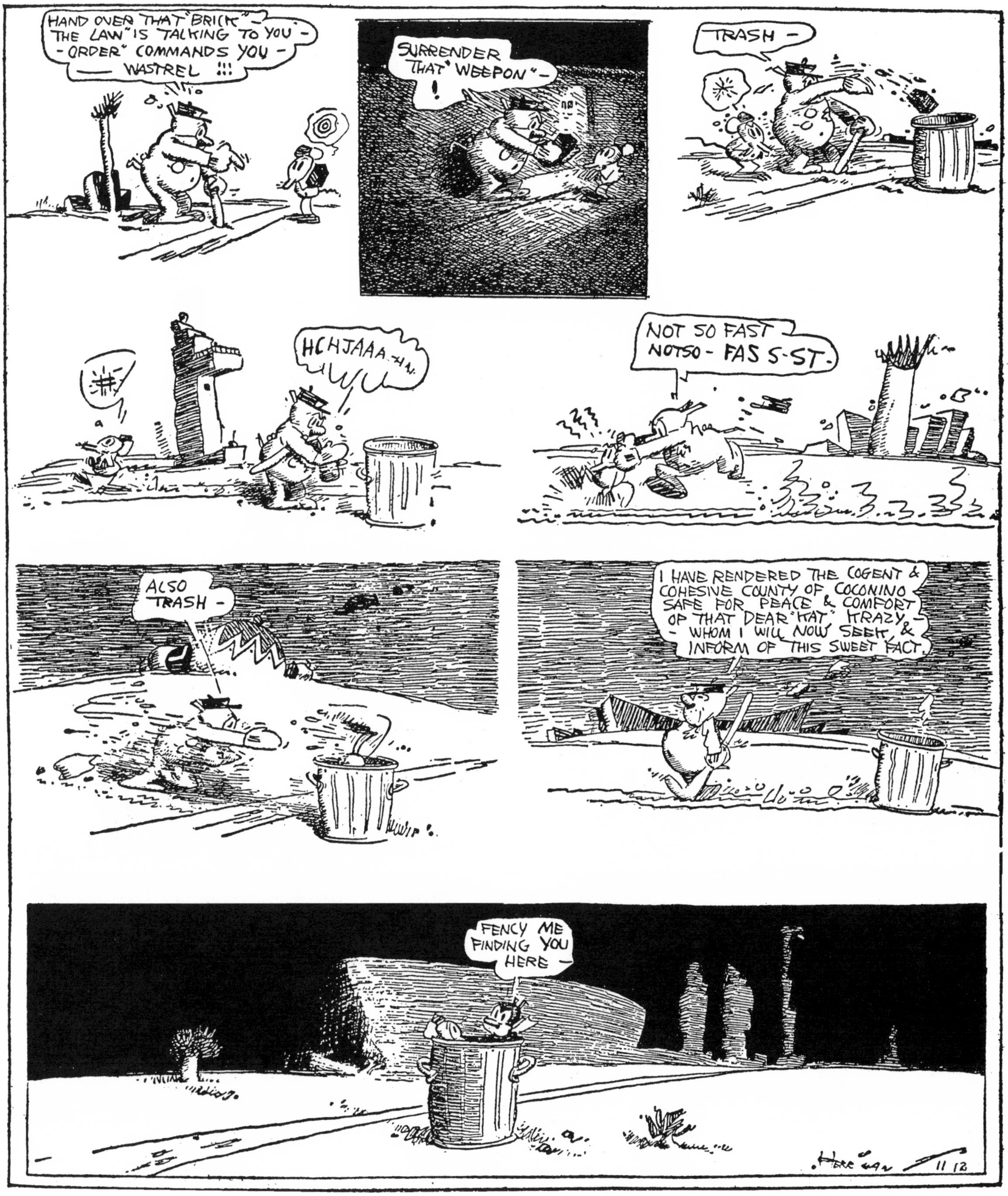

HAND OVER THAT "BRICK" - THE "LAW" IS TALKING TO YOU - "ORDER" COMMANDS YOU - — WASTREL !!!
SURRENDER THAT "WEEPON" - !
TRASH -
HCHJAAA-
NOT SO FAST NOTSO - FAS S-ST -
ALSO TRASH -
I HAVE RENDERED THE COGENT & COHESIVE COUNTY OF COCONINO SAFE FOR PEACE & COMFORT OF THAT DEAR "KAT" KRAZY - WHOM I WILL NOW SEEK & INFORM OF THIS SWEET FACT.
FENCY ME FINDING YOU HERE -

November 12th, 1933.

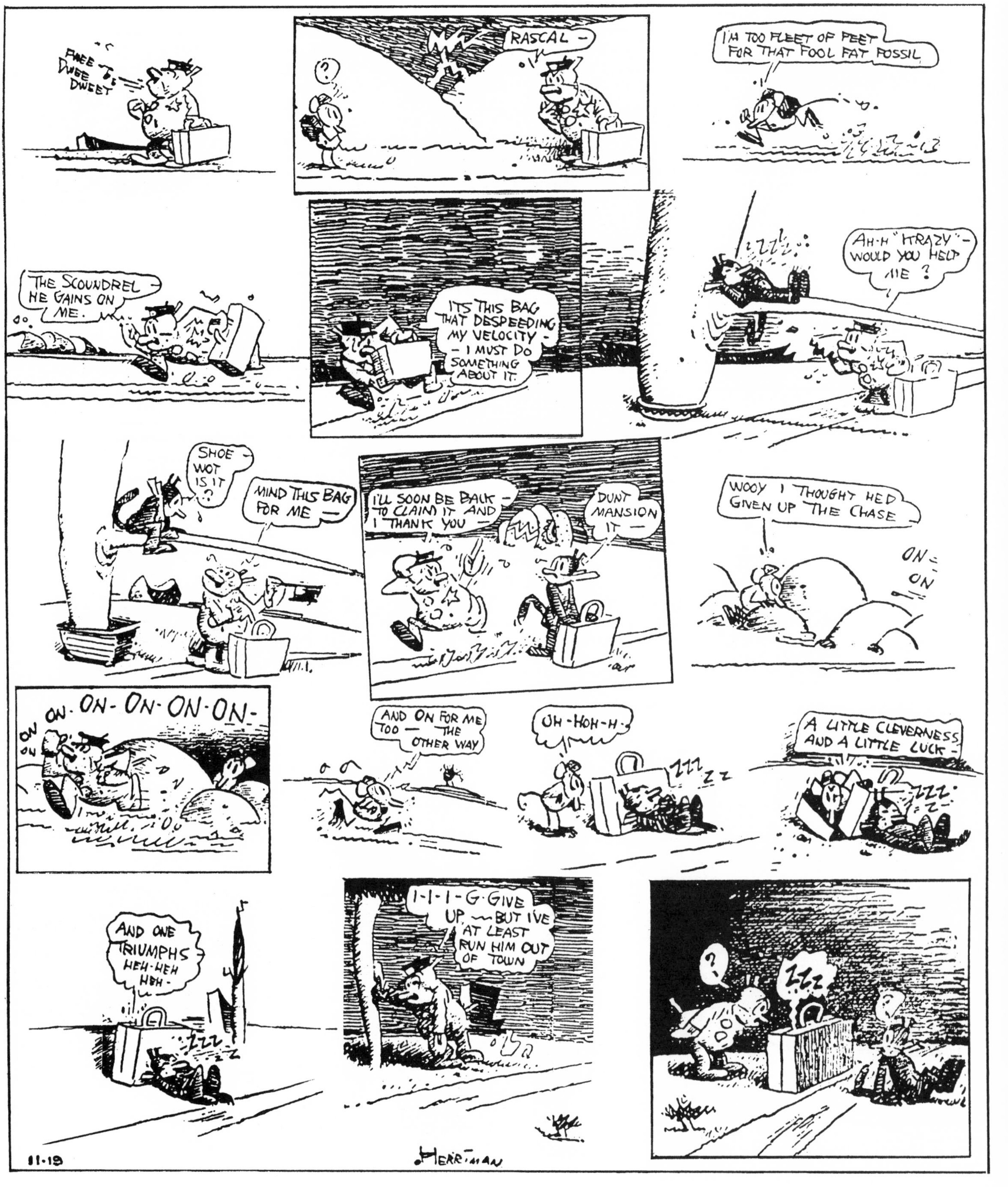
FWEE DWEE DWEET
RASCAL
I'M TOO FLEET OF FEET FOR THAT FOOL FAT FOSSIL
THE SCOUNDREL HE GAINS ON ME.
ITS THIS BAG THAT DESPEEDING MY VELOCITY - I MUST DO SOMETHING ABOUT IT.
AH-H "KRAZY" - WOULD YOU HELP ME ?
SHOE WOT IS IT ?
MIND THIS BAG FOR ME
I'LL SOON BE BACK TO CLAIM IT AND I THANK YOU
DUNT MANSION IT
WOOY I THOUGHT HE'D GIVEN UP THE CHASE
ON ON
ON ON ON - ON - ON - ON - ON -
AND ON FOR ME TOO - THE OTHER WAY
OH - HOH - H
A LITTLE CLEVERNESS AND A LITTLE LUCK
AND ONE TRIUMPHS HEH-HEH HEH
I-I-I-G GIVE UP, BUT I'VE AT LEAST RUN HIM OUT OF TOWN
?
ZZZ
11-19
HERRIMAN

November 19th, 1933.

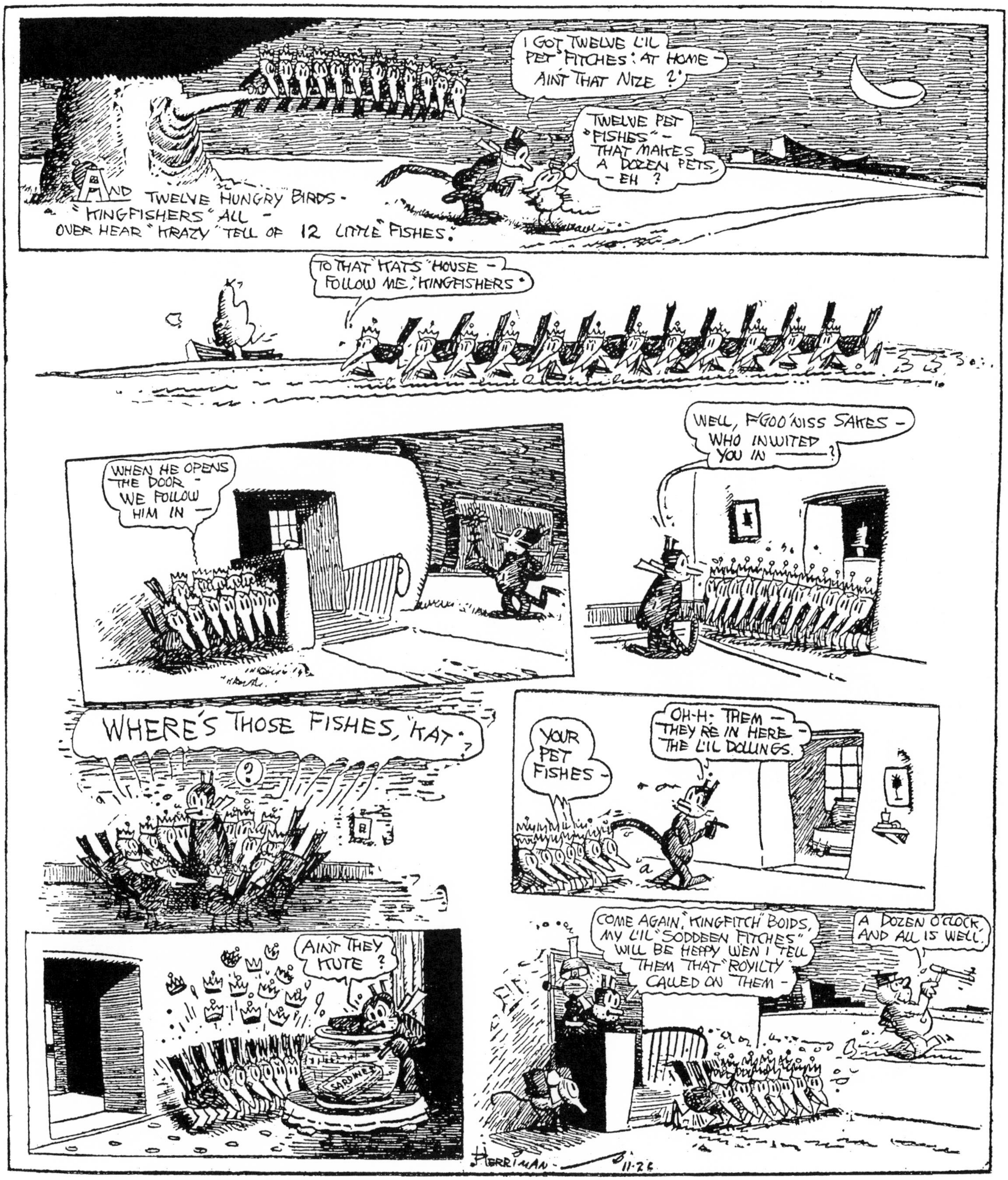
I GOT TWELVE L'IL PET FITCHES AT HOME - AIN'T THAT NIZE ?
TWELVE PET "FISHES" - THAT MAKES A DOZEN PETS, - EH ?
AND TWELVE HUNGRY BIRDS - "KINGFISHERS" ALL - OVER HEAR "KRAZY" TELL OF 12 LITTLE FISHES.
TO THAT KAT'S HOUSE - FOLLOW ME, KINGFISHERS
WHEN HE OPENS THE DOOR - WE FOLLOW HIM IN -
WELL, F'GOO'NISS SAKES - WHO INWITED YOU IN ?
WHERE'S THOSE FISHES, KAT ?
YOUR PET FISHES -
OH-H: THEM - THEY'RE IN HERE THE L'IL DOLLINGS.
AIN'T THEY KUTE ?
SARDINES
COME AGAIN, "KINGFITCH" BOIDS, MY L'IL "SODDEEN FITCHES" WILL BE HEPPY WEN I TELL THEM THAT "ROYILTY" CALLED ON THEM -
A DOZEN O'CLOCK AND ALL IS WELL.
HERRIMAN 11-26

November 26th, 1933.

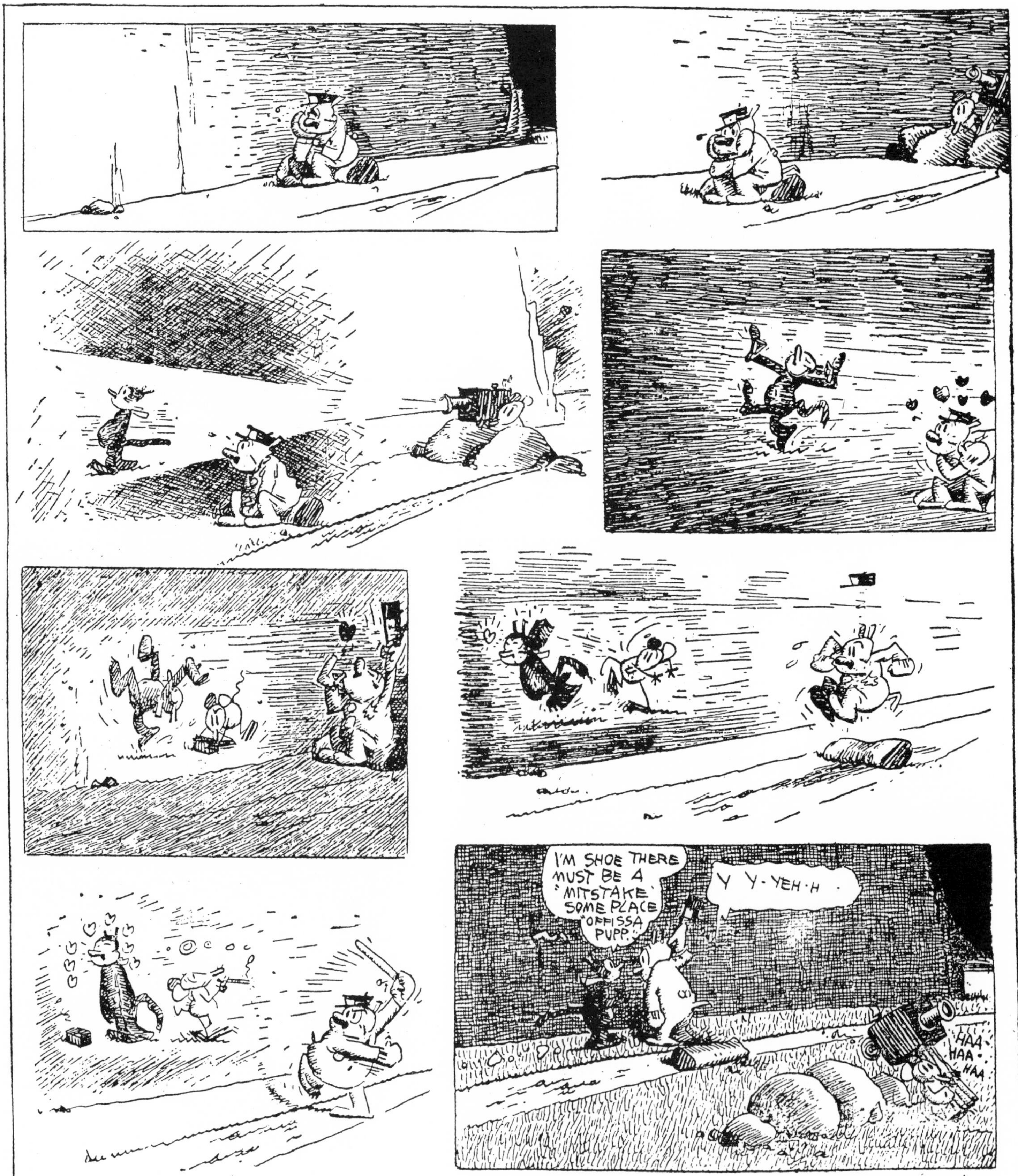
I'M SHOE THERE MUST BE A "MITSTAKE" SOME PLACE "OFFISSA PUPP."
Y Y-YEH-H
HAA HAA HAA
HERRIMAN
123

December 3rd, 1933.

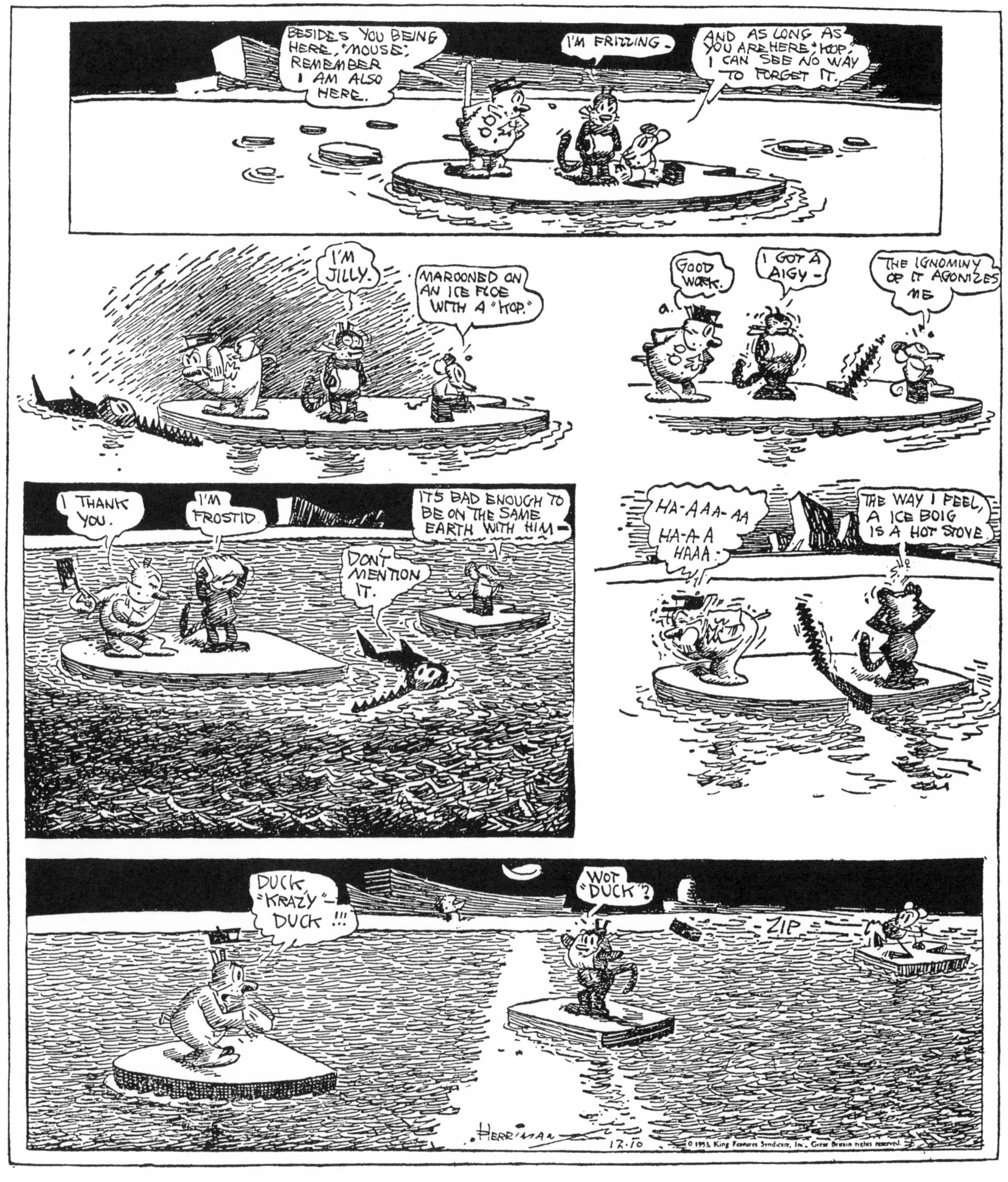
BESIDES YOU BEING HERE, "MOUSE," REMEMBER I AM ALSO HERE.
I'M FRIZZING -
AND AS LONG AS YOU ARE HERE, "KOP," I CAN SEE NO WAY TO FORGET IT.
I'M JILLY.
MAROONED ON AN ICE FLOE WITH A "KOP."
GOOD WORK.
I GOT A AIGY -
THE IGNOMINY OF IT AGONIZES ME
I THANK YOU.
I'M FROSTID.
IT'S BAD ENOUGH TO BE ON THE SAME EARTH WITH HIM -
DON'T MENTION IT.
HA-AAA-AA HA-A-A HAAA.
THE WAY I FEEL, A ICE BOIG IS A HOT STOVE.
DUCK, "KRAZY" - DUCK !!!
WOT "DUCK"?
ZIP
HERRIMAN
12-10
© 1933, King Features Syndicate, Inc. Great Britain rights reserved.

December 10th , 1933.

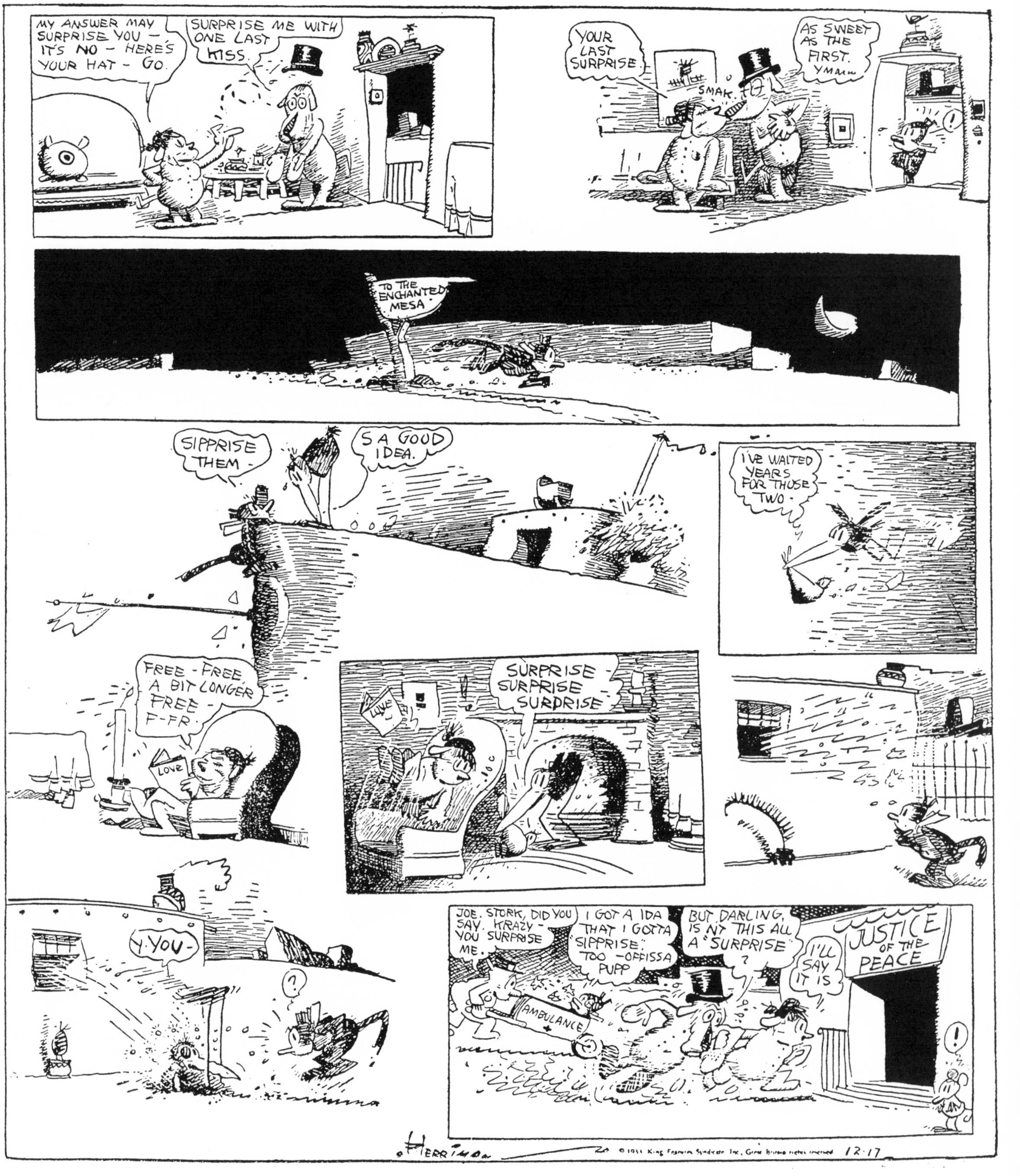
MY ANSWER MAY SURPRISE YOU — IT'S NO — HERE'S YOUR HAT - GO.
SURPRISE ME WITH ONE LAST KISS.
YOUR LAST SURPRISE
AS SWEET AS THE FIRST.
SMAK
TO THE ENCHANTED MESA
SIPPRISE THEM
S A GOOD IDEA.
I'VE WAITED YEARS FOR THOSE TWO -
FREE - FREE A BIT LONGER FREE - F-FR
LOVE
SURPRISE SURPRISE SURPRISE
LOVE
Y-YOU-
?
JOE. STORK, DID YOU SAY. KRAZY - YOU SURPRISE ME.
I GOT A IDA THAT I GOTTA SIPPRISE, TOO — OFFISSA PUPP
BUT, DARLING, IS N'T THIS ALL A "SURPRISE"?
I'LL SAY IT IS
JUSTICE OF THE PEACE
AMBULANCE
!
Herriman
12·17

December 17th, 1933.

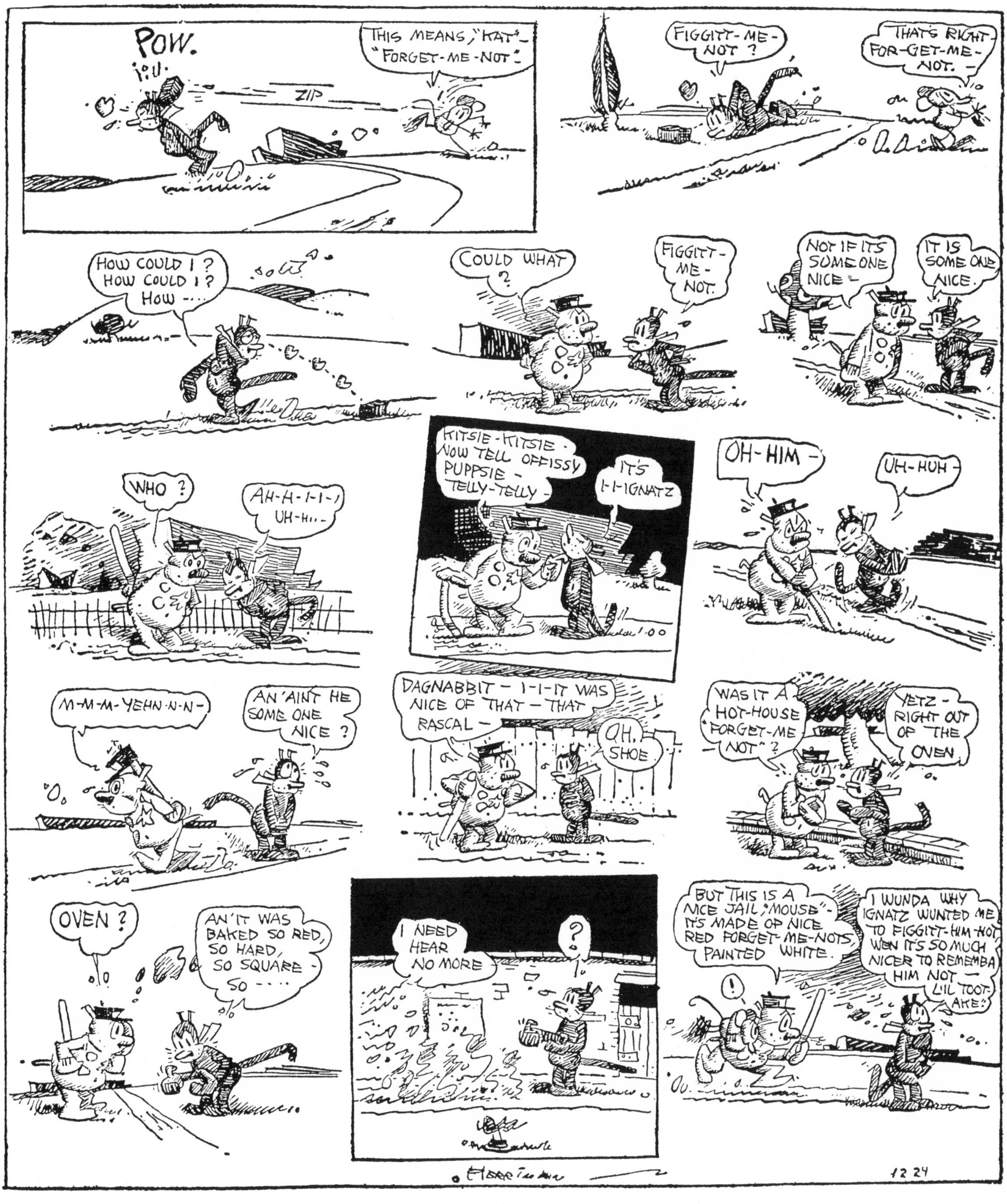

POW.
ZIP
THIS MEANS, "KAT" — "FORGET-ME-NOT".
FIGGITT-ME-NOT?
THAT'S RIGHT FOR-GET-ME-NOT.
HOW COULD I? HOW COULD I? HOW —...
COULD WHAT?
FIGGITT-ME-NOT.
NOT IF ITS SOME ONE NICE —
IT IS SOME ONE NICE.
WHO?
AH-H-I-I-I UH-HI...
KITSIE-KITSIE NOW TELL OFFISSY PUPPSIE — TELLY-TELLY —
IT'S I-I-IGNATZ
OH-HIM —
UH-HUH —
M-M-M-YEHN-N-N —
AN' AIN'T HE SOME ONE NICE?
DAGNABBIT — I-I-IT WAS NICE OF THAT — THAT RASCAL —
OH, SHOE
WAS IT A HOT-HOUSE "FORGET-ME-NOT"?
YETZ — RIGHT OUT OF THE OVEN
OVEN?
AN' IT WAS BAKED SO RED, SO HARD, SO SQUARE — SO —...
I NEED HEAR NO MORE
?
BUT THIS IS A NICE JAIL, "MOUSE" — IT'S MADE OF NICE RED FORGET-ME-NOTS, PAINTED WHITE.
!
I WUNDA WHY IGNATZ WUNTED ME TO FIGGITT-HIM-NOT WEN IT'S SO MUCH NICER TO REMEMBA HIM NOT — LIL TOOT-AKE!

December 24th, 1933.

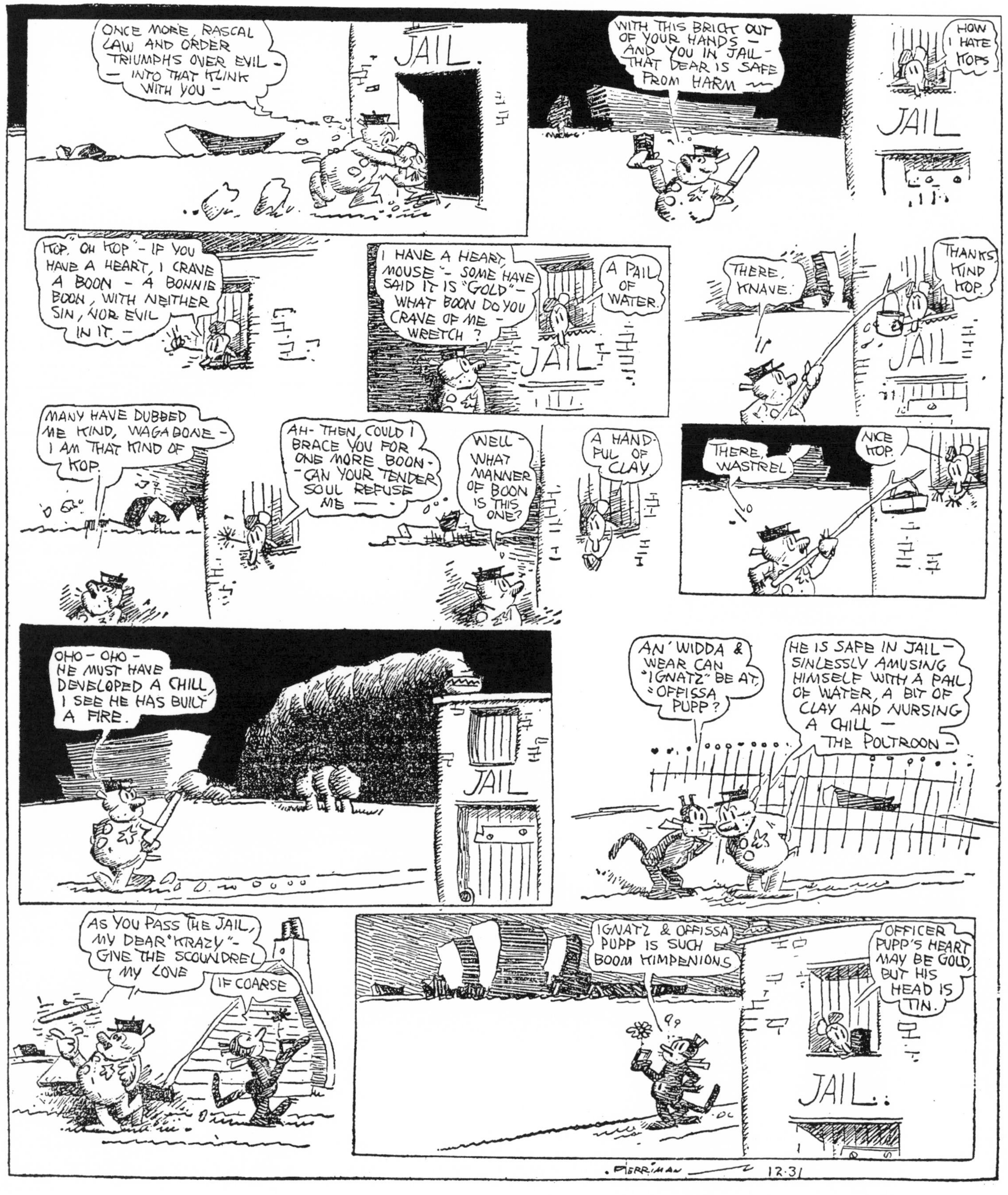

ONCE MORE, RASCAL LAW AND ORDER TRIUMPHS OVER EVIL — INTO THAT KLINK WITH YOU —
JAIL.
WITH THIS BRICK OUT OF YOUR HANDS — AND YOU IN JAIL — THAT DEAR IS SAFE FROM HARM
HOW I HATE KOPS
JAIL
KOP, OH KOP — IF YOU HAVE A HEART, I CRAVE A BOON — A BONNIE BOON, WITH NEITHER SIN, NOR EVIL IN IT. —
I HAVE A HEART, MOUSE — SOME HAVE SAID IT IS "GOLD" — WHAT BOON DO YOU CRAVE OF ME — WRETCH ?
A PAIL OF WATER.
JAIL
THERE, KNAVE.
THANKS, KIND KOP.
JAIL
MANY HAVE DUBBED ME KIND, WAGABONE — I AM THAT KIND OF KOP.
AH — THEN, COULD I BRACE YOU FOR ONE MORE BOON — CAN YOUR TENDER SOUL REFUSE ME —
WELL — WHAT MANNER OF BOON IS THIS ONE?
A HAND-FUL OF CLAY
THERE, WASTREL
NICE KOP.
OHO — OHO — HE MUST HAVE DEVELOPED A CHILL, I SEE HE HAS BUILT A FIRE.
JAIL
AN' WIDDA & WEAR CAN "IGNATZ" BE AT, OFFISSA PUPP?
HE IS SAFE IN JAIL — SINLESSLY AMUSING HIMSELF WITH A PAIL OF WATER, A BIT OF CLAY AND NURSING A CHILL — THE POLTROON —
AS YOU PASS THE JAIL, MY DEAR "KRAZY" — GIVE THE SCOUNDREL MY LOVE
IF COARSE
IGNATZ & OFFISSA PUPP IS SUCH BOOM KIMPENIONS
OFFICER PUPP'S HEART MAY BE GOLD, BUT HIS HEAD IS TIN.
JAIL.
HERRIMAN 12-31

December 31st, 1933.

1934.

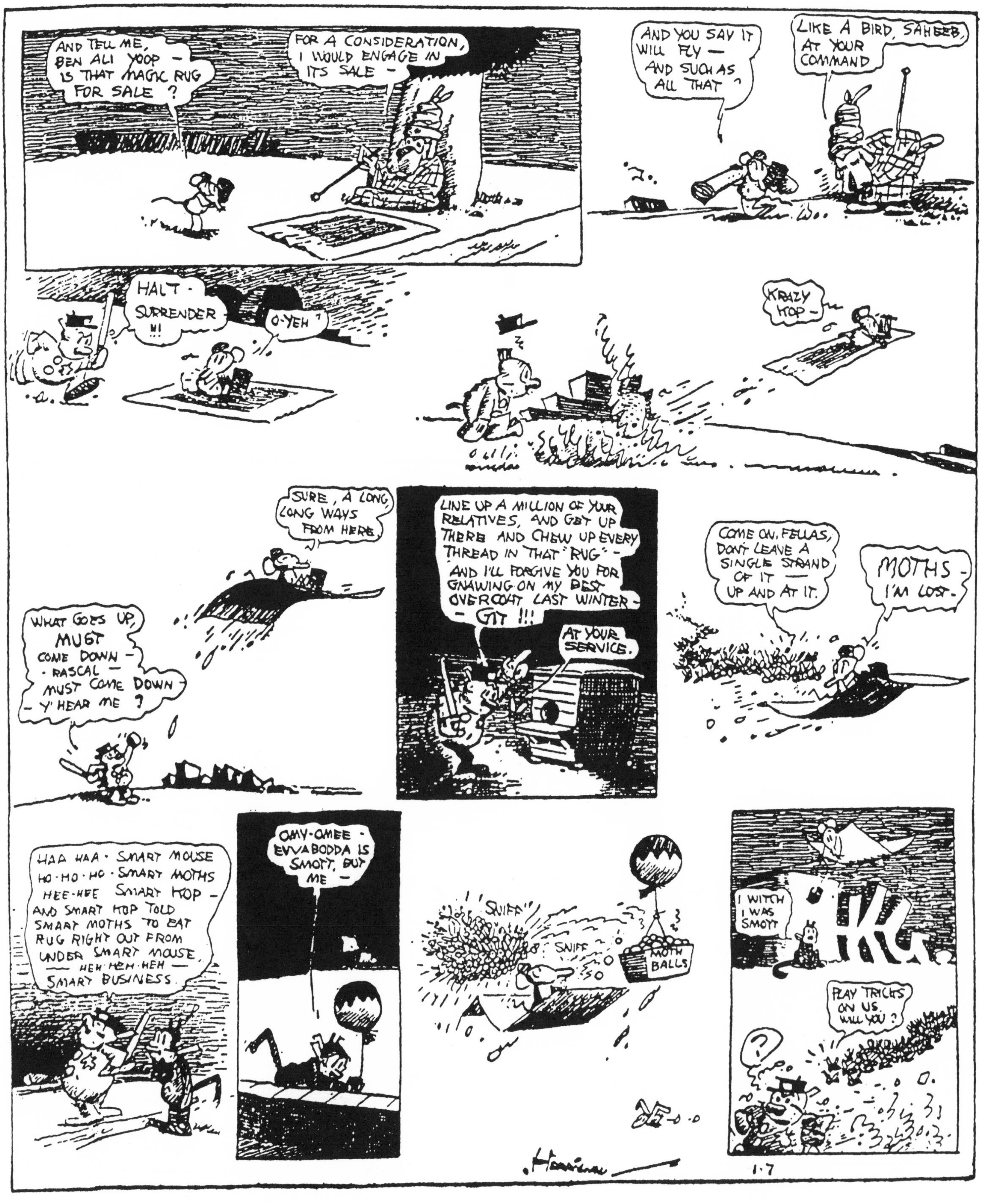
AND TELL ME, BEN ALI YOOP - IS THAT MAGIC RUG FOR SALE ?
FOR A CONSIDERATION, I WOULD ENGAGE IN ITS SALE -
AND YOU SAY IT WILL FLY - AND SUCH AS ALL THAT ?
LIKE A BIRD, SAHEEB, AT YOUR COMMAND
HALT - SURRENDER !!!
O-YEH
KRAZY KOP -
SURE, A LONG, LONG WAYS FROM HERE.
WHAT GOES UP, MUST COME DOWN - - RASCAL - MUST COME DOWN - Y' HEAR ME ?
LINE UP A MILLION OF YOUR RELATIVES, AND GET UP THERE AND CHEW UP EVERY THREAD IN THAT RUG - AND I'LL FORGIVE YOU FOR GNAWING ON MY BEST OVERCOAT LAST WINTER - GIT !!!
AT YOUR SERVICE.
COME ON, FELLAS, DON'T LEAVE A SINGLE STRAND OF IT - UP AND AT IT.
MOTHS - I'M LOST -
HAA HAA - SMART MOUSE HO-HO-HO - SMART MOTHS HEE-HEE SMART KOP - AND SMART KOP TOLD SMART MOTHS TO EAT RUG RIGHT OUT FROM UNDER SMART MOUSE. - HEH HEH HEH - SMART BUSINESS.
OAKY-OMEE - EVVABODDA IS SMOTT, BUT ME -
SNIFF
SNIFF
MOTH BALLS
I WITCH I WAS SMOTT
KG
PLAY TRICKS ON US, WILL YOU ?
?
Herriman
1-7

January 7th, 1934.

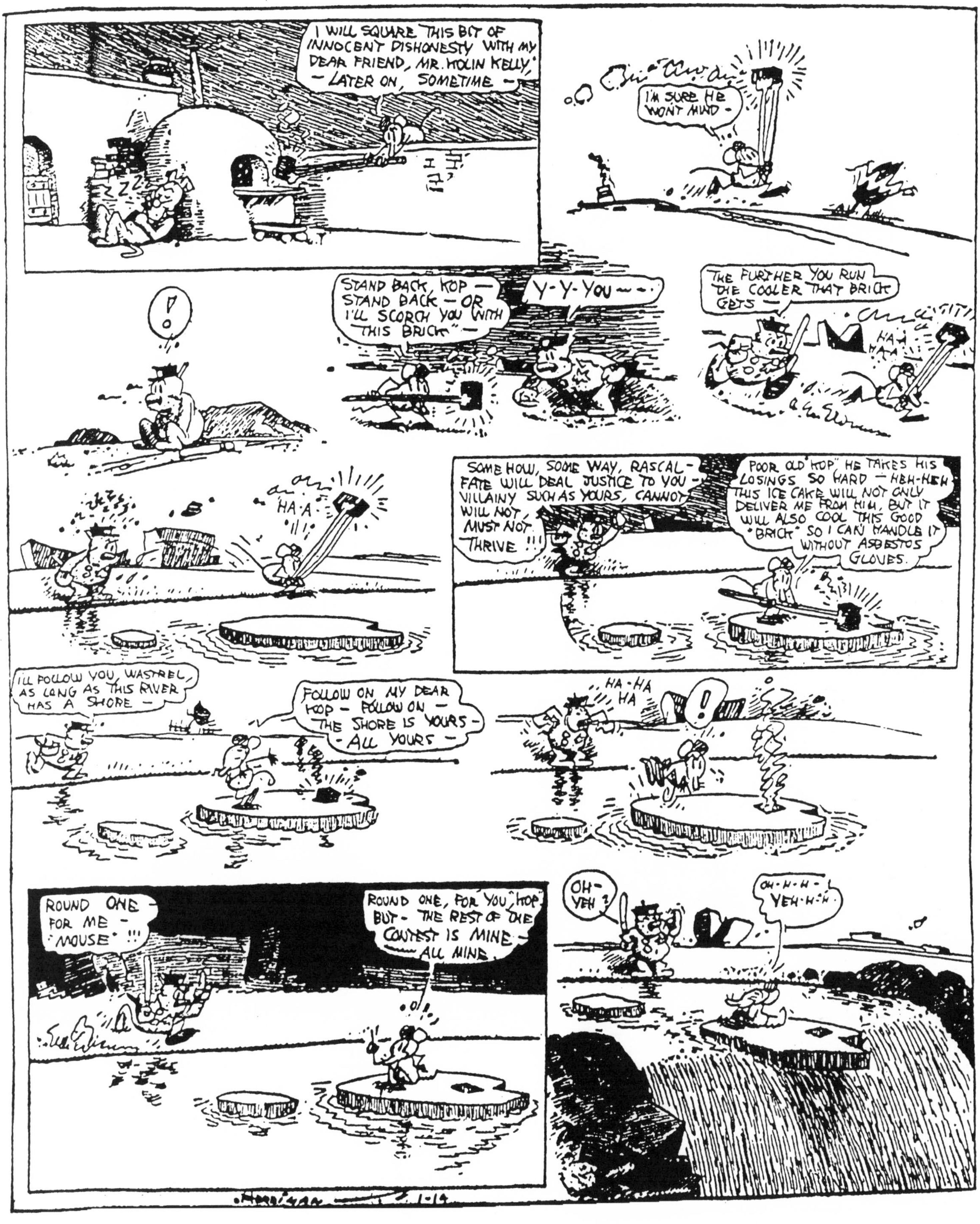
I WILL SQUARE THIS BIT OF INNOCENT DISHONESTY WITH MY DEAR FRIEND, MR. KOLIN KELLY — LATER ON, SOMETIME —
I'M SURE HE WON'T MIND —
STAND BACK, KOP — STAND BACK — OR I'LL SCORCH YOU WITH THIS BRICK —
Y-Y-YOU — — .
THE FURTHER YOU RUN THE COOLER THAT BRICK GETS —
HA HAA
HA-A
SOME HOW, SOME WAY, RASCAL — FATE WILL DEAL JUSTICE TO YOU — VILLAINY SUCH AS YOURS, CANNOT, WILL NOT, MUST NOT THRIVE !!!
POOR OLD "KOP," HE TAKES HIS LOSINGS SO HARD — HEH-HEH THIS ICE CAKE WILL NOT ONLY DELIVER ME FROM HIM, BUT IT WILL ALSO COOL THIS GOOD "BRICK" SO I CAN HANDLE IT WITHOUT ASBESTOS GLOVES.
I'LL FOLLOW YOU, WASTREL, AS LONG AS THIS RIVER HAS A SHORE —
FOLLOW ON MY DEAR KOP — FOLLOW ON — THE SHORE IS YOURS — ALL YOURS —
HA-HA HA
ROUND ONE FOR ME — MOUSE !!!
ROUND ONE, FOR YOU, "KOP" BUT — THE REST OF THE CONTEST IS MINE — ALL MINE
OH-YEH ?
OH-H-H — YEH-H-H
Herriman 1-14

January 14th, 1934.

AND WHO IS THIS LITTLE "BEE", MR. BUM BILL BEE ?
OH, HE'S JUST SO SO, Y'KNOW, NOT ONE OF OUR BEST -
PFEEP -
DID HE SAY THAT L'IL BEE WAS JUST "SOW SOW" - MAYBE HE MENDED THAT HE WAS A "SOWING" BEE
YES, I GUESS HE MEANT HE WAS A "SEWING BEE"
I'LL HELP HIM - I'LL GIVE HIM SOMETHING TO SEW.
ME, TOO, I'LL GIVE HIM ALSO SOMETHING TO "SOW."
OF COURSE, I DID NOT INTRODUCE YOU - WHY SHOULD I ? - YOU, A LOAFER - A LOWLIFE, A "DRONE" - I SHOULD SAY NOT -
PFUF
PFAAAA-
AH-H-HMMM
ZZZZZZ
"THESE" HAVE BEEN IN NEED OF A PATCH FOR SOMETIME - IT WILL MEAN AN HONEST PENNY OR TWO FOR THAT POOR LITTLE "SEWING BEE" TO MEND THEM.
I NID THIS WEET TO MAKE ME SOME "WEET-CAKES" BUT THAT POO' LI'L "SOWING BEE" NIDS IT MO' - TO SOW & SELL FOR TWO HONEST PENNIES OR SO -
WHEAT.
WELL !!! WHY SHOULD ONE WORK, WHEN FOOD & RAIMENT COMES TO ONE - PROOF ON THOSE "BUSY" BEES.
WHEAT.
JUST AS I WAS GETTING QUITE HUNGRY AND VERY CHILLY.
WHEAT
I GAVE THAT L'IL "SOWING BEE" SOMETHING TO SOW, AND I'M GOING TO SEE IF HE DONE IT.
I GAVE HIM SOMETHING TO "SEW," TOO I'M GOING, TOO.
I'LL GO WITH YOU.
ME, TOO
HERRIMAN 1-28

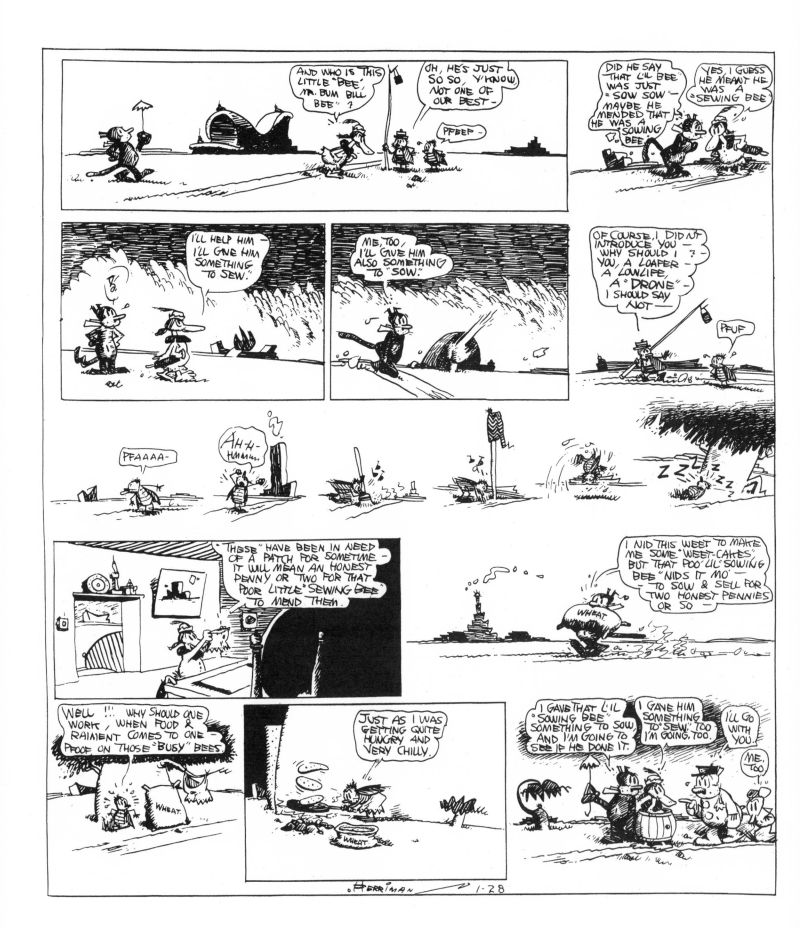

January 28th, 1934.

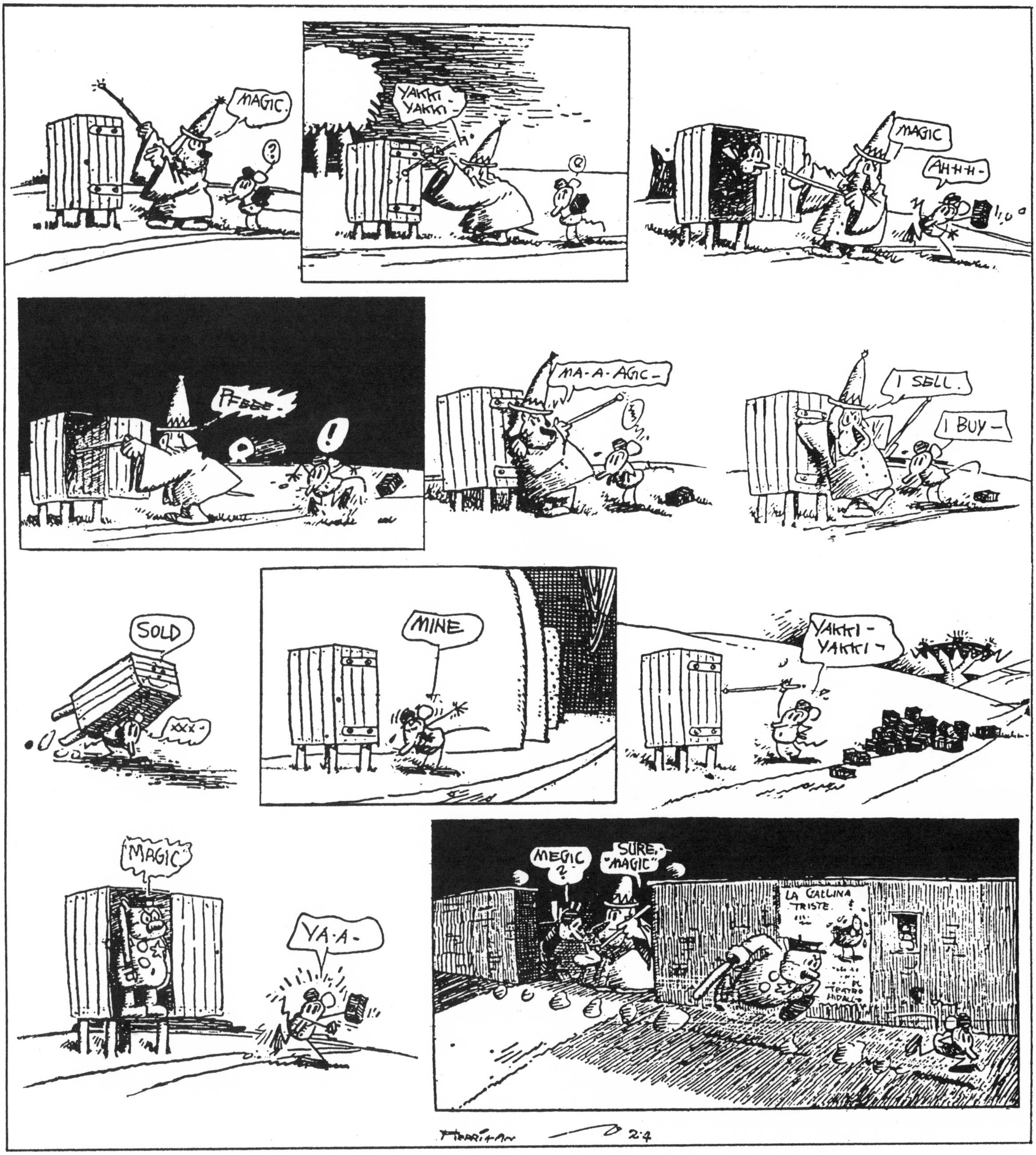
MAGIC.
YAKKI YAKKI
MAGIC
AH-H-H-
PFBBB
!
MA-A-AGIC-
I SELL.
I BUY-
SOLD
XXX
MINE
YAKKI-YAKKI-
MAGIC
YA-A-
MEGIC ?
SURE "MAGIC"
LA GALLINA TRISTE
TEATRO HIDALGO
HERRIMAN 2-4

February 4th, 1934.

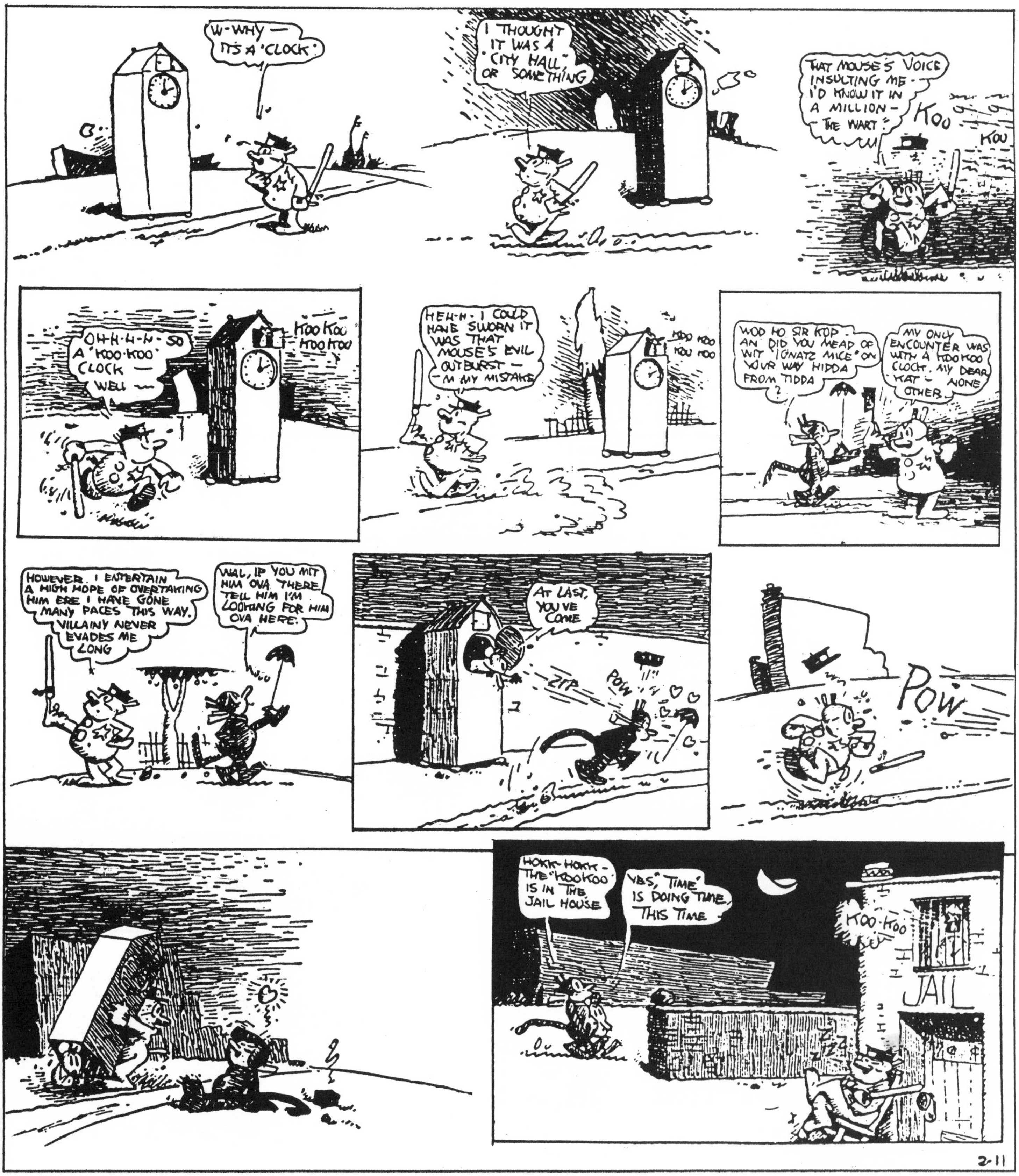
W-WHY— IT'S A 'CLOCK'
I THOUGHT IT WAS A "CITY HALL" OR SOMETHING
THAT MOUSE'S VOICE INSULTING ME - I'D KNOW IT IN A MILLION - THE WART
KOO KOO
OH-H-H-H- SO A 'KOO-KOO' CLOCK — WELL —
KOO KOO KOO KOO
HEH-H- I COULD HAVE SWORN IT WAS THAT MOUSE'S EVIL OUTBURST — M MY MISTAKE
KOO KOO KOO KOO
WOD HO SIR KOP. AN' DID YOU MEAD OF WIT 'IGNATZ MICE' ON YOUR WAY HIDDA FROM TIDDA ?
MY ONLY ENCOUNTER WAS WITH A KOO KOO CLOCK. MY DEAR KAT - NONE OTHER.
HOWEVER, I ENTERTAIN A HIGH HOPE OF OVERTAKING HIM ERE I HAVE GONE MANY PACES THIS WAY. VILLAINY NEVER EVADES ME LONG
WAL, IF YOU MIT HIM OVA THERE, TELL HIM I'M LOOKING FOR HIM OVA HERE.
AT LAST, YOU'VE COME
ZIP
POW
POW
HOKK-HOKK- THE "KOOKOO" IS IN THE JAIL HOUSE
YES, "TIME" IS DOING TIME, THIS TIME
KOO-KOO
JAIL
2-11

February 11th, 1934.

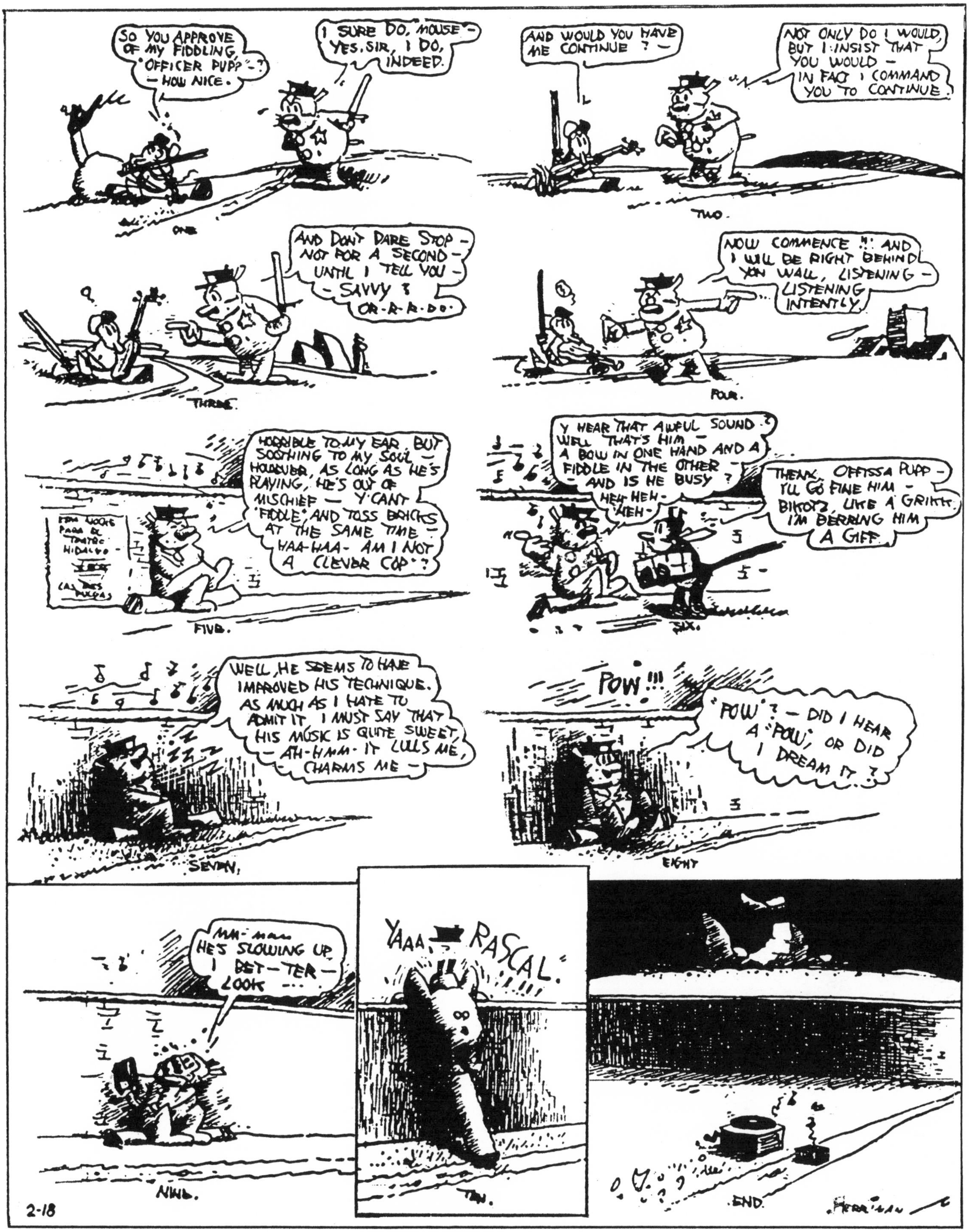
SO YOU APPROVE OF MY FIDDLING, OFFICER PUPP? – HOW NICE.
I SURE DO, MOUSE – YES, SIR, I DO, INDEED.
ONE.
AND WOULD YOU HAVE ME CONTINUE ? –
NOT ONLY DO I WOULD, BUT I INSIST THAT YOU WOULD – IN FACT I COMMAND YOU TO CONTINUE.
TWO.
AND DON'T DARE STOP – NOT FOR A SECOND – UNTIL I TELL YOU – SAVVY? OR-R-R-D-O.
THREE.
NOW COMMENCE !! AND I WILL BE RIGHT BEHIND YON WALL, LISTENING – LISTENING INTENTLY.
FOUR.
HORRIBLE TO MY EAR, BUT SOOTHING TO MY SOUL – HOWEVER, AS LONG AS HE'S PLAYING, HE'S OUT OF MISCHIEF – Y CAN'T "FIDDLE" AND TOSS BRICKS AT THE SAME TIME – HAA-HAA – AM I NOT A CLEVER COP?
FIVE.
Y HEAR THAT AWFUL SOUND? WELL THAT'S HIM – A BOW IN ONE HAND AND A FIDDLE IN THE OTHER – AND IS HE BUSY? HEH HEH – HEH –
THENK, OFFISSA PUPP – YU GO FINE HIM – BIKOTZ, LIKE A GRIKH, I'M BERRING HIM A GIFF.
SIX.
WELL, HE SEEMS TO HAVE IMPROVED HIS TECHNIQUE. AS MUCH AS I HATE TO ADMIT IT, I MUST SAY THAT HIS MUSIC IS QUITE SWEET, – AH-HMM – IT LULLS ME, CHARMS ME –
SEVEN.
POW!!!
"POW"? – DID I HEAR A "POW," OR DID I DREAM IT?
EIGHT
MM-MM HE'S SLOWING UP, I BET-TER LOOK –...
NINE.
YAAA – RASCAL.
TEN.
END.
HERRIMAN
2-18

February 18th, 1934.

February 25th, 1934.

HALT, WORM
WHAT DO YOU SUPPOSE I GOT UP EARLY FOR - HEH?
"EARLY MORN", EARLY KATBIRD" EARLY WORM"
WELL, IF I DONT GET YOU, THE EARLY "KATFISH" WILL.
SAVED.
YOU SAVED ME
YES, AND NOW - WHAT ?
YOU'VE COME JUST IN TIME, "OFFICER PUPP" YOU'LL NOTICE THAT THAT "MOUSE" HAS SOMETHING IN THAT DIPPER.
OHO-
AND WE TRUST YOU HAVE SOME IDEA WHAT HE HAS IN THAT DIPPER - "OFFICER".
THE WATER IS WET AND DEEP AND COLD - BUT "DUTY" CALLS !!!
OH, WELL, THERE'S ANOTHER EARLY MORN TOMORROW
NO, MY DEAR "OFFICER PUPP" NO, NOT A "BRICK" - JUST A POOR LITTLE WORM SAVED FROM THAT EARLY KATBIRD & EARLY KATFISH BY BEING EARLIER THAN THEY WERE.
OH.
LATE HOP
GONE, GONE, MY ENTIRE REGALIA - GONE.
FENCY GETTING UP OILY AN FINDING A POLEETZ MIN'S UNIFORM - MAYBE IF I GET UP OILY TIMORRA I'LL FIND A EDMIRIL'S UNIFORM OR MAYBE A JENERIL'S - WHO KNOWS?
HERRIMAN. 3-4

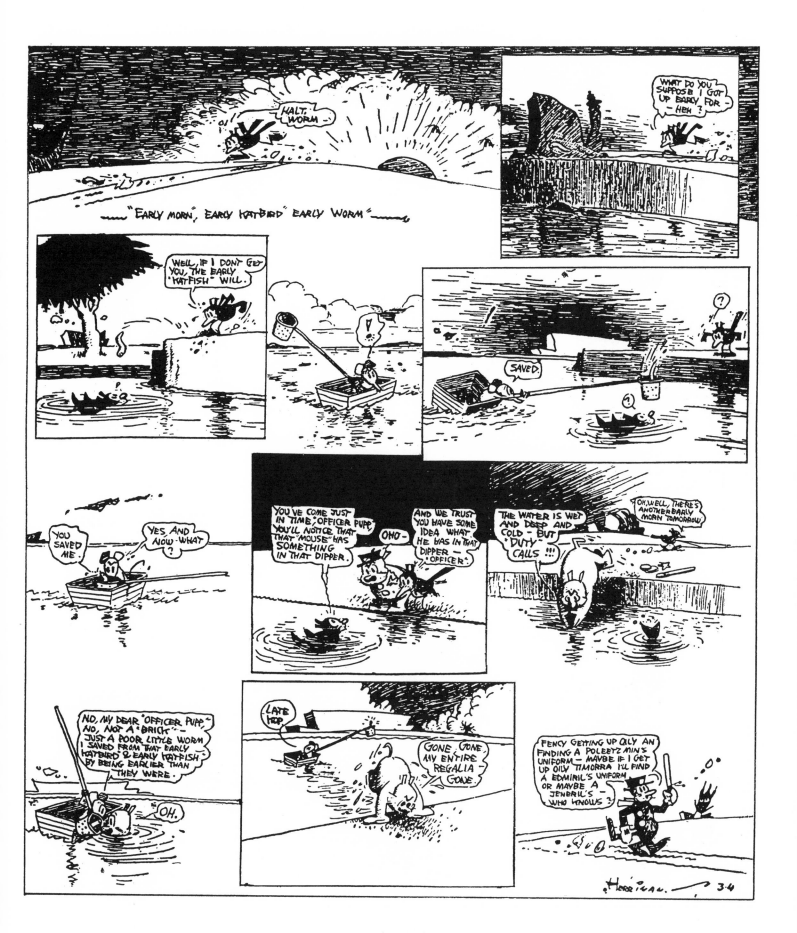

March 4th, 1934.

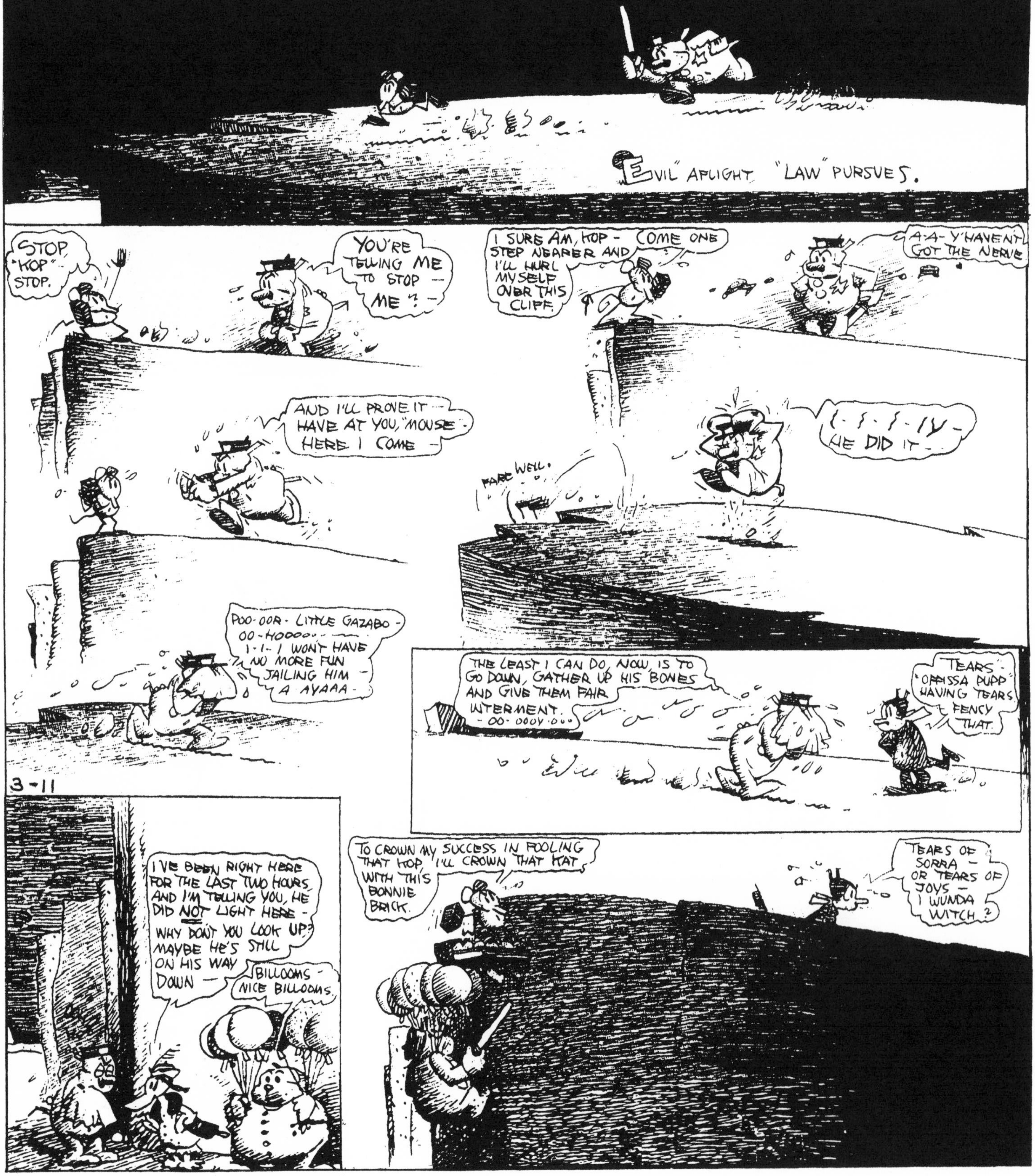
"Evil" aflight "Law" pursues.
Stop "Kop" stop.
You're telling me to stop -- me ?--
I sure am, Kop - come one step nearer and I'll hurl myself over this cliff.
A-A- Y'haven't got the nerve
And I'll prove it - have at you, "mouse" - here I come -
Fare well.
I-I-I-Iy- he did it -
Poo-oor- little gazabo - oo-hoooo.... I-I-I won't have no more fun jailing him - a ayaaa -
3-11
The least I can do, now, is to go down, gather up his bones and give them fair interment. -oo-oooy-o...
Tears - Offissa Pupp having tears - fency that.
I've been right here for the last two hours, and I'm telling you, he did not light here - why don't you look up? maybe he's still on his way down -
Billooms - nice billooms.
To crown my success in fooling that Kop, I'll crown that Kat with this bonnie brick.
Tears of sorra - or tears of joys - I wunda witch?

March 11th, 1934.

THERE NOW, THOSE "AUTO HORNS" ARE ON YOUR FUTILE FEET - AS THOUGH THEY GREW ON THEM - "MOUSE" -
GO, SINNER GO AND AS EVERY STEP YOU TAKE WILL EMIT A "HONK", I WILL AT ALL TIMES KNOW JUST WHERE YOU ARE
HONK
HONK
HAA-HAA-HAAA - - ONCE UPON A TIME YOU "MICE" THOUGHT YOU WERE PRETTY "SMART" TO TIE A "BELL" ON A "CAT" - REMEMBER - HAA-HAA - HAAAAA - -
PFUI -
HONK
HONK
DID I HEAR A OTTO HARM "TOOT", OFFISSA PUPP - OR DID MY "YEARS" DISSIVE ME ?
YOUR PRETTY EARS DID NOT DECEIVE YOU, MY DEAR "KRAZY" - I HAVE THIS DAY WREAKED A WITFUL WREAKMENT UPON THAT WASTREL "IGNATZ" - THE "AUTO HORNS" YOU HEARD, ARE TIED TO HIS SINFUL FEET.
BUT WUNT THAT MAKE HIM TOOT WEN EVVA HE WALKS ?
SURE - THAT'S JUST WHAT I WANT HIM TO DO -
NO -
YEH
HAAA HAAA HAAA
THAT WAS AWFIL NICE OF YOU, OFFISSA PUPP - BECAUSE NOW I WILL ALWAYS KNOW WEN HE'S COMING -
AND SO WILL I, MY DEAR "KRAZY", SO WILL I - - REMEMBER THAT -
I'LL HEAR A HONK, AN' A TOOT AN' THERE WILL BE "IGNATZ" - HOW SWITT.
AND THERE WILL BE, ME - TOO -
HA HA HA
HO HO HO HO HO HO
POW.
AND THEN - HE'LL HONK, AND TOOT TO JAIL -
HAW HAW HOOO
BUT WOT IF HE DOES N'T HONK AN' TOOT WEN HE COMES ?
DON'T MAKE ME LAUGH ANY MORE, KRAZY - I'VE LAUGHED ENOUGH TO DAY.
3.18
HERRIMAN

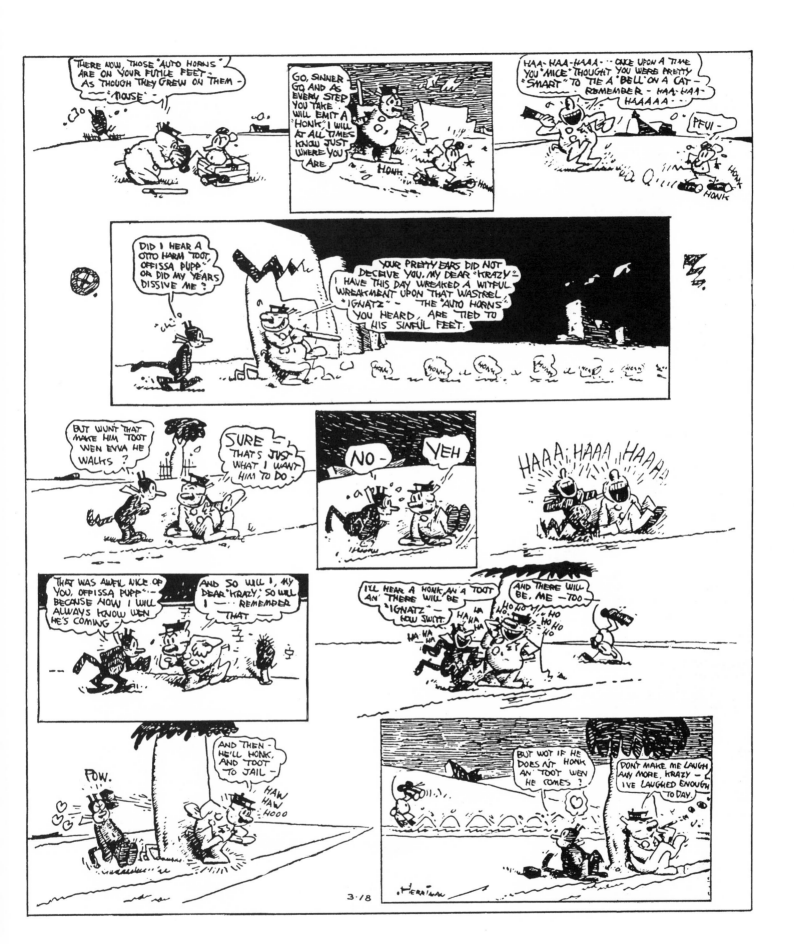

March 18th, 1934.

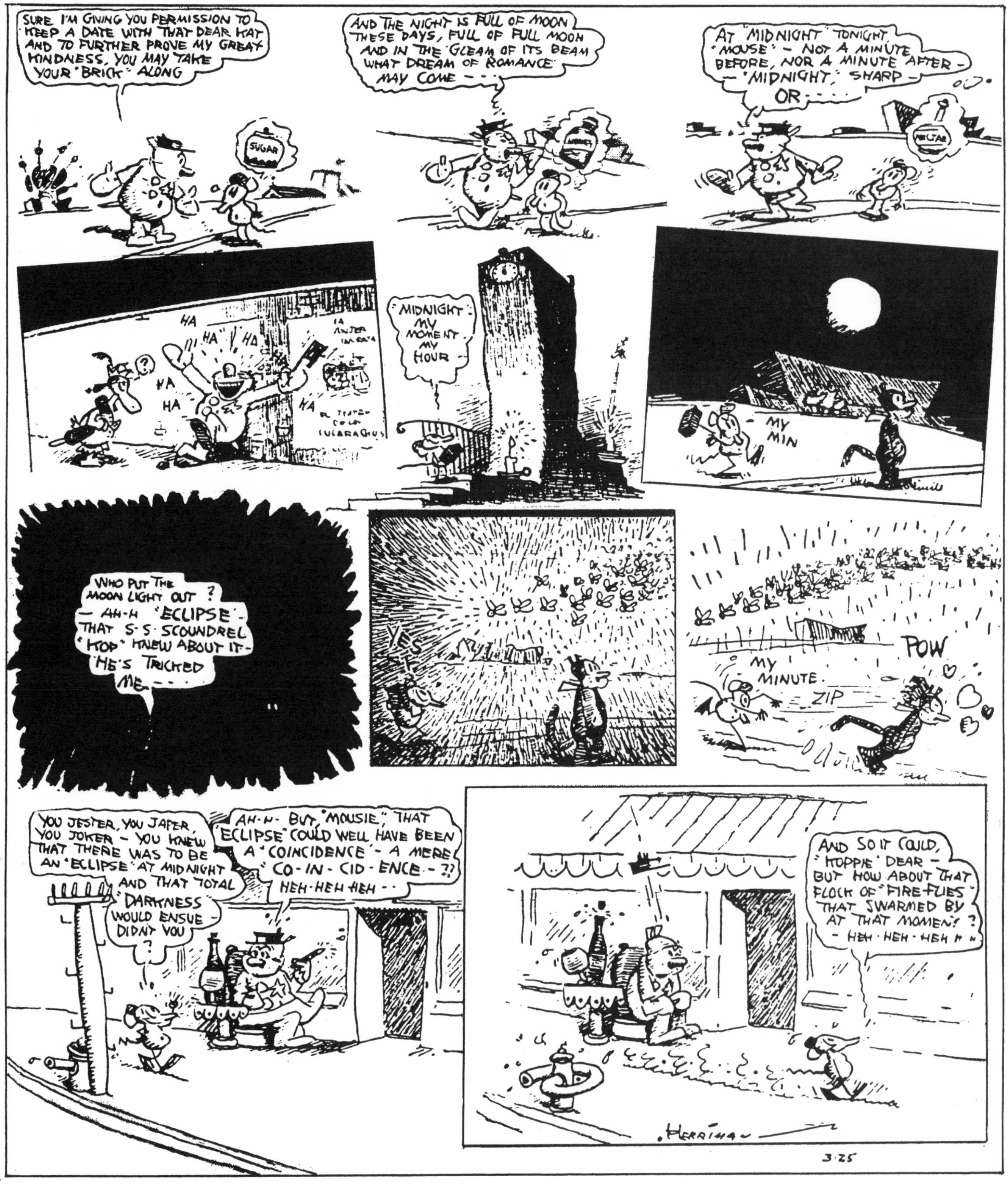
SURE I'M GIVING YOU PERMISSION TO KEEP A DATE WITH THAT DEAR KAT AND TO FURTHER PROVE MY GREAT KINDNESS, YOU MAY TAKE YOUR "BRICK" ALONG
SUGAR
AND THE NIGHT IS FULL OF MOON THESE DAYS, FULL OF FULL MOON AND IN THE "GLEAM OF ITS BEAM" WHAT DREAM OF ROMANCE MAY COME - - -
AT "MIDNIGHT" TONIGHT, "MOUSE" - NOT A MINUTE BEFORE, NOR A MINUTE AFTER - - "MIDNIGHT" SHARP - OR - - -
HA
HA
HA
HA
HA
HA
MIDNIGHT MY MOMENT MY HOUR
MY MIN
WHO PUT THE MOON LIGHT OUT ? - AH-H "ECLIPSE" - THAT S-S-SCOUNDREL "KOP" KNEW ABOUT IT - HE'S TRICKED ME - - -
YES
MY MINUTE
ZIP
POW
YOU JESTER, YOU JAPER, YOU JOKER - YOU KNEW THAT THERE WAS TO BE AN "ECLIPSE" AT MIDNIGHT AND THAT TOTAL "DARKNESS" WOULD ENSUE - DIDN'T YOU ?
AH-H - BUT, "MOUSIE," THAT "ECLIPSE" COULD WELL HAVE BEEN A "COINCIDENCE" - A MERE "CO-IN-CID-ENCE" - ?? HEH-HEH-HEH - -
AND SO IT COULD, "KOPPIE" DEAR - BUT HOW ABOUT THAT FLOCK OF "FIRE-FLIES" THAT SWARMED BY AT THAT MOMENT ? - HEH - HEH - HEH H H
HERRIMAN
3-25

March 25th, 1934.

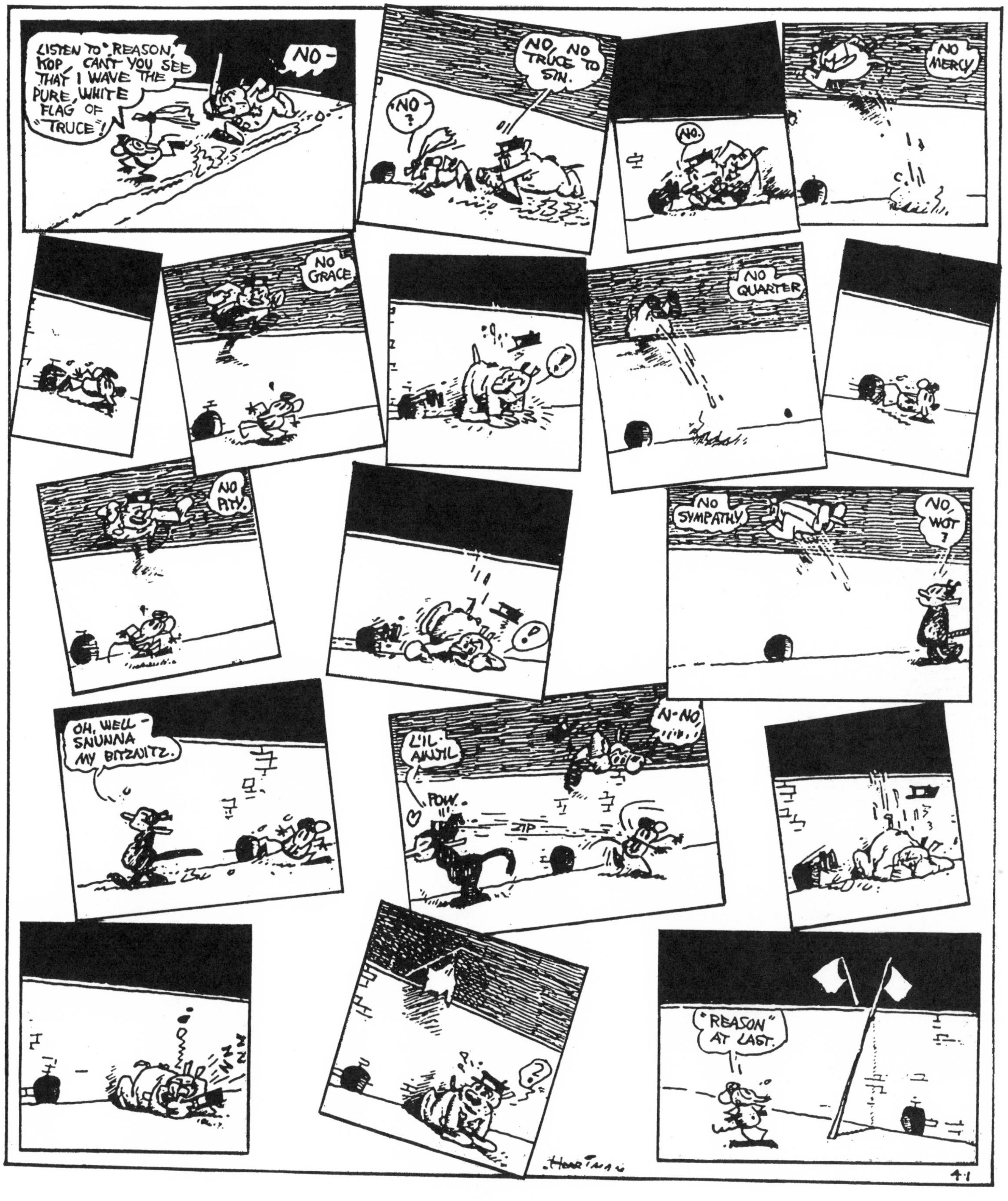

LISTEN TO "REASON," KOP, CAN'T YOU SEE THAT I WAVE THE PURE, WHITE FLAG OF "TRUCE"!
NO-
NO ?
NO, NO TRUCE TO SIN.
NO.
NO MERCY
NO GRACE
NO QUARTER
NO PITY.
NO SYMPATHY
NO, WOT ?
OH, WELL - SNUNNA MY BITZWITZ.
L'IL AINJIL
POW
ZIP
N-NO
"REASON" AT LAST.
HERRIMAN
4-1

April 1st, 1934.

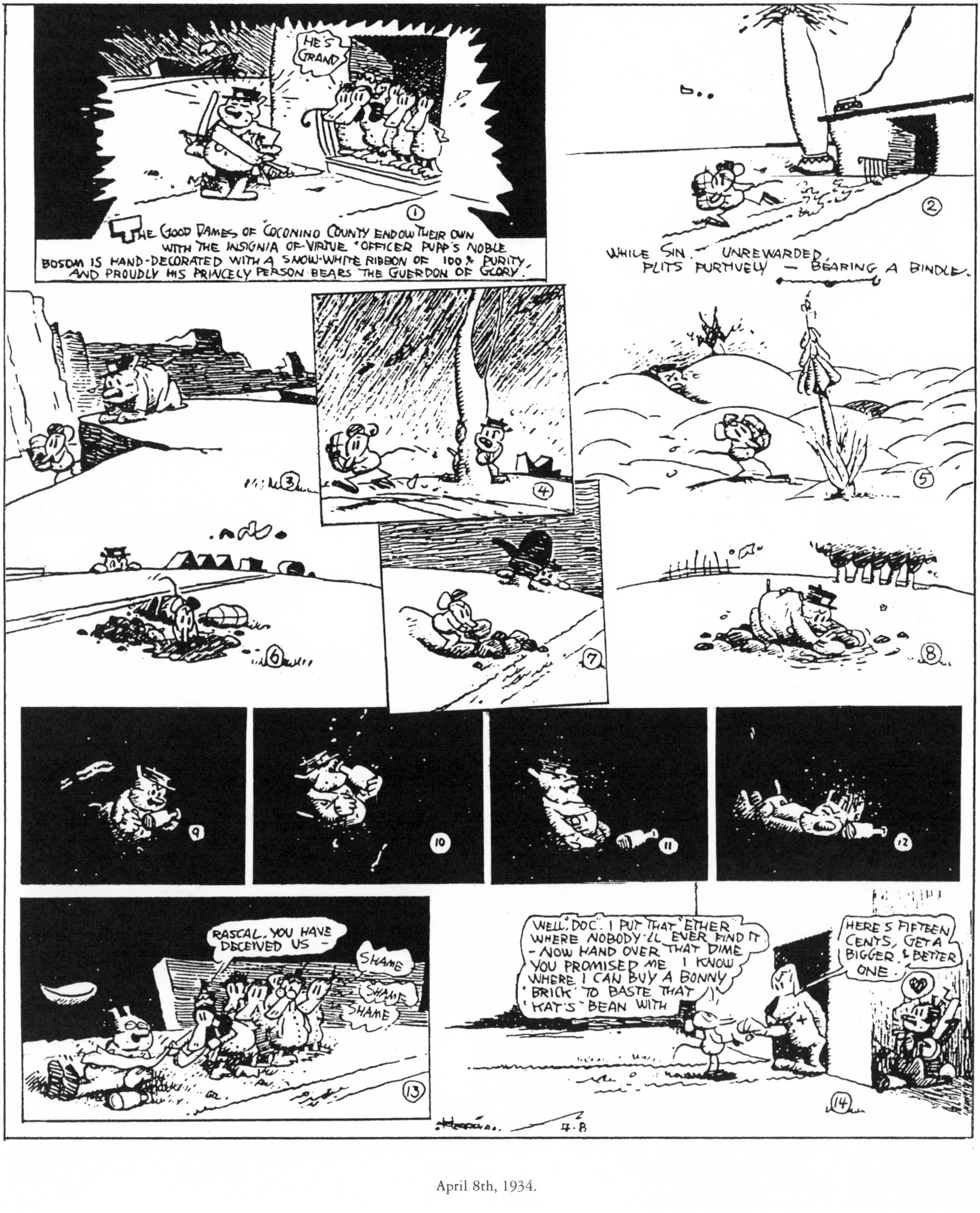
HE'S GRAND
THE GOOD DAMES OF COCONINO COUNTY ENDOW THEIR OWN WITH THE INSIGNIA OF VIRTUE 'OFFICER PUPP'S NOBLE BOSOM IS HAND-DECORATED WITH A SNOW-WHITE RIBBON OF 100% PURITY. AND PROUDLY HIS PRINCELY PERSON BEARS THE GUERDON OF GLORY.
WHILE SIN, UNREWARDED, FLITS FURTIVELY — BEARING A BINDLE.
RASCAL, YOU HAVE DECEIVED US -
SHAME
SHAME
SHAME
WELL, DOC. I PUT THAT ETHER WHERE NOBODY'LL EVER FIND IT - NOW HAND OVER THAT DIME YOU PROMISED ME. I KNOW WHERE I CAN BUY A BONNY 'BRICK' TO BASTE THAT 'KAT'S' BEAN WITH
HERE'S FIFTEEN CENTS, GET A BIGGER & BETTER ONE.
4-8

April 8th, 1934.

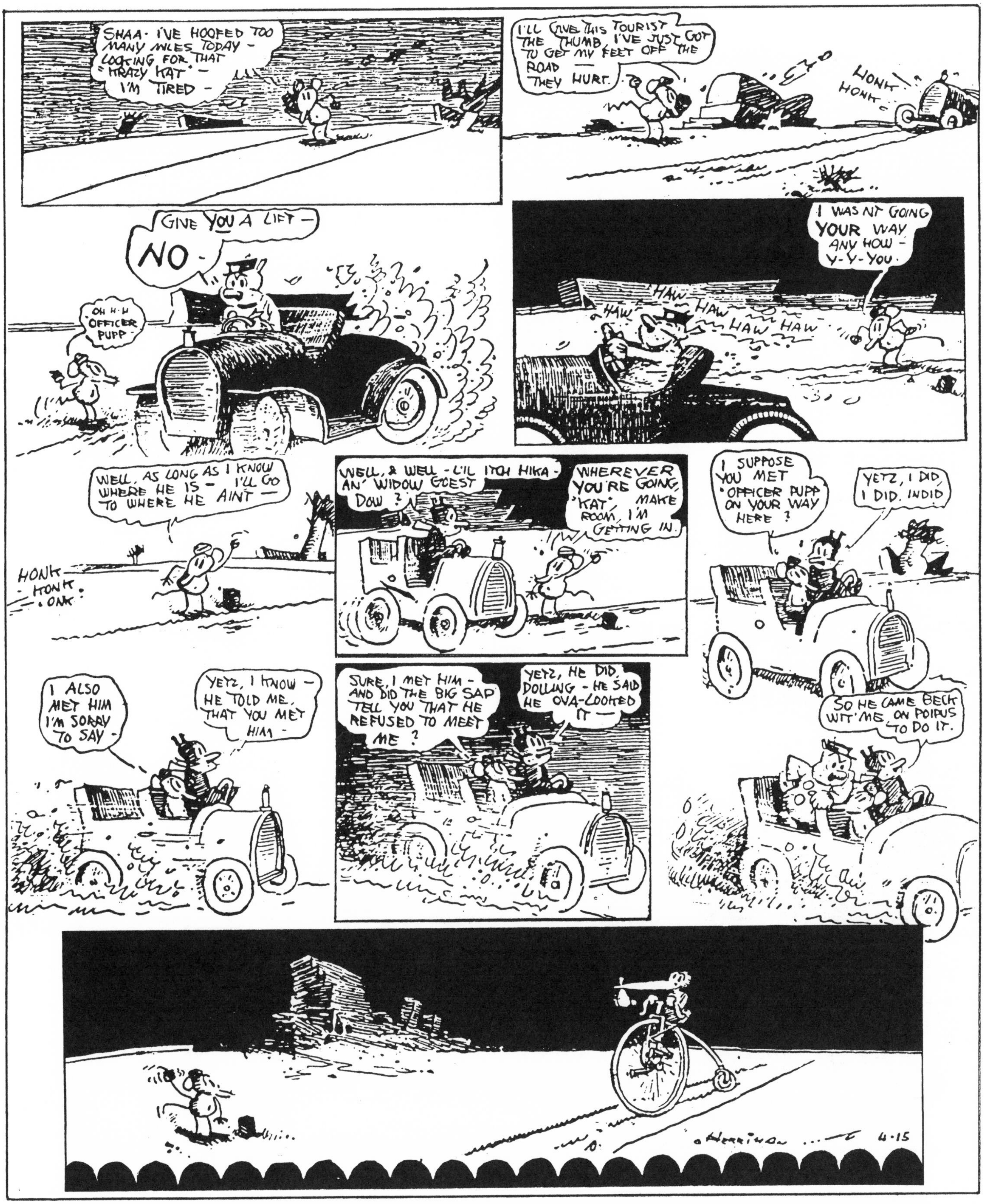
SHAA- I'VE HOOFED TOO MANY MILES TODAY - LOOKING FOR THAT KRAZY KAT - I'M TIRED -
I'LL GIVE THIS TOURIST THE THUMB, I'VE JUST GOT TO GET MY FEET OFF THE ROAD — THEY HURT.
HONK HONK
GIVE YOU A LIFT -
NO -
OH H-H "OFFICER PUPP"
I WAS N'T GOING YOUR WAY ANY HOW - Y-Y-YOU.
HAW HAW HAW HAW HAW
WELL, AS LONG AS I KNOW WHERE HE IS - I'LL GO TO WHERE HE AIN'T —
HONK - HONK - ONK
WELL, & WELL - L'IL ITCH HIKA - AN' WIDOW GOEST DOW ?
WHEREVER YOU'RE GOING, 'KAT', MAKE ROOM, I'M GETTING IN.
I SUPPOSE YOU MET "OFFICER PUPP" ON YOUR WAY HERE ?
YETZ, I DID, I DID. INDID
I ALSO MET HIM I'M SORRY TO SAY -
YETZ, I KNOW - HE TOLD ME. THAT YOU MET HIM -
SURE, I MET HIM - AND DID THE BIG SAP TELL YOU THAT HE REFUSED TO MEET ME ?
YETZ, HE DID, DOLLING - HE SAID HE OVA-LOOKED IT —
SO HE CAME BECK WIT ME, ON POIPUS TO DO IT.
4-15

April 15th, 1934.

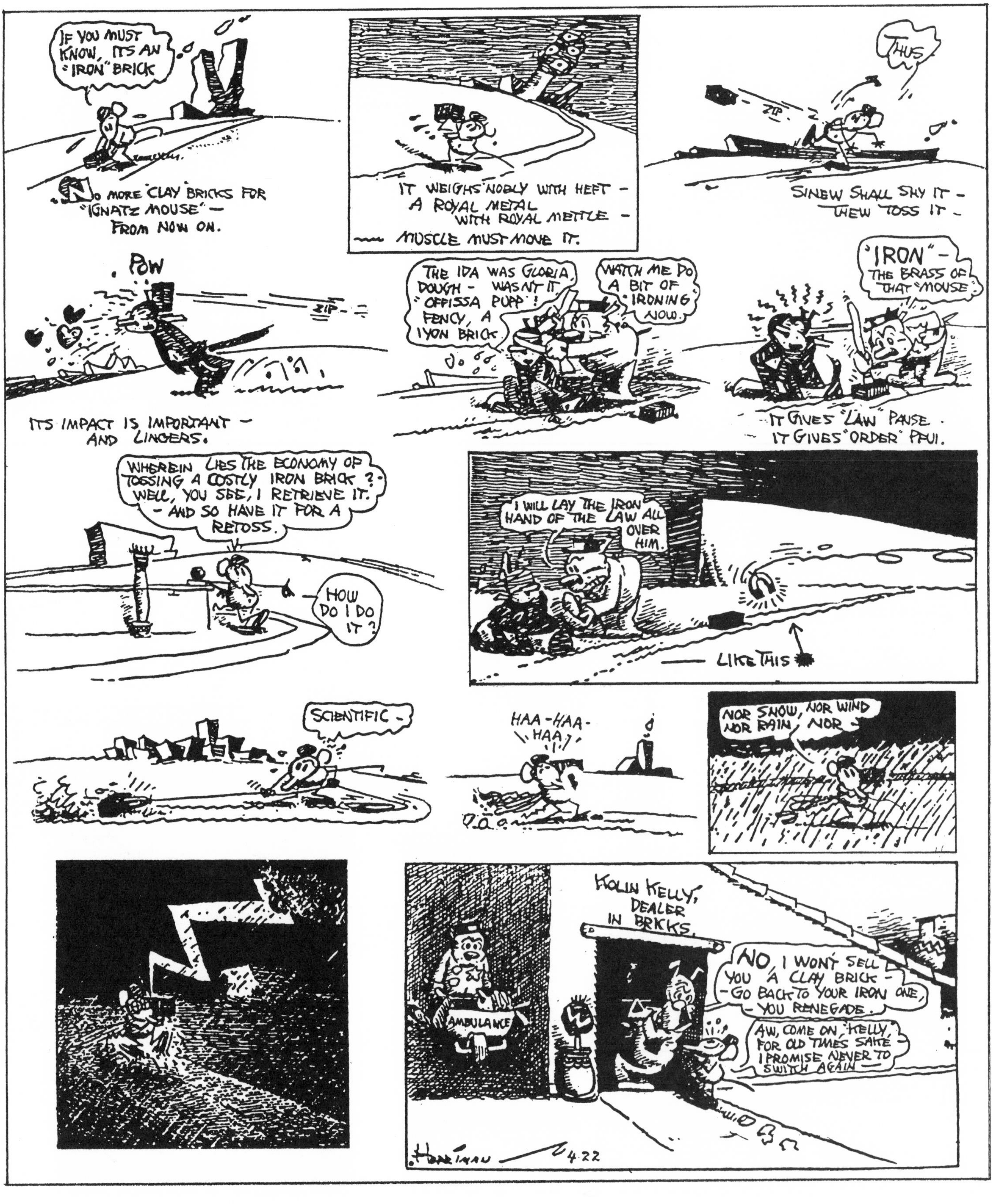

IF YOU MUST KNOW, ITS AN "IRON" BRICK
No more "CLAY" BRICKS FOR "IGNATZ MOUSE" — FROM NOW ON.
IT WEIGHS NOBLY WITH HEFT — A ROYAL METAL WITH ROYAL METTLE —
— MUSCLE MUST MOVE IT.
THUS
ZIP
SINEW SHALL SHY IT — THEW TOSS IT —
POW
ZIP
ITS IMPACT IS IMPORTANT — AND LINGERS.
THE IDA WAS GLORIA DOUGH — WASN'T IT "OFFISSA PUPP"! FENCY, A IYON BRICK
WATCH ME DO A BIT OF IRONING NOW.
"IRON" — THE BRASS OF THAT "MOUSE"
IT GIVES "LAW" PAUSE. — IT GIVES "ORDER" PFUI.
WHEREIN LIES THE ECONOMY OF TOSSING A COSTLY IRON BRICK? — WELL, YOU SEE, I RETRIEVE IT. — AND SO HAVE IT FOR A RETOSS.
HOW DO I DO IT?
I WILL LAY THE IRON HAND OF THE LAW ALL OVER HIM.
— LIKE THIS
SCIENTIFIC —
HAA-HAA-HAA
NOR SNOW, NOR WIND NOR RAIN, NOR —
KOLIN KELLY, DEALER IN BRKKS.
AMBULANCE
NO, I WON'T SELL YOU A CLAY BRICK — GO BACK TO YOUR IRON ONE, — YOU RENEGADE.
AW, COME ON, "KELLY," FOR OLD TIMES SAKE I PROMISE NEVER TO SWITCH AGAIN —
HERRIMAN 4-22

April 22nd, 1934.

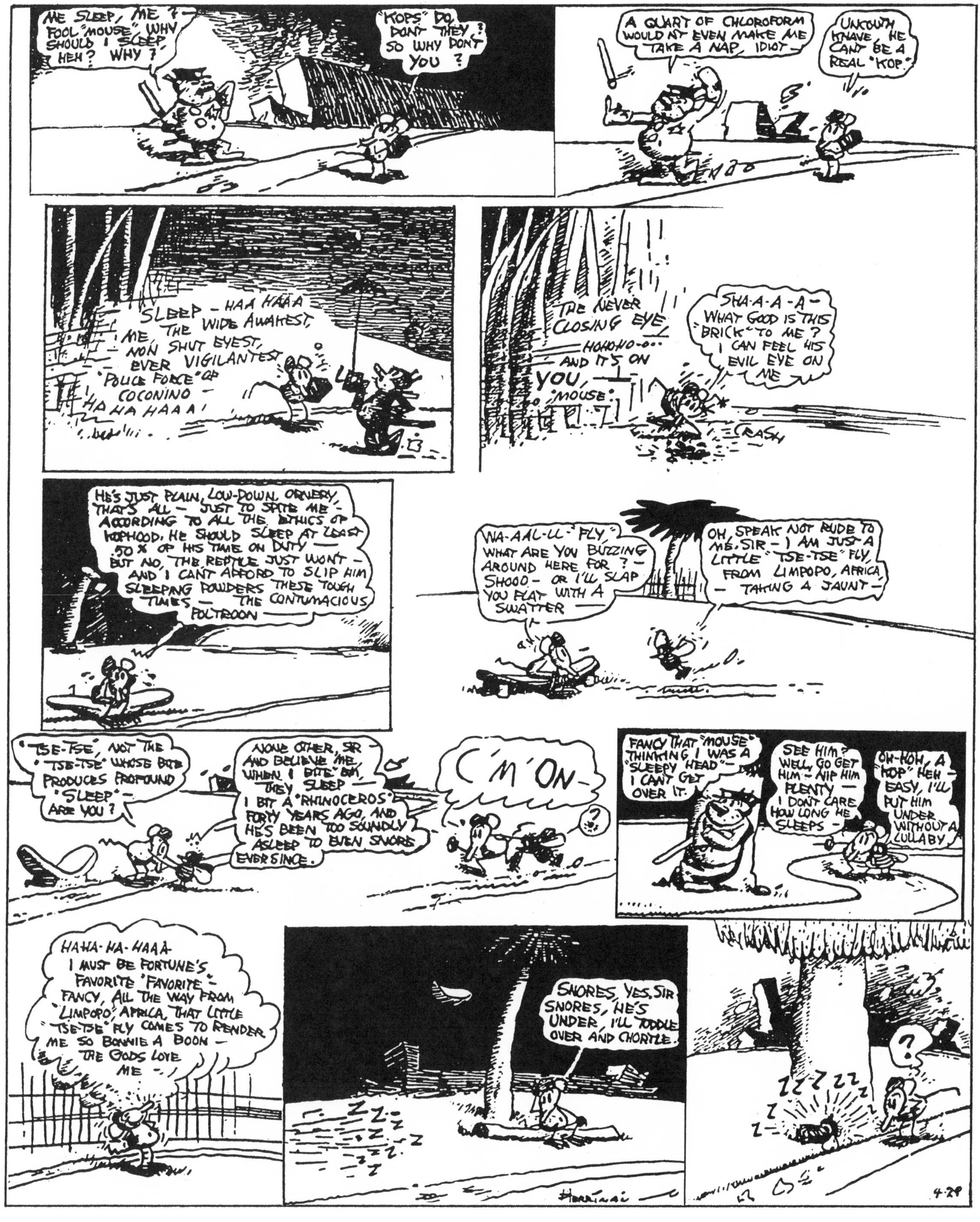
ME SLEEP, ME ? FOOL "MOUSE" WHY SHOULD I SLEEP HEH? WHY?
"KOPS" DO, DON'T THEY? SO WHY DON'T YOU?
A QUART OF CHLOROFORM WOULD N'T EVEN MAKE ME TAKE A NAP, IDIOT —
UNKOUTH KNAVE, HE CAN'T BE A REAL "KOP."
SLEEP — HAA HAAA ME, THE WIDE AWAKEST, NON SHUT EYEST, EVER VIGILANTEST "POLICE FORCE" OF COCONINO — HA HA HAAA!
THE NEVER CLOSING EYE — HOHOHO-O- AND IT'S ON YOU, "MOUSE"
SHA-A-A-A — WHAT GOOD IS THIS "BRICK" TO ME? I CAN FEEL HIS EVIL EYE ON ME
CRASH
HE'S JUST PLAIN, LOW-DOWN, ORNERY, THAT'S ALL — JUST TO SPITE ME — ACCORDING TO ALL THE ETHICS OF KOPHOOD, HE SHOULD SLEEP AT LEAST 50% OF HIS TIME ON DUTY — BUT NO, THE REPTILE JUST WON'T — AND I CAN'T AFFORD TO SLIP HIM SLEEPING POWDERS THESE TOUGH TIMES — THE CONTUMACIOUS POLTROON
WA-AAL-LL" FLY, WHAT ARE YOU BUZZING AROUND HERE FOR? SHOOO — OR I'LL SLAP YOU FLAT WITH A SWATTER
OH, SPEAK NOT RUDE TO ME, SIR — I AM JUST A LITTLE "TSE-TSE" FLY, FROM LIMPOPO, AFRICA, — TAKING A JAUNT —
"TSE-TSE", NOT THE "TSE-TSE" WHOSE BITE PRODUCES PROFOUND "SLEEP" — ARE YOU?
NONE OTHER, SIR AND BELIEVE ME, WHEN I BITE 'EM, THEY SLEEP — I BIT A "RHINOCEROS" FORTY YEARS AGO, AND HE'S BEEN TOO SOUNDLY ASLEEP TO EVEN SNORE EVER SINCE.
C'M'ON
?
FANCY THAT "MOUSE" THINKING I WAS A "SLEEPY HEAD" — I CAN'T GET OVER IT.
SEE HIM? WELL, GO GET HIM — NIP HIM PLENTY — I DON'T CARE HOW LONG HE SLEEPS —
OH-HOH, A "KOP" HEH — EASY, I'LL PUT HIM UNDER WITHOUT A LULLABY
HA-HA-HA-HAAA I MUST BE FORTUNE'S FAVORITE "FAVORITE" FANCY, ALL THE WAY FROM "LIMPOPO", AFRICA, THAT LITTLE "TSE-TSE" FLY COMES TO RENDER ME SO BONNIE A BOON — THE GODS LOVE ME —
SNORES, YES, SIR SNORES, HE'S UNDER, I'LL TODDLE OVER AND CHORTLE.
?
Herriman
4-29

April 29th, 1934.

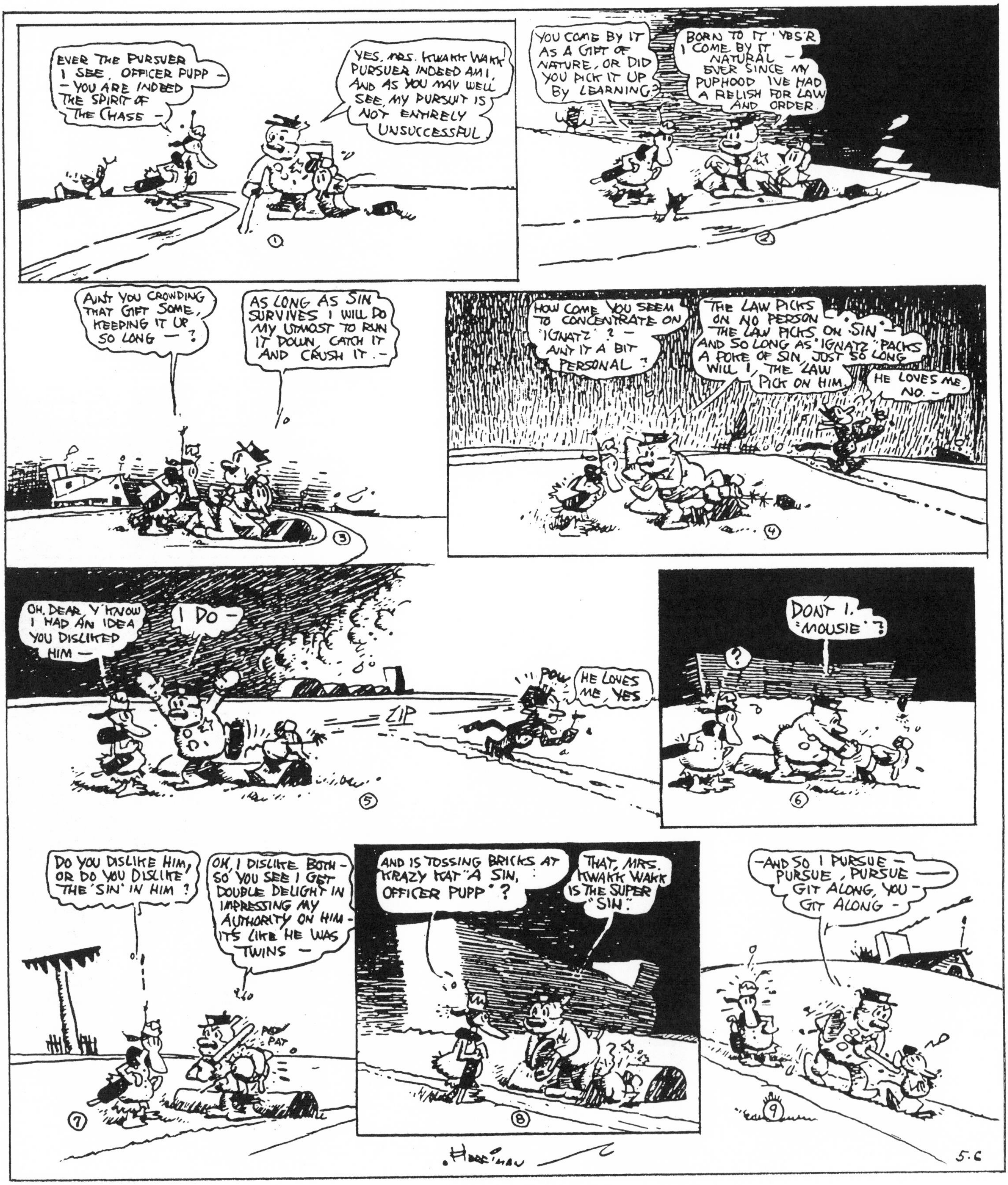
EVER THE PURSUER I SEE, OFFICER PUPP — YOU ARE INDEED THE SPIRIT OF THE CHASE —
YES, MRS. KWAKK WAKK! PURSUER INDEED AM I, AND AS YOU MAY WELL SEE, MY PURSUIT IS NOT ENTIRELY UNSUCCESSFUL
YOU COME BY IT AS A GIFT OF NATURE, OR DID YOU PICK IT UP BY LEARNING?
BORN TO IT, YES'R I COME BY IT NATURAL — EVER SINCE MY PUPHOOD I'VE HAD A RELISH FOR LAW AND ORDER
AIN'T YOU CROWDING THAT GIFT SOME, KEEPING IT UP SO LONG — ?
AS LONG AS SIN SURVIVES I WILL DO MY UTMOST TO RUN IT DOWN, CATCH IT AND CRUSH IT. —
HOW COME YOU SEEM TO CONCENTRATE ON "IGNATZ"? — AIN'T IT A BIT PERSONAL?
THE LAW PICKS ON NO PERSON — THE LAW PICKS ON "SIN" — AND SO LONG AS "IGNATZ" PACKS A POKE OF SIN, JUST SO LONG WILL I, THE LAW, PICK ON HIM.
HE LOVES ME. NO. —
OH, DEAR, Y'KNOW I HAD AN IDEA YOU DISLIKED HIM —
I DO —
ZIP
POW
HE LOVES ME, YES
DON'T I, "MOUSIE"?
DO YOU DISLIKE HIM, OR DO YOU DISLIKE THE "SIN" IN HIM?
OH, I DISLIKE BOTH — SO YOU SEE I GET DOUBLE DELIGHT IN IMPRESSING MY AUTHORITY ON HIM — IT'S LIKE HE WAS TWINS —
PAT PAT
AND IS TOSSING BRICKS AT "KRAZY KAT" A SIN, OFFICER PUPP?
THAT, MRS. KWAKK WAKK IS THE SUPER "SIN".
—AND SO I PURSUE — PURSUE, PURSUE — GIT ALONG, YOU — GIT ALONG —
HERRIMAN
5-6

May 6th, 1934.

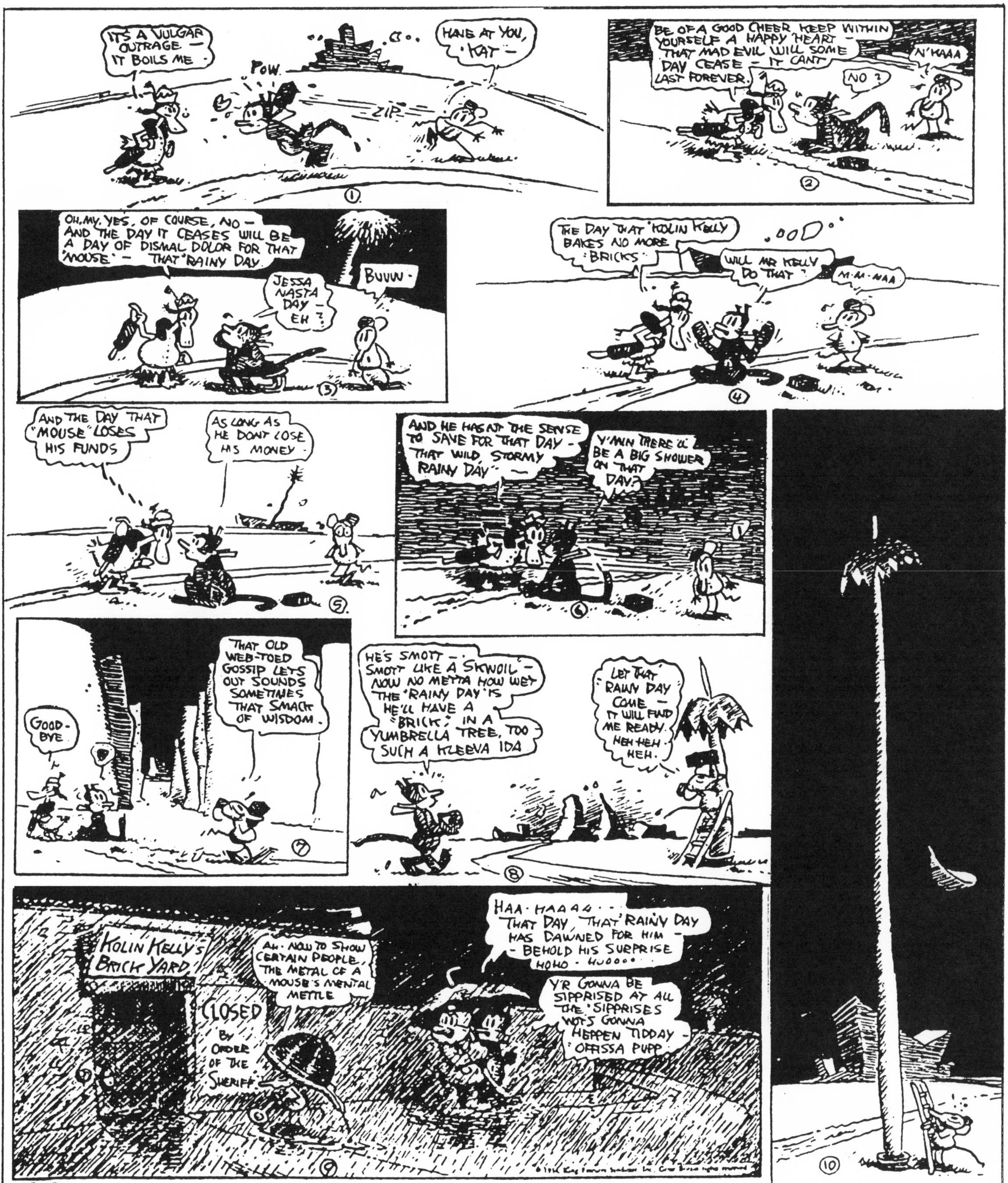

IT'S A VULGAR OUTRAGE — IT BOILS ME.
POW.
ZIP
HANG AT YOU, "KAT" —
BE OF A GOOD CHEER. KEEP WITHIN YOURSELF A HAPPY HEART — THAT MAD EVIL WILL SOME DAY CEASE — IT CAN'T LAST FOREVER.
NO ?
N'HAAA
OH, MY, YES, OF COURSE, NO — AND THE DAY IT CEASES WILL BE A DAY OF DISMAL DOLOR FOR THAT "MOUSE" — THAT "RAINY DAY."
JESSA NASTA DAY — EH ?
BUUW.
THE DAY THAT "KOLIN KELLY" BAKES NO MORE "BRICKS"
WILL MR KELLY DO THAT ?
M·M·NAA
AND THE DAY THAT "MOUSE" LOSES HIS FUNDS
AS LONG AS HE DONT LOSE HIS MONEY
AND HE HAS NT THE SENSE TO SAVE FOR THAT DAY — THAT WILD, STORMY RAINY DAY —
Y'AIN THERE'LL BE A BIG SHOWER ON THAT DAY?
GOOD-BYE
THAT OLD WEB-TOED GOSSIP LETS OUT SOUNDS SOMETIMES THAT SMACK OF WISDOM.
HE'S SMOTT — SMOTT LIKE A SKWOIL — NOW NO METTA HOW WET THE "RAINY DAY" IS HE'LL HAVE A "BRICK" IN A YUMBRELLA TREE, TOO — SUCH A KLEEVA IDA
LET THAT RAINY DAY COME — IT WILL FIND ME READY. HEH HEH HEH.
KOLIN KELLY'S BRICK YARD
CLOSED BY ORDER OF THE SHERIFF
AH — NOW TO SHOW CERTAIN PEOPLE, THE METAL OF A MOUSE'S MENTAL METTLE
HAA · HAAAA · · THAT DAY, THAT "RAINY DAY" HAS DAWNED FOR HIM — BEHOLD HIS SURPRISE HOHO · HUOOOO ·
Y'R GONNA BE SIPPRISED AT ALL THE "SIPPRISES" WOT'S GONNA HEPPEN TIDDAY — "OFFISSA PUPP"
5·13

May 13th, 1934.

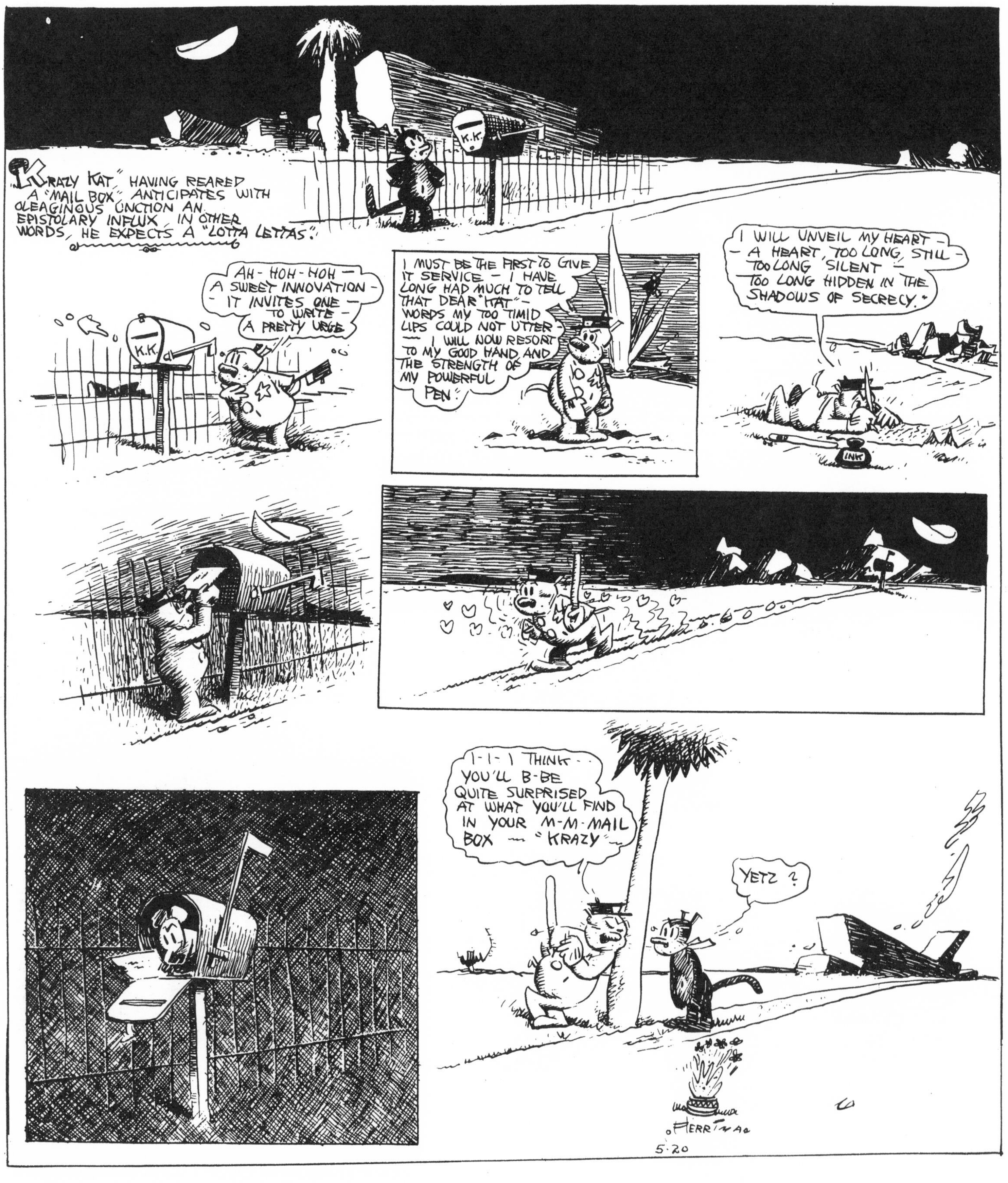
"Krazy Kat" having reared a "mail box" anticipates with oleaginous unction an epistolary influx in other words, he expects a "Lotta Lettas".
K.K.
AH - HOH - HOH — A SWEET INNOVATION — IT INVITES ONE — TO WRITE A PRETTY URGE
I MUST BE THE FIRST TO GIVE IT SERVICE — I HAVE LONG HAD MUCH TO TELL THAT DEAR "KAT" — WORDS MY TOO TIMID LIPS COULD NOT UTTER — I WILL NOW RESORT TO MY GOOD HAND AND THE STRENGTH OF MY POWERFUL PEN.
I WILL UNVEIL MY HEART — A HEART, TOO LONG, STILL — TOO LONG SILENT — TOO LONG HIDDEN IN THE SHADOWS OF SECRECY.
INK
I-I-I THINK YOU'LL B-BE QUITE SURPRISED AT WHAT YOU'LL FIND IN YOUR M-M-MAIL BOX — "KRAZY"
YETZ ?
HERRIMAN
5·20

May 20th, 1934.

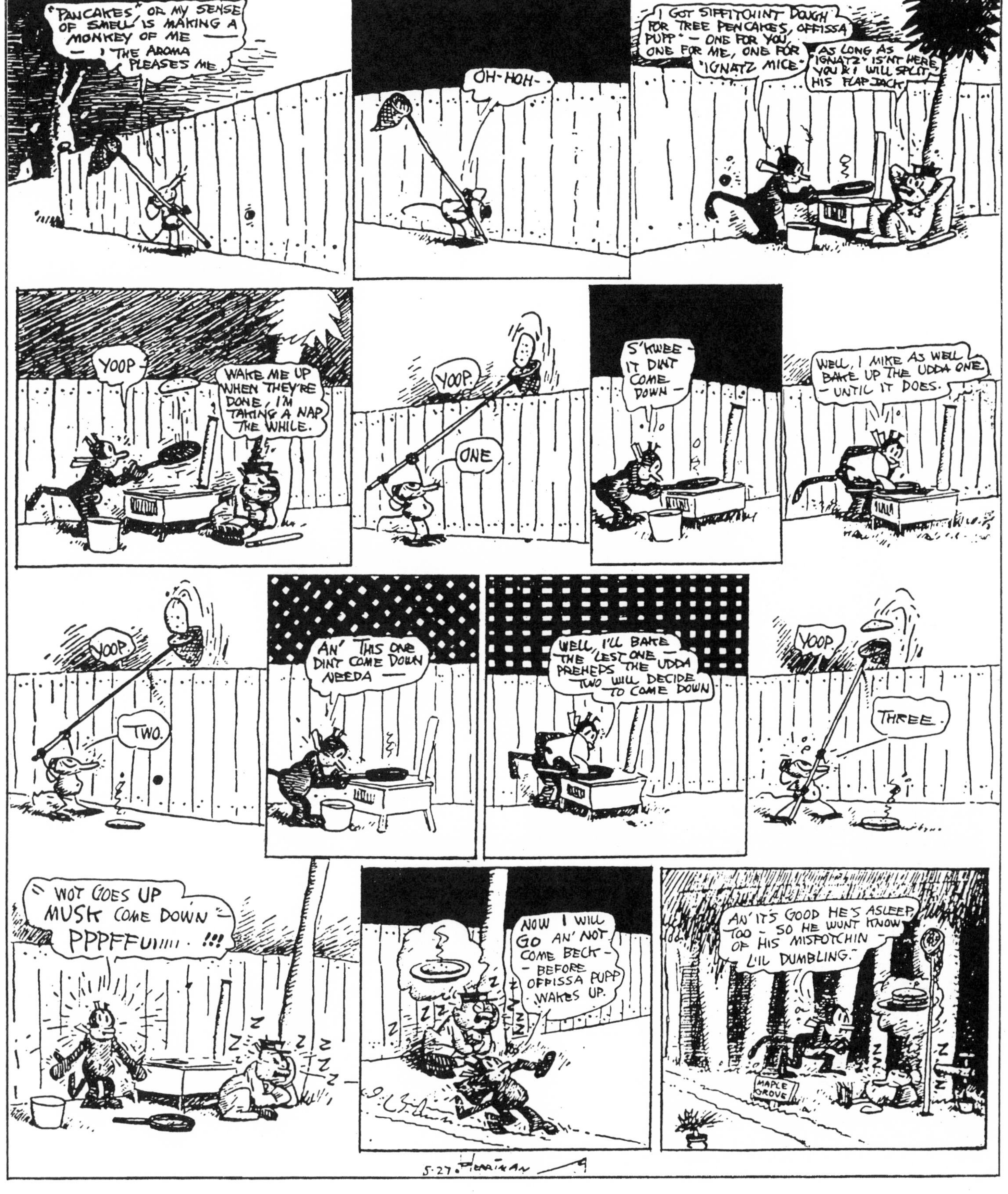
"PANCAKES" OR MY SENSE OF SMELL IS MAKING A MONKEY OF ME — I THE AROMA PLEASES ME.
OH-HOH-
I GOT SIFFITCHINT DOUGH FOR TREE PENCAKES, OFFISSA PUPP" — ONE FOR YOU, ONE FOR ME, ONE FOR "IGNATZ MICE"
AS LONG AS "IGNATZ" ISN'T HERE, YOU & I WILL SPLIT HIS FLAP JACK.
YOOP -
WAKE ME UP WHEN THEY'RE DONE, I'M TAKING A NAP THE WHILE.
YOOP.
ONE
S'KWEE - IT DINT COME DOWN -
WELL, I MIKE AS WELL BAKE UP THE UDDA ONE - UNTIL IT DOES.
YOOP.
TWO.
AN' THIS ONE DINT COME DOWN NEEDA —
WELL, I'LL BAKE THE LEST ONE - PREHEPS THE UDDA TWO WILL DECIDE TO COME DOWN
YOOP.
THREE.
WOT GOES UP MUSK COME DOWN - PPPFFU!!!!! !!!
NOW I WILL GO AN' NOT COME BECK - BEFORE OFFISSA PUPP WAKES UP.
AN' IT'S GOOD HE'S ASLEEP TOO - SO HE WUNT KNOW OF HIS MISFOTCHIN - L'IL DUMBLING."
MAPLE GROVE
5·27. HERRIMAN

May 27th, 1934.

GIMME IT NOW, IT'S MY TURN -
HEY, I WANT ANOTHER WHIFF OF THAT TORPEDO
PUFF
PUFF
PUFF
I'VE GOT TO PUT A STOP TO THIS SINFUL ORGY RIGHT NOW - THOSE KIDS ARE SHOWING SIGNS OF GROWING UP TO BE JUST LIKE THEIR WICKED 'FATHER' - I WONT HAVE IT.
AINT YOU ASHAMED OF YOURSELVES YOU, MILTON; YOU, MARSHAL, & YOU IRVING? — AINT IT ENOUGH THAT I'VE GOT TO HANDLE YOUR SINFUL DAD'S MORALS, WITHOUT YOU LITTLE RASCALS ADDING TO MY WORRIES? — HAAAA?
AND WHAT'S MORE, DONT YOU KNOW THAT THIS CIGAR WILL MAKE YOU SICK, RUIN YOUR HEALTH, STUNT YOUR GROWTH - YOUR MINDS, YOUR SOULS - HEH-H-H
DO YOU WANT TO GET DIZZY? DO YOU WANT A HEAD ACHE? DO YOU WANT TO GET GREEN? DO YOU WANT SPOTS BEFORE YOUR EYES - ? I ASK YOU -
NO, I BET A THOUSAND MILLION DOLLARS, Y' DONT, OF COURSE, NO — AND REMEMBER, I MAY BE YOUR PUSILLANIMOUS PAPPY'S WORST ENEMY, BUT I'M YOUR BEST FRIEND — YEH-H-H-H.
UHM—
SNIFF
UHMMMM
AHHHH
FPFFF
OOHH
WELL
UH-H-YMM
HE LOVES ME, NO.
HE LOVES ME, YETZ.
POW
ZIP
WHY, PAP, THAT'S OUR'N.
YOU DONT TELL ME
PULL IN UNISON JUNIORS PUFF FAIR -
I WUNDA IF THOSE SPOTS IS BEFORE HIS EYE, OR MINE ?
Herriman 6-3

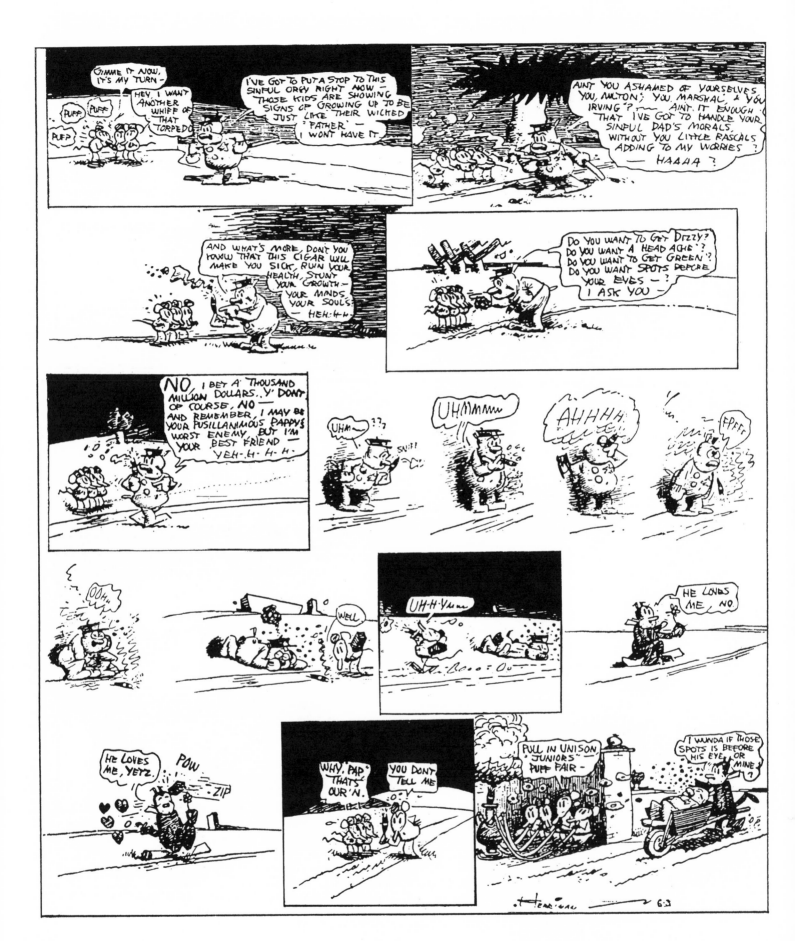

June 3rd, 1934.

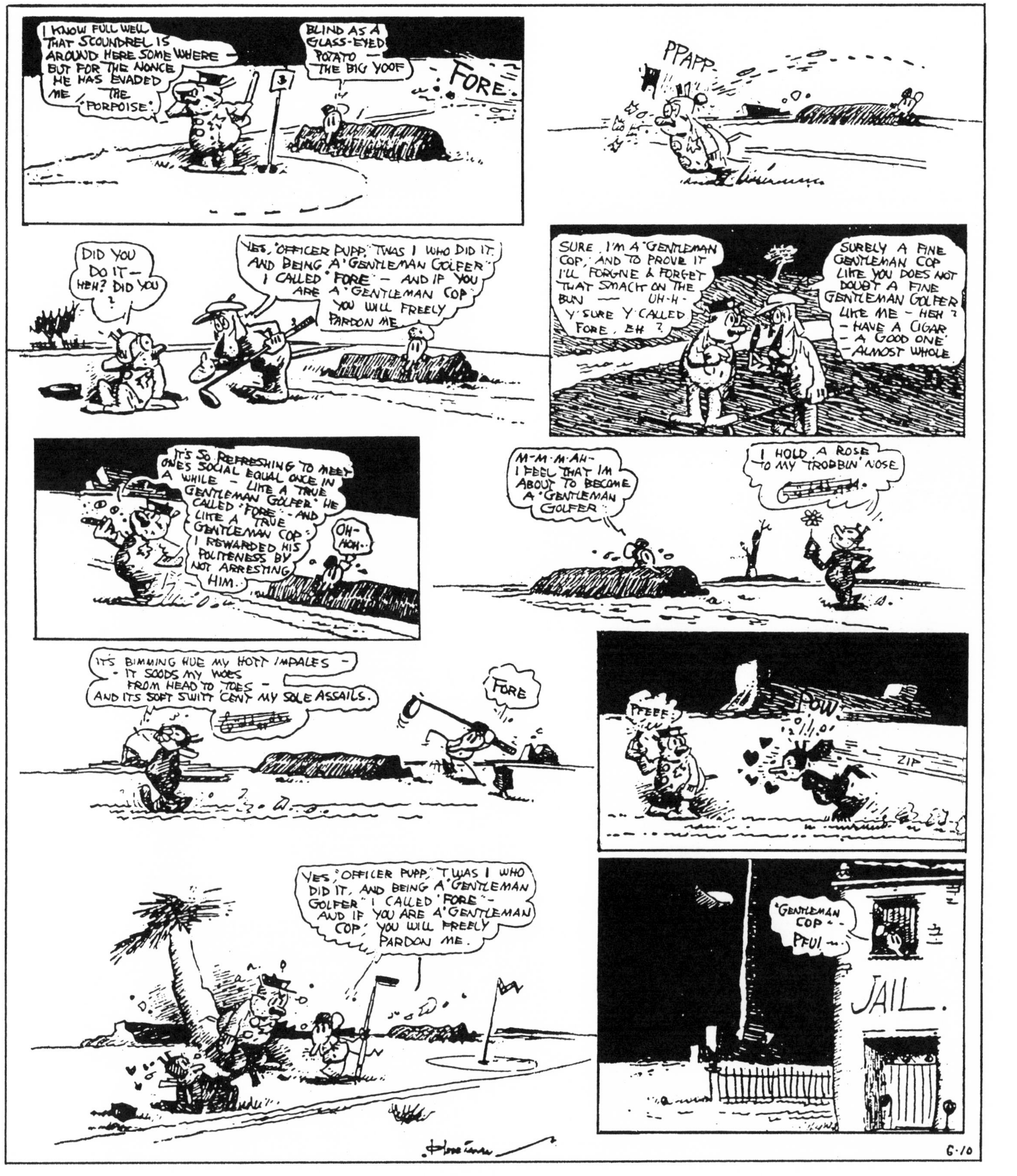
I KNOW FULL WELL THAT SCOUNDREL IS AROUND HERE SOME WHERE BUT FOR THE NONCE HE HAS EVADED ME — THE "PORPOISE"
BLIND AS A GLASS-EYED POTATO — THE BIG YOOF
FORE
PPAPP
DID YOU DO IT — HEH? DID YOU ?
YES, OFFICER PUPP, TWAS I WHO DID IT. AND BEING A "GENTLEMAN GOLFER" I CALLED "FORE" — AND IF YOU ARE A "GENTLEMAN COP" YOU WILL FREELY PARDON ME.
SURE I'M A "GENTLEMAN COP," AND TO PROVE IT I'LL FORGIVE & FORGET THAT SMACK ON THE BUN — UH-H — Y'SURE Y' CALLED FORE, EH ?
SURELY A FINE GENTLEMAN COP LIKE YOU DOES NOT DOUBT A FINE GENTLEMAN GOLFER LIKE ME — HEH ? — HAVE A CIGAR — A GOOD ONE — ALMOST WHOLE
IT'S SO REFRESHING TO MEET ONE'S SOCIAL EQUAL ONCE IN A WHILE — LIKE A TRUE GENTLEMAN GOLFER HE CALLED "FORE" — AND LIKE A TRUE GENTLEMAN COP I REWARDED HIS POLITENESS BY NOT ARRESTING HIM.
OH-HOH..
M-M-M-AH — I FEEL THAT I'M ABOUT TO BECOME A "GENTLEMAN GOLFER"
I HOLD A ROSE TO MY TRODBIN' NOSE
IT'S BIMMING HUE MY HOTT IMPALES — IT SOODS MY WOES FROM HEAD TO TOES — AND ITS SOFT SWITT CENT MY SOLE ASSAILS.
FORE
PFEEE
POW
ZIP
YES, OFFICER PUPP, T'WAS I WHO DID IT. AND BEING A "GENTLEMAN GOLFER" I CALLED "FORE" — AND IF YOU ARE A "GENTLEMAN COP" YOU WILL FREELY PARDON ME.
"GENTLEMAN COP" — PFUI —
JAIL.
6-10

June 10th, 1934.

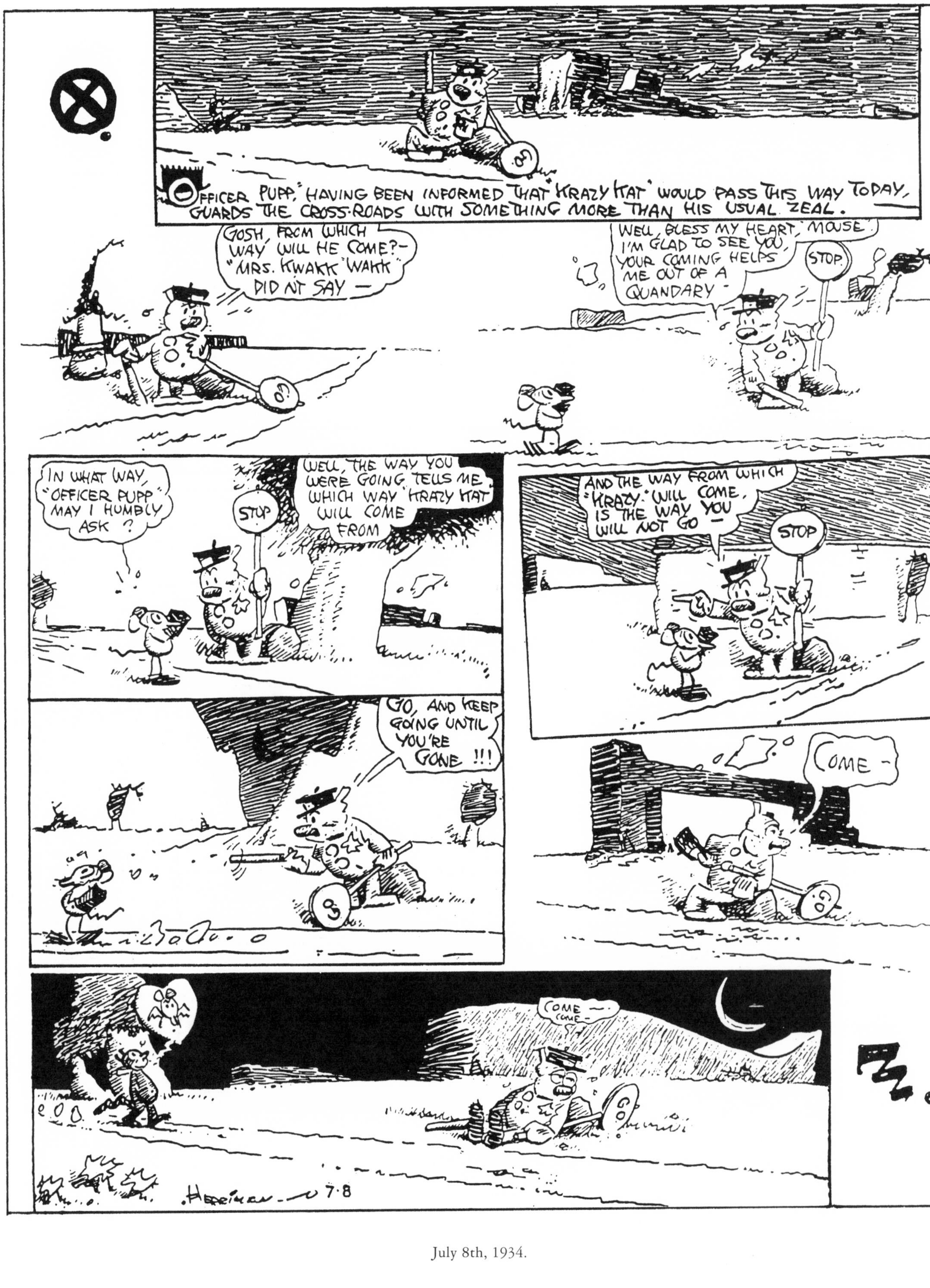
Officer Pupp, having been informed that "Krazy Kat" would pass this way today, guards the cross-roads with something more than his usual zeal.
Gosh, from which way will he come?- "Mrs. Kwakk Wakk" did n't say -
Well, bless my heart, "mouse" I'm glad to see you, your coming helps me out of a quandary -
Stop
In what way, "Officer Pupp" may I humbly ask ?
Well, the way you were going tells me which way "Krazy Kat" will come from
Stop
And the way from which "Krazy" will come, is the way you will not go -
Stop
Go, and keep going until you're gone !!!
Go
Come -
Go
Come - come -
Go
Herriman - 7-8

July 8th, 1934.

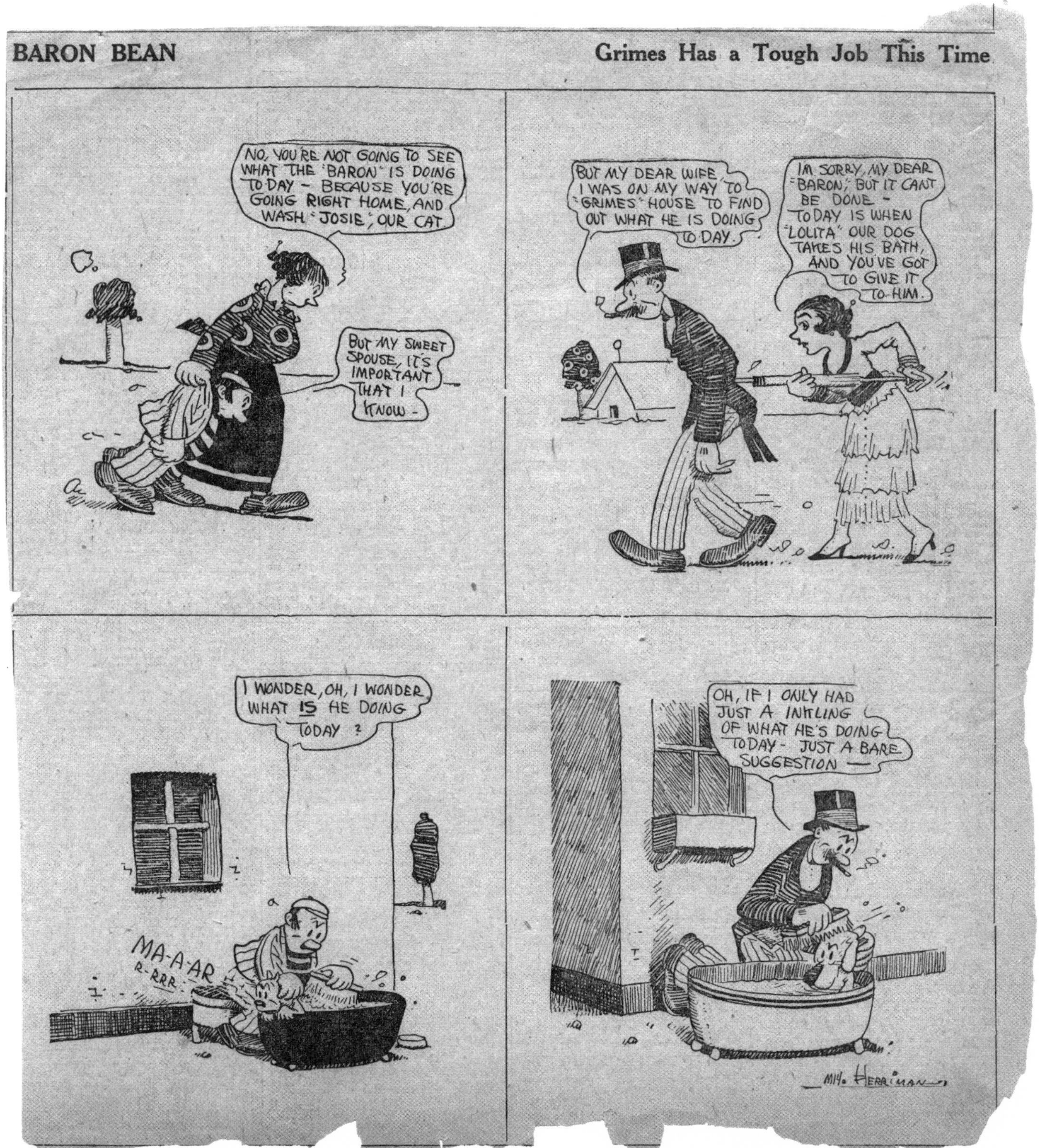
BARON BEAN
Grimes Has a Tough Job This Time
NO, YOU'RE NOT GOING TO SEE WHAT THE "BARON" IS DOING TO-DAY - BECAUSE YOU'RE GOING RIGHT HOME, AND WASH "JOSIE," OUR CAT.
BUT MY SWEET SPOUSE, IT'S IMPORTANT THAT I KNOW -
BUT MY DEAR WIFE, I WAS ON MY WAY TO "GRIMES" HOUSE TO FIND OUT WHAT HE IS DOING TO DAY.
I'M SORRY, MY DEAR "BARON," BUT IT CAN'T BE DONE - TO DAY IS WHEN "LOLITA" OUR DOG TAKES HIS BATH, AND YOU'VE GOT TO GIVE IT TO HIM.
I WONDER, OH, I WONDER WHAT IS HE DOING TODAY ?
MA-A-AR
R-RRR
OH, IF I ONLY HAD JUST A INKLING OF WHAT HE'S DOING TODAY - JUST A BARE SUGGESTION -
HERRIMAN

Baron Bean, undated, c. 1917-1919, from an unidentified paper.
This, however, appears to be "the real Herriman."
Collection C. Ware.

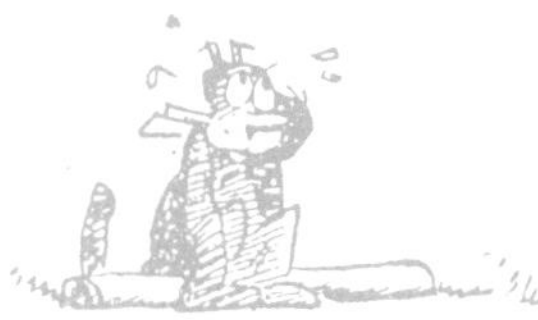

The IGNATZ MOUSE DEBAFFLER PAGE.

1/29/33: In most cases we allow Herriman's Tower-of-Babble puns to stand unexplained for readers to puzzle over, but this one caused enough konsternation even among ye humble polyglot editors to kindly share with you its solution: The "kee veev" in "he's on the kee veev" is a phonetic rendition of the French expression *qui vive*, meaning he's on high alert. Simple, *non*?

2/26/33: Don Kiyoti co-starred in an earlier Herriman Sunday strip with a short, pudgy pig named Sancho Pansy. The setting was apparently Mexican, but the ambience was very much Coconino. An example can be seen on Peter Campbell's excellent Coconino County website — a site to behold!

3/19/33: A surprising "social consciousness" episode, possibly reflecting the growing public realization of national wrack and ruin in the 1933 "depth of the Great Depression." (There are actually quite a few Spanish speaking women named Marihuana, just as there are Anglo women named Mary Jane.)

4/9/33: Another quite obscure linguistic gymnastic: When the pinnut wender says "May Woy," it almost certainly means he's Spanish and is saying *Me voy* ("I am leaving.")

1/7/34: Here Garge delights one fan with the initials, KG, or — possibly — IGK, and mystifies the rest of us forever. Maybe it's just we're not smott enuf to figga it oudt.

Additional DeBaffling by Derya Ataker: The following 46 Sunday pages were reconstructed from mutilated "daily-formatted" strips salvaged from the *New York Evening Journal* (for details, see the introduction beginning on page 6):

1933: January 1, 8, 15, 22, 29; February 12, 19, 26; March 5, 19, 26; April 2, 16, 23, 30; May 7, 14; June 4, 11, 18; July 2, 9, 30; August 6, 13, 20, 27; September. 3; and November 19.

1934: February 4, 11, 18, 25; March 4, 18; April 1, 8, 15, 22, 29; May 6, 13, 27; June 3, 10; and July 8.

In the previous volume, *Krazy & Ignatz: 1931-1932*, ten pages were reconstructed in this manner as well: In 1931, March 15, May 10, 24, August 30, and September 6; in 1932, June 12, and December 4, 11, and 18.

It also bears mentioning that any skipped dates (both for that volume and the present one) reflected dates upon which the official syndicate release, so far as can be ascertained, consisted of a re-presentation of an earlier strip. Since these had perforce all been collected in prior *Krazy + Ignatz* volumes, we saw no need to redundantly re-represent them (but we were remiss in not reminding readers anew of that fact, to shoo away suspicions that we had merely forgot to run them, or been umable to locate them).

In 1931, these instances of (as Krazy him/herself might put it) "day-jar voo" occurred on all four Sundays in January, February 1 and 8, April 5 and 12, July 19 and 26, August 2 and 9, November 22 and 29. In 1932, July 24 and 31, August 7, 21, and 28, September 4, and November 13 were likewise recycled.

As for the volume you hold in your hands, there were, in 1933, surprisingly enough, no reprints at all — 53 strips drawn, 53 strips printed, 53 strips found and presented here for your delectation! In the first five months of 1934 only one date was a reprint (January 21). However, the penultimate new black-and-white Sunday, June 10th, was followed by three consecutive reprints, after which the July 8th strip, the last known original before the color revival, was followed by four straight reprints (July 15, 22, 29 and August 5), and then nothing. Did Herriman continue to draw Sunday strips that either were never published or of which no copies survive? Or did *Krazy Kat* go into reprints until the color revival of 1935?

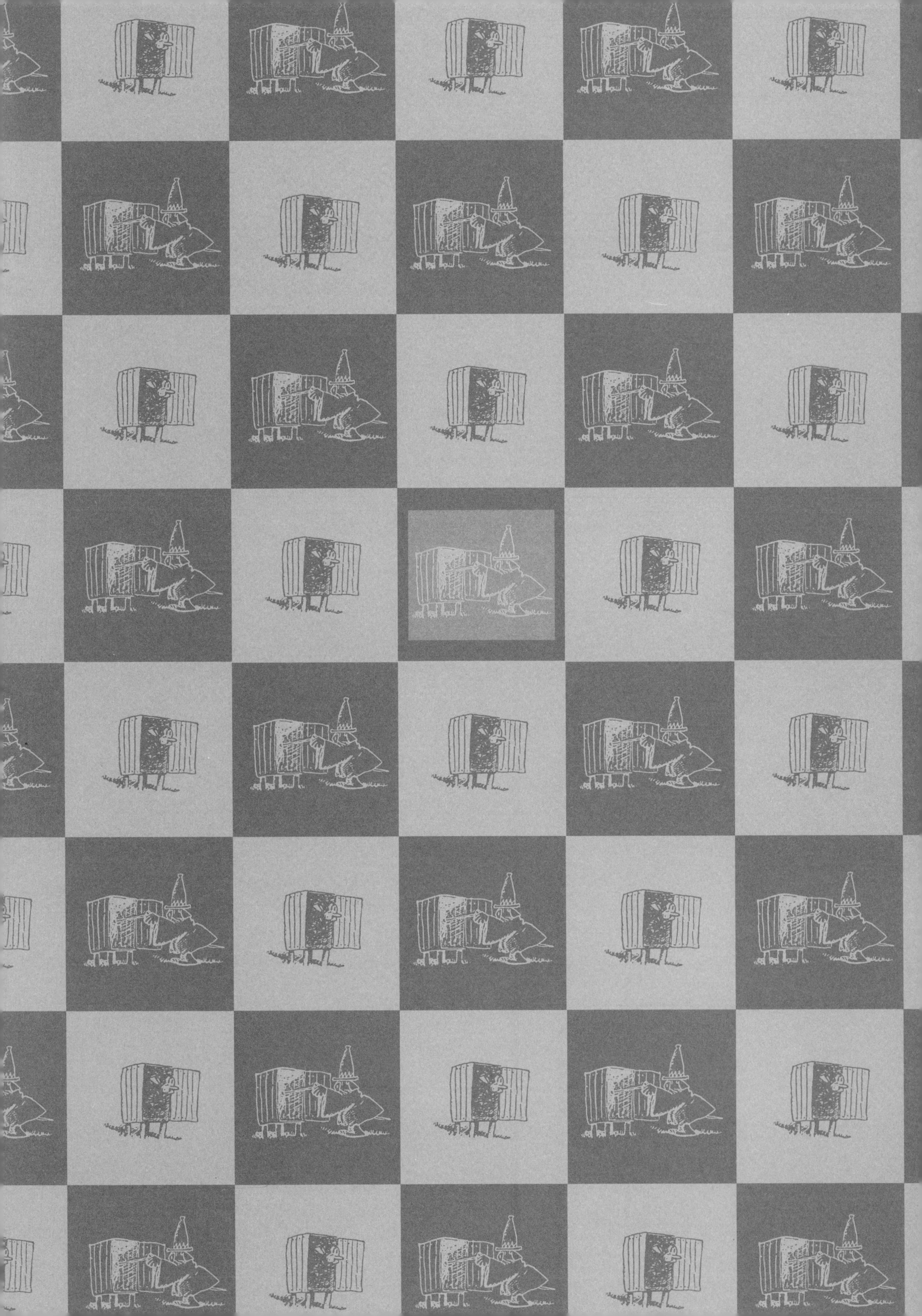